IT'S ♥ BRIDGE,
BABY

IT'S BRIDGE, BABY

HOW TO BE A PLAYER IN TEN EASY LESSONS

· JEFF BAYONE ·

Owner of the Manhattan Bridge Club

with AMANDA BEESLEY

RIVERHEAD BOOKS · NEW YORK

Riverhead Books
Published by The Berkley Publishing Group
A member of Penguin Putnam Inc.
200 Madison Avenue
New York, New York 10016

First edition: July 1998

The Penguin Putnam Inc. World Wide Web site address is
http://www.penguinputnam.com

Library of Congress Cataloging-in-Publication Data

Bayone, Jeff.
    It's bridge, baby : how to be a player in ten easy lessons / Jeff
Bayone ; with Amanda Beesley.—1st ed.
        p.   cm.
    ISBN 1-57322-678-5 (pbk.)
    1. Contract bridge.   I. Beesley, Amanda.   II. Title.
GV1282.3.B364   1998
795.41'5—dc21   98-11424
                                                            CIP

Printed in the United States of America

10   9   8   7   6   5   4   3   2   1

CONTENTS

♠CKNOWLEDGMENTS

Tom Ng runs the novice program at the Manhattan Bridge Club, and is the best there is at making the game come alive. Many of the ideas and examples in this book are the direct result of our years of collaboration.

Thanks to Charles Nurse for managing the club for the months I needed to be otherwise occupied, and to my wife, Barbara, for managing the rest of my life for those same months.

Special thanks to the Strauss family—Anita, for giving advice; Doug, for not; and Ariel, simply because she wanted to be mentioned.

I'll certainly miss those knock-down-drag-out sessions with Julie Grau, my editor. Every concept, every statement, every hand, was scrutinized until she was satisfied that they were clear and understandable. She was unrelenting. The book is much the better for it.

I'd like to dedicate this book to Sara (Squeak), my delightful daughter.

INTRODUCTION

Picture this. I am six-feet-four-inches tall. One hundred ninety pounds. I have a moustache. My name is Jeff. And I am your mother.

At least for the purposes of this book I am.

You see, until now, all books about bridge have assumed that you bring to the table a fair amount of knowledge about the game. Even the books that purport to be for beginners assume that you know at least a little something before you open to page one. And to be honest, until recently, most readers did. I should know; I was one of them.

Like many of my generation, I learned bridge at home by watching my mother and her friends as they held tense auctions, battled, laughed their way through hand after hand and tallied up the scores amid the arguments and celebrations of teammates and opponents. But after twenty-one years of teaching, I've begun to notice a change—a revolution, even—in American bridge culture. People are coming to the game with no knowledge or experience whatsoever, attracted simply by the chance to play the smartest, most exciting and social card game ever invented. Too old for Twister and too young for Bingo, a new breed of beginner is showing up at the club, drawn to the game by strong word of mouth. Bridge is starting to seem, well, *trendy*. As most don't have a bridge-playing mother handy to show them the ropes, I have adopted them—as I now offer to adopt you. I am your mother. And I will tell you all about bridge, baby.

In effect, you will learn bridge at your mother's knee, the way the best bridge players all over the world always have: without tedious memorization, mind-boggling charts or baffling jargon. The technique I've developed, over the course of decades teaching bridge, replicates the best of this "bridge by osmosis" method, and is based purely on common sense. If you happen to have that, a deck of cards and a willingness to learn and have fun, then you're ready to begin.

What you are about to experience are the same ten lessons that I use to instruct absolute beginners at the club. Ten lessons that will gently transform you from a blank-slate novice to a bridge player with the ability, and eagerness, to sit down at a table and play the game. You will be competent at all four aspects of bridge—declarer play, defense, bidding and scoring—and, even more important, I guarantee you will enjoy them. All after just ten simple lessons. Does Mother know best, or what?

My own journey to expertise started long after I sat in for Aunt Flo at my mother's weekly game. As I grew, bridge began to seem square and outdated, so I turned to chess, "the game of kings." In college, I joined the chess team. The team practiced in the same room as the bridge team, and I found myself watching them scornfully. Bridge! An old lady's game! One day we were preparing for a chess tournament when we suddenly realized that we were one short of the five players needed to field a team. Gesturing to one of the bridge players, the captain of our team said, "Maybe we can get that guy Ron to fill in."

"Ron? The *bridge* player?" I said. "Are you joking?"

It turned out that Ron the bridge player also happened to be Ron the former New York State Junior Chess Champion. Having discovered bridge the year before, he dropped chess like a hot potato. He found bridge just as challenging, but more engaging, faster paced and more interactive than chess. That's when I decided bridge was worth a second look.

After nearly thirty years of play, I'm still madly in love with the game. (How many men can say the same for their college sweethearts?) I'm also in love with teaching it. Right from the start I try to make the game come alive to my students. Furiously cramming all sorts of rules and regulations gets you further away from a true understanding of the game, not closer. By taking a commonsense approach based on a grasp of how the cards work and what the bids mean, beginners can start playing almost immediately. Before they know it, they are developing a feel for the game that confers on them an expertise that is more valuable than by any rote training sessions. And once they're playing, my job is easy. They respond to the beauty of the game by wanting to know more.

This is why other beginner books have failed to win over new converts and why I was anxious to take up the challenge in a book of my own. If only I could convey the same excitement, the passion for the game that comes through in the classroom—the silent conversations with a loyal partner, the thrill of exploiting an opponent's hidden weakness, of unleashing a secret weapon and hatching brilliant and devious plans. There is a poetry to the game of bridge that is accessible even to beginners.

These ten lessons should be approached with an open mind and, above all, at your own pace. Some of the concepts introduced will be easy, and some will require more concentration. The practice hands that follow most chapters will help clarify the lessons and begin to approximate the rhythm of the game.

If you already know a little something about the game (a closet bridge player?) and are coming to this book for a refresher course, you'll find vigorous exercises and new takes on old ideas.

There's a glossary of terms at the back of the book, a summary of bids (a cheat sheet, if you please) and directions on where to go to further your knowledge of the game once you've mastered the principles of this book. Oh yes, bridge mastery is a long ways away, but I can assure you that every step has its own rewards and every hand you play will bring you closer to bridge enlightenment. So don't ever get discouraged, have fun with the game and remember me on Mother's Day.

♠1 WINNING TRICKS

Let's *begin with your childhood.* **When you** were a kid, did you ever play a card game called war? For those of you who didn't, or if you can't remember that far back, this is how it would go: you'd split a deck of cards in two, put one half facedown in front of you and the other half facedown in front of your buddy. Then you picked the top card from your pile and flipped it over. Your friend would do the same thing. Whoever had the higher card would win. The winner would take the two cards and put them at the bottom of his pile. You didn't know it at the time, but the two cards—one contributed from each player at the table—constituted a trick. There are fifty-two cards in a deck, therefore twenty-six tricks. The game ended when someone won all the tricks.

Like war, bridge is a game of tricks. But unlike war, bridge lets you actually *see* your cards before you play them. That makes a big difference. It's not just plain luck but vision, common sense, logic, and experience that determine which cards get played and in what order.

It takes four players to play the game of bridge. Each trick requires four cards, one from each player.

With fifty-two cards in a deck, that means there are thirteen tricks in the war we call bridge. The object of the game, in its most basic terms, is to win as many tricks as you can. A bridge **hand** ends when all thirteen tricks have been played. Before we go any further, it's not a bad idea for you to get a deck of bridge or regular playing cards. Bridge cards are the same as regular playing cards in every way except they are slightly smaller in size, so that each player can more easily hold thirteen cards in his or her hand at once.

▪ THE LINGO

Lawyers, cooks, cops and musicians all have their own unique language. It should come as no surprise that bridge players do, too. Let's listen to one of them discussing a game played earlier in the day:

"Remember that hand lefty doubled you in four hearts? You held stiff queen, ace king sixth, four baby, king-jack tight. You dropped the doubleton queen of diamonds offside to make an overtrick! Don't you think his partner should have pulled to four spades?"

Yes, we really do talk that way. And soon you will too.

Let's start with a few basic terms. In a standard deck of fifty-two cards, there are four **suits: spades (♠), hearts (♥), diamonds (♦)**, and **clubs (♣)**. Each suit consists of thirteen cards. Let's examine one suit, say diamonds. Spread them out. Notice that some of the cards have diamonds in the center. The two has two diamond **spots** on it, the three has three spots, . . . all the way to the ten, the highest one of these numbered cards, which has ten spots that look like diamonds. Now, whether these spots happen to be shaped like spades, hearts, diamonds, or clubs, do you know what we call them? **Spot cards.** (Did you think this was rocket science?)

Next come three cards with faces on them, the jack (J),

queen (Q), and the king (K), the **face cards**. The ace (A) is
called the ace. It is the most powerful and highest-ranking
card in the suit. In order of strength, strongest to weakest,
we have the ace, the king, the queen, the jack, the ten, the
nine, etc., all the way down to the lowly deuce (2). The ace
beats any other card in the suit, the king beats every other
card but the ace, and so on down to the two, which loses to
every other card in the suit. As the highest cards in the
game, the ace, the face cards, and the ten hold an honored
position in bridge—they are your **honors**.

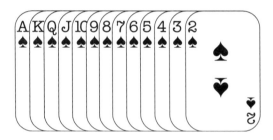

When describing a bridge hand, we always name the
cards from the highest on down to a nine, but we rarely
mention the smaller cards by name. Smaller spot cards are
less important and so are usually mentioned simply as part
of the total number of cards in the suit.

For example, you would describe ♠A 8 3 2 as "ace fourth
of spades," since it features an ace and a total of four spade
cards. Your ♥K J 9 6 4 would be "king jack nine fifth of
hearts." ♦A K 5 would be "ace king third of diamonds."

When you only have one lowly card in a suit, you call it
a **singleton**. For example, ♣7 is "singleton club." If you have
two, they would be a **doubleton**—or, if you want to get
cooler, **two little**, or even **two baby**. Three cards in a suit
would be a **tripleton**, or **three little** or **three baby**. When
you're talking about an honor card that's all alone in its suit

(say, a ♠K without any other spades) you call it **stiff**. When you're describing two honor cards that rank right next to each other with no other honors around them (say, the ♦Q and ♦J), you say they are **tight**.

Now let's put it all together.

Example 1.

HOW THE HAND LOOKS	HOW THE HAND SOUNDS
♠ A 6 5	"ace third of spades"
♥ Q J 7 5 2	"queen jack fifth of hearts"
♦ K Q	"king queen tight of diamonds"
♣ 6 5 4	"tripelton club"

Example 2.

HOW THE HAND LOOKS	HOW THE HAND SOUNDS
K 10 9 7	"king ten nine fourth"
A 6	"ace and one"
K Q J	"king queen jack tight"
10 9 4 2	"ten nine fourth"

Notice that in Example 2 I didn't name each suit as I went through. This is because we always describe the suits in the same order: first spades, then hearts, then diamonds, and finally clubs. (You don't have to memorize this; just know that the cards are in reverse alphabetical order: S, H, D, C, or ♠♥♦♣.)

Here are a couple for you to try:

Q: How would you describe all of the suits in the following
   hand, one by one:
   ♠ K
   ♥ A J 7 4 3 2
   ♦ 8 7 5
   ♣ Q 9 2

A: ♠K   = "stiff king" of spades
   ♥ A J 7 4 3 2   = "ace jack sixth" (six cards
                       altogether) of hearts
   ♦ 8 7 5   = "three baby" (or "three little")
                       of diamonds
   ♣ Q 9 2   = "queen nine third" of clubs

Q: How about this one? Careful, it's tricky.
   ♦ 9 5
   ♥ Q 10 6 4 3
   ♠ A K 7 2
   ♣ K Q

A: ♠ A K 7 2   = "ace king fourth"
   ♥ Q 10 6 4 3   = "queen ten fifth"
   ♦ 9 5   = "nine and one" (or "nine
                       doubleton")
   ♣ K Q   = "king queen tight"

Did you remember to put the suits in the right order before
saying them?

   Don't worry about trying to memorize these terms. Just
use them whenever you can, and they will soon become second nature.
   Now you're ready for your first bridge joke. Four bridge
players are on safari. One day the leader of the group steps
into quicksand. As his friends approach, he's already in it
up to his neck. He yells out, "Quick, give me a hand!" "Okay,"

one of them says. "You're looking at ace king fourth, jack third . . ."

▪ SETTING UP

Bridge is played by four people sitting around a table. The person opposite you is your partner. You work together as a team. The players to your left and right are your opponents. They also work as a team. At the bridge table you always have two opponents, one friend.

In order to discuss the various players at the table let's give them names. We'll base them on where they're sitting. Assigning each seat a direction, we refer to one team as **North–South** and the other as **East–West**.

Bridge is played in a clockwise direction, so, for example, if we start with North, the order of play will be North, East, South, and then West.

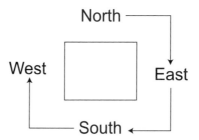

From South's vantage, North is his partner. West is his **left-hand opponent (LHO)**; East is his **right-hand opponent (RHO)**.

So let's begin. First our players will decide on partnerships, and then one of them will deal.

▪ PICKING PARTNERS

There are two ways to decide who plays with whom in a bridge game:

Formal method: Each person picks a card out of the deck. The person with the highest card sits wherever he or she wants, the next highest card becomes that first person's partner, and the other two players become the opposing pair.

Informal method: Everyone sits wherever they want. Whoever sits across from you at the table is your partner.

▪ DEALING THE CARDS

Who deals first?

Formal method: The person who drew the highest card deals first.

Informal method: Whoever wants to deal gets to deal.

The dealer shuffles the cards and deals one card at a time around the table in a clockwise direction starting with the person immediately to the dealer's left, until all fifty-two cards are distributed. This will produce four **hands** of thirteen cards each.

Now each player picks up his cards and arranges them into suits.

▪ THE PLAY

Whenever you see a description of a bridge game in the newspaper or a book, you get to see all four hands at once. There are no secrets. But when you're playing a real game of bridge, three hands are hidden and only one is visible to all players. This open hand is called the **dummy** and it goes on the table for everyone to see. The person who sits behind the dummy hand is not involved in the play (I'll explain how the dummy is determined in chapter 4). The person across from the dummy plays both his own cards and those of the dummy for the partnership. This person is called the **declarer.** The two opponents of the dummy and the declarer are the **defenders.** The three players look at their hands and the hand on the table and attempt to **visualize** what cards the other players are holding and how and when to play the cards in their own hands. In essence they become detectives.

This is how a complete deal might be displayed in your local newspaper's bridge column:

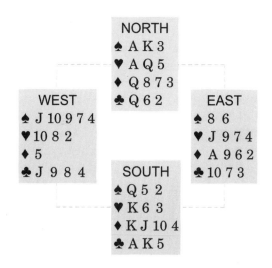

```
               NORTH
               ♠ A K 3
               ♥ A Q 5
               ♦ Q 8 7 3
               ♣ Q 6 2
   WEST                        EAST
   ♠ J 10 9 7 4                ♠ 8 6
   ♥ 10 8 2                    ♥ J 9 7 4
   ♦ 5                         ♦ A 9 6 2
   ♣ J 9 8 4      SOUTH        ♣ 10 7 3
               ♠ Q 5 2
               ♥ K 6 3
               ♦ K J 10 4
               ♣ A K 5
```

For consistency, North is almost always the dummy. The declarer is therefore South. East and West are the defenders. **The person to the left of the declarer always makes the opening lead.**

The order of the suits is important. They are displayed the same way we say them. Spades first (on top), followed by hearts, then diamonds, then clubs. All four hands are always displayed in the same fashion, although later in the book you may see the cards set up this way:

> ♠ ♥ ♦ ♣
> A A 3 Q
> J 10 2 7
> 9 9
> 8 3
> 4

You'd read this hand up and down rather than right to left, but it's basically the same principle.

When you look in the paper, it's up to you to imagine a real game of bridge where only the North hand, the dummy, would be visible to everyone. Each player at the table would see his thirteen cards and the dummy's thirteen cards—only twenty-six of the fifty-two total cards.

Fifty-two cards are a lot to contend with, I know. Where do you begin? What are you supposed to do? What should you be thinking about?

Hyperventilating yet?

Allow me to simplify the learning process. I'll ease you in rather than throw you in. Instead of starting with fifty-two cards, thirteen to each hand, we'll start with four cards, just one to a hand. Instead of twenty-six hidden cards, we'll put everything on the table.

Feeling better?

Okay, students, let us now go to Bridge Detective School, where you'll learn a few "tricks" of the trade.

THREE BASIC WAYS OF WINNING TRICKS

▪ I. HIGH CARDS TAKE TRICKS

From your deck of cards take out the 4, 6, 7 and 9 of diamonds. Give yourself (South) the 9. Give North the 4, East the 6, and West the 7, like so:

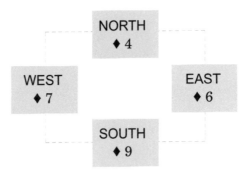

West, your opponent, happens to be the first person to play a card. We say West is **on lead.** West plays his 7, which means he puts it faceup in the middle of the table. Going in a clockwise direction, the person who plays next would be North. She follows with her 4. So far, West is winning the trick. He has the higher card. East now contributes the 6, no change. But now you gleefully produce the 9, the highest card played to the trick. You, South, **take** or win the trick.

Look at the cards again. Couldn't you have guessed right away that South would win the trick, simply because she happened to hold the highest card? But it isn't just South who wins. North wins as well, because North and South are partners.

Got the idea?

Following Suit

What if more than one suit is involved in a trick? Let's look carefully at an example in which the highest card on the table *doesn't* win a trick:

Exchange your ♦9 with the ♥9:

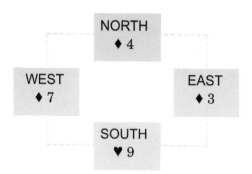

NORTH
♦ 4

WEST
♦ 7

EAST
♦ 3

SOUTH
♥ 9

Q: Say West is on lead. Do you think East–West will win a trick?

A: West leads the seven, North plays the four, and East plays the three. So far West is winning. But then South plays her nine, thinking that she is going to win the trick: after all, she holds the highest card at the table, right?

Wrong. Even though the nine is a higher card than West's 7, it cannot win the trick. Why? **Because the suit that's led is the only suit that can win the trick.** That ♥9 is not stronger than West's ♦7; in fact, it's irrelevant in this battle, which was announced with West's opening card to be a battle of diamonds. If you cannot follow suit and you are forced to play a card of another suit, we say that this card gets **discarded.**

This brings us to our first Basic Rule of Bridge: **The highest card of the suit that was led will win the**

trick. If you can follow suit, you must follow suit. If you cannot, you choose a card of any other suit to discard.

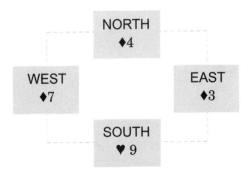

Q: Working with the same cards, who would win the trick if South were on lead?

A: South would. No other player has a card higher than the card that South led. No one else has a card in that suit. In fact, if South's ♥9 were the meager ♥2, it would still win the trick, beating out all the other cards.

■ CHOOSING A CARD TO LEAD

Now we'll make things a little more challenging by adding a few more cards. Lay out the ♠ A K Q J 10 9 3 2 on the table like this:

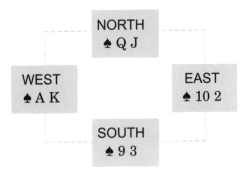

Let's say that North is on lead with the Q J tight of spades. How does she choose which card to play first?

When two cards are right next to each other like this, or in **sequence,** they should always be considered to be of equal strength. Here's why: as far as North is concerned, what are the only cards out on the table that can beat her ♠Q? The ♠A and the ♠K. And what are the only cards that can beat her ♠J? Again, the ♠A and the ♠K. In the playing of the hand, there is no difference between the queen and the jack.

When you're on lead, however, and hold two cards in sequence like this, you should **lead the higher** of the two cards (we'll learn why later). Therefore, North will lead her Q. East's cards are both lower than the Q, but he still has a choice. Should he play the 10 or the 2? Since he knows that neither of his cards will take the trick, he plays the 2; after all, he will want to save the more powerful 10 for a subsequent trick where it may have a chance of winning. South plays the 3, and West will play his A or K to win the trick (since West is not on lead, he is not restricted to playing the higher of these two sequential cards but can play either one because they both outrank the Q). West collects the cards and places them facedown in front of him.

The cards now look like this:

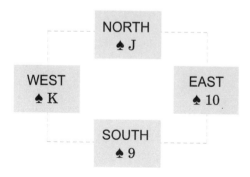

Basic Rule Number Two: **Whoever wins the trick gets to lead to the next trick.**

West won the last trick and now leads the K, the new highest card, which wins the second trick. We call the highest card left in a suit the **master card.** Until the ace gets played, it is always the master card for nothing can beat it. And once it gets played the next highest card, in this case the K, gets **promoted** to the new master card.

Now, let's switch the 2 and the K from the previous example.

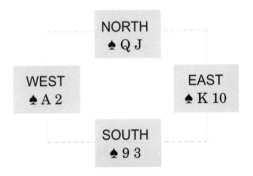

NORTH
♠ Q J

WEST
♠ A 2

EAST
♠ K 10

SOUTH
♠ 9 3

Q: If North leads her Q, can East–West win two tricks?

A: Use your common sense here. East–West are a team. In the previous example West had the A K, and East had the 10 2. The cards may be switched around, but East–West still holds the two highest cards. (Remember, for this example everyone can see all the cards.) So when North leads her Q, East has a choice. If he chooses to play, or **commit**, his K, then what will West do when his turn comes? He will see that his partner's K is higher than either of the opponents' cards. East's K has already won this trick for the partnership, so West will play his deuce and save his A for the following trick.

So the answer to the question is yes. If everyone plays as well as they can, East–West will win both tricks.

Let's look at one more example of how high cards win tricks. Lay out eight cards like this:

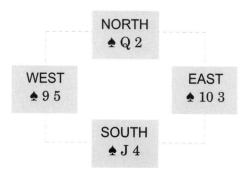

Q: With North on lead, can North–South win both tricks?

A: The ace and king are gone, so the queen is the new master card, and it must win. It can't be helped: the master card will take the trick. So if North will lead her queen, South will save his jack and play the 4, and North's queen will win the first trick.

The cards now look like this:

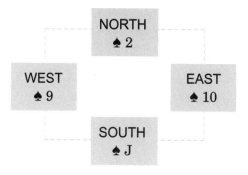

North is on lead again, since her queen took the first trick. When the cards are played, South's jack, the new master card, will take the second trick.

If you managed to figure this out without touching the cards, good for you. You have just exercised your growing powers of visualization. If you needed to play the cards to answer the question, that's fine too. But try laying the cards out again, and this time do all the work in your head rather than by moving the cards around.

The process of visualization is crucial. In bridge, as in most games, once you make your move, you've made your move. If you're unhappy with the outcome, you cannot take it back and try another card. "Look" (visualize) before you leap (play)" is a good bridge adage.

Try another visualization game:

Q: West is on lead and plays the ace. Who wins the first trick? How about the second trick?

A: The ace, being the master card, wins the first trick, no problem. Now the cards look like this:

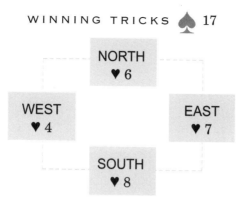

The new master card, South's 8, will take the second trick.

Memory, believe it or not, plays only a minor role in bridge. In the previous example, the trick is not to memorize the ♥A ♥4 ♥6 ♥3 ♥7 ♥2 ♥8 ♥5 as random cards. Try remembering the *story* of the two tricks. The ace of hearts took the first trick; the new master card, the lowly ♥8, took the second. See how much easier that is?

Let's look at another example with more than one suit involved:

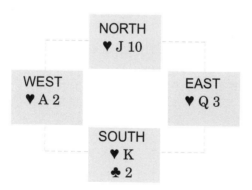

Q: If West leads his ace, how many tricks will East–West win? Visualize the outcome.

A: Two tricks. In the first trick, West plays the ace, North plays the 10, East plays the 3, and South, as much as she doesn't want to, plays her king. She hates to play her king, because she knows that West's ace, the master card, will beat it. But she has no choice, because *she must follow suit.*

This is what the cards look like at the beginning of the second trick:

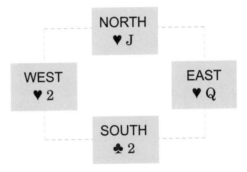

NORTH
♥ J

WEST
♥ 2

EAST
♥ Q

SOUTH
♣ 2

The new master card is East's queen. West, having won the first trick, is on lead. Can you see that East will win this second trick with that new master card, that queen?

This time I'm going to throw three different suits into the puzzle:

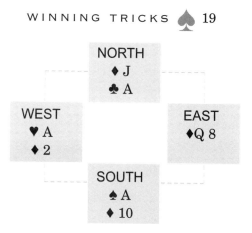

Q: If East is on lead and plays the ♦Q, who wins the first trick? How about the second trick? (Remember, if you *can* follow suit, you *must* follow suit.)

A: East wins the first trick with the ♦Q, and since East will still be on lead he will win the second trick with the ♦8. In this case, even though North, South and West are all holding aces, they are unable to follow suit. East's ♦8 beats out all those aces!

■ STOPPERS

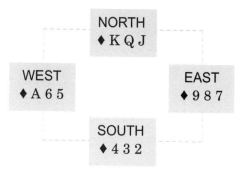

Say North leads with the ♦K. How many tricks do you think North–South can win? What is North's objective in leading the king?

If North leads with the ♦K and West plays the ace, North–South will lose the first trick to the master card. We call the ace a **stopper,** a card that is standing in the way of an opponent's trick-taking ability. By playing the king, North has forced West to relinquish his ace. Once the ace is out of the way, North's queen and jack become promoted to master cards.

Here are two new bridge terms to add to your vocabulary:

A **quick trick** is a card that can win a trick immediately. In the example above, West's ace is a quick trick, because it can win the first trick without a problem.

Potential is the ability to *develop* tricks in a suit. Potential does not mean instant victories, but rather promoting cards of lesser rank to master-card strength. In the above example, North–South have no quick tricks, but they do have two tricks in potential (two **slow tricks**). Before the queen and the jack become real tricks, though, North must knock out West's stopper, the ace. East–West, on the other hand, have one quick trick in the suit but no slow winners, no potential, no ability to win any subsequent tricks in the suit.

So then, describing the players' holdings in the above example, we would say that East–West has one quick trick and no potential, whereas North–South has no quick tricks and two potential tricks.

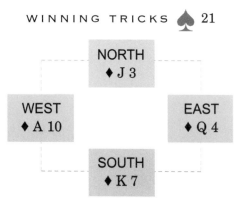

NORTH
♦ J 3

WEST
♦ A 10

EAST
♦ Q 4

SOUTH
♦ K 7

Q: With West on lead, how many tricks can E–W win?

A: West has a choice of leads. West has the master card, the ace. South has the next highest card, the king. After West's ace is gone, South's king will be promoted to the new master card. So whether West leads the ace or the ten, West will win one trick and South will win the other.

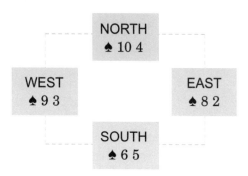

NORTH
♠ 10 4

WEST
♠ 9 3

EAST
♠ 8 2

SOUTH
♠ 6 5

Q: With North on lead, how many tricks can N–S win?

A: This is the same as the previous exercise, except with spot cards. N–S wins with the master card—the ♠10. E–W wins one with the ♠9, the card that becomes promoted to the master card after the ♠10 is played.

NORTH
♣ A Q 3

WEST
♣ J 9 4

EAST
♣ 7 6 5

SOUTH
♣ K 10 8

Q: North is on lead. How many tricks can N–S win?

A: Three. In this example, the three highest cards are held by N–S. If we switched South's king and North's 3, you would immediately see that North would win all three tricks:

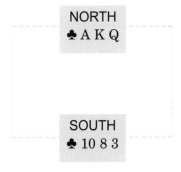

NORTH
♣ A K Q

SOUTH
♣ 10 8 3

North and South work as a partnership. An experienced player sees the North–South combination of cards as a group. This is another example of visualization. As combinations of cards get more difficult, you will increasingly need to fall back on the technique of seeing how the cards work before you play them.

■ TRANSPORTATION

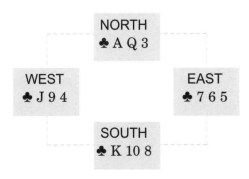

NORTH
♣ A Q 3

WEST
♣ J 9 4

EAST
♣ 7 6 5

SOUTH
♣ K 10 8

Lay out these cards faceup on the table. As an exercise, play the three North cards in random order and see how this affects the play of the South cards. If we start with North's ♣3, the trick might go like this:

Trick 1.	N–♣3	E–♣5	S–♣K	W–♣4
Trick 2.	S–♣8	W–♣9	N–♣A	E–♣6
Trick 3.	N–♣Q	E–♣7	S–♣10	W–♣J

See how the lead **travels** to South on the first trick, with South winning the first trick and taking the lead away from North? Then the lead travels back to North, with North taking the second trick with the ♣A. It is as if there is an invisible **bridge** between the two hands that allows the lead to shuttle back and forth between the two partners. The ability to move back and forth between two hands is so central to the game that the word "bridge" may owe its name to this concept.

Q: East is on lead. How many tricks can E–W make?

A: You know that East will win the first two tricks, since East is holding the A K. The important trick is therefore the third trick. Visualize how the cards will look on the third trick and you will have your answer:

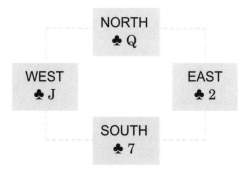

East will still be on lead. North wins trick three. So the answer is that E–W can win two tricks.

NORTH
♣ J 2

WEST
♦ 10 3

EAST
♥ Q
♣ 10

SOUTH
♥ J
♣ 5

Q: With South on lead, can N–S win two tricks?

A: Only if he leads the ♣5. If he leads the ♥J, even though it's his higher card, East will win with the ♥Q. Visualize what happens if South leads the ♣5. West cannot follow suit, so he discards the ♦3. North, seeing East's ♣10, goes up with his ♣J to win this trick. East must now follow suit with the ♣10. North's ♣2 is the only remaining club, and since he is on lead, the ♣2 wins the second trick.

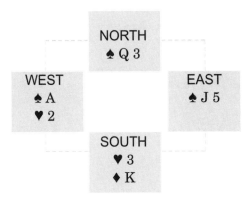

NORTH
♠ Q 3

WEST
♠ A
♥ 2

EAST
♠ J 5

SOUTH
♥ 3
♦ K

Q: West leads the ♠A. What card should South discard?

A: The ♦K! Even though it beats the tar out of the lowly
♥3, what card will West be leading at trick two? That's
right, the ♥2. To beat the ♥2, you need any heart higher
than the ♥2. So you save the ♥3.

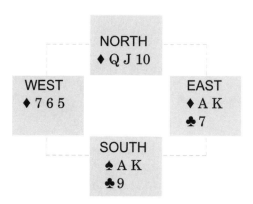

NORTH
♦ Q J 10

WEST
♦ 7 6 5

EAST
♦ A K
♣ 7

SOUTH
♠ A K
♣ 9

Q: West leads the ♦7. What card should South save?

A: The ♣9. Visualize the third trick. After East's ♦A and ♦K
have won the first two tricks, East will still be on lead
with only the ♣7 left. Save the ♣9 to beat the ♣7.

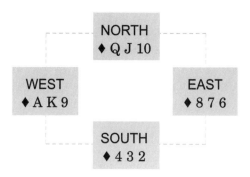

NORTH
♦ Q J 10

WEST
♦ A K 9

EAST
♦ 8 7 6

SOUTH
♦ 4 3 2

Q: Which pair has more *potential* in this suit, N–S or E–W?

A: North–South. While it is true that E–W have the two
master cards and can win two quick tricks, their lesser

cards offer no hope of winning a third trick. N–S, on the other hand, have no quick winners, but they do own the next three highest cards and therefore have the ability to win a slow trick, the third trick in the suit. Slow winners (those that become promoted to master cards) are another way of looking at what it is to have potential.

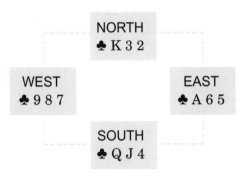

Q: How many tricks do N–S have in potential?

A: Two. After East's ace is played, N–S have the two highest cards.

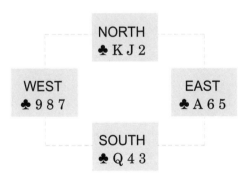

The North and South cards are slightly different in this setup, but N–S still has two tricks in potential.

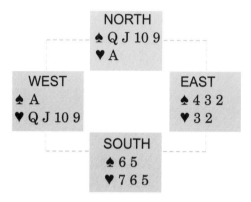

Q: How many tricks can E–W win with West on lead? (Do this one in your head.)

A: West should lead the ♥Q (top of a sequence), knocking out North's ♥A stopper and promoting his ♥J, ♥10 and ♥9 to winners.

When North tries to promote spade winners for himself, he must lose the lead to West's ♠A stopper. West then takes his three heart winners. West wins one spade and three hearts.

If West first led the ♠A instead, then switched to hearts, he would find that his side would only win one trick. By spending his quick trick too soon, West (a) promoted all of North's spades to winners immediately and (b) deprived himself of an entry to his hearts once they were promoted to winners.

Therefore it makes sense to go after your side's potential first. Your stoppers are needed to stop the opponents from playing and winning (**cashing**) their slow-trick winners and to provide entries to your hand once you've set up (**established**) slow-trick winners for yourself.

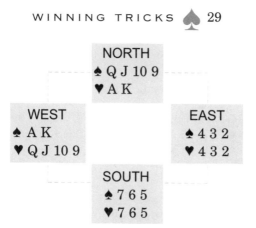

NORTH
♠ Q J 10 9
♥ A K

WEST
♠ A K
♥ Q J 10 9

EAST
♠ 4 3 2
♥ 4 3 2

SOUTH
♠ 7 6 5
♥ 7 6 5

Q: West is on lead. How many tricks can E–W win?

A: Four. Again West must lead with her potential, which is in hearts. Trick one: the ♥Q lures out one of North's stoppers (say the ♥K). Trick two: North now switches to the suit that offers his side the most potential, which is spades. His ♠Q knocks out one of West's stoppers (say the ♠K). Trick three: West now shifts back to hearts, flushing out her opponent's last stopper. Trick four: The opponents lead a spade, and West regains the lead with the ♠A. In tricks five and six she plays and wins with her two promoted (established) hearts. West makes two spade tricks and two heart tricks.

Back up and visualize what would happen if West first led one of her two spade stoppers. It would then be too late to switch to hearts and hope to establish tricks in that suit. Say West leads with the ♠A, winning the first trick, then switches to the ♥Q. North wins with the ♥K, plays back a spade and uses up West's last stopper. West continues hearts, but North immediately wins with his ♥A stopper and then cashes his two spade winners. West wins only two spade tricks.

Where did she go wrong? She played one of her stoppers too soon, so she was beaten to the punch. North was able to establish his potential winners before West was able to establish hers. In bridge terms, by cashing a winner too soon, West **lost a tempo** (the vernacular is "she got tempoed out"), and it cost her dearly.

▪ II. LENGTH TAKES TRICKS

Now that you've begun to learn how high cards take tricks, I'd like to introduce you to a second powerful way of taking tricks in bridge: **length**.

Let's take a look at how length in a suit can take tricks:

Example 1.

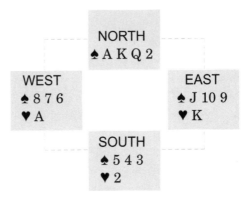

NORTH
♠ A K Q 2

WEST
♠ 8 7 6
♥ A

EAST
♠ J 10 9
♥ K

SOUTH
♠ 5 4 3
♥ 2

Q: With North on lead, how many tricks can N–S win?

Here we are presented with a complete suit (spades) of thirteen cards. Thirteen is a prime number and cannot be divided evenly; 4-3-3-3 is about as evenly as we can divide thirteen four ways. In the above example, let's give North four spades. Everyone else has three spades and one other card, in this case a heart.

Try to visualize what happens when North plays the ♠A, then the ♠K, then the ♠Q, and finally, on the fourth trick, the ♠2.

Trick one: North plays the ♠A and wins the trick.

Trick two: The new master card is the ♠K. North is on lead since she won the last trick. She plays the ♠K. Again everyone follows.

Trick three: North now cashes the ♠Q. Everyone follows. What is now left in everyone's hand? Visualize . . .

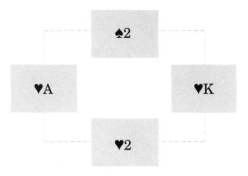

Trick four: North plays her last card, the ♠2. Everyone else has run out of spades. North's ♠2 therefore wins the last trick as everyone else is forced to discard.

See how North's spade length—four cards in a suit—won all those tricks? Nobody could stop her. She plowed through her spades, depleting her opponents until her lowly deuce remained as the most powerful card at the table. Length makes Goliaths of Davids and winners of low-ranking cards.

Taking tricks with length is not always quite this straightforward. Many times the suits don't prove to be cooperative. Here is a particularly nasty example:

Example 2.

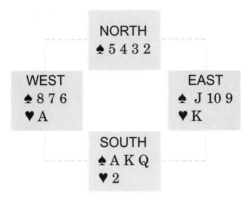

NORTH
♠ 5 4 3 2

WEST
♠ 8 7 6
♥ A

EAST
♠ J 10 9
♥ K

SOUTH
♠ A K Q
♥ 2

The honors in the South hand are alone, stripped of any spot cards. (Remember we call these honors **tight**).

Q: With either North or South on lead, how many tricks can N–S take?

A: Only three. South will take the first three tricks with her powerful spade suit. Can they win another? Visualize the fourth trick. The key is who has the lead. Since she won the last trick, South has the lead. North's ♠5 is a winner, as it's the lone remaining spade, but it is in the wrong hand. We can't get there from here. We say North's hand is **entryless.**

When a suit is divided so that we cannot enjoy the fruits of its length, we say that suit is **blocked**. In this example, the spade suit was **naturally blocked,** that is, we played no part in it, the cards were simply dealt that way. Here, N–S were naturally blocked from reaching their fourth spade trick.

We must take pains not to block a suit ourselves.

Example 3.

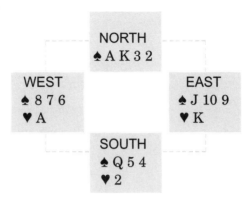

NORTH
♠ A K 3 2

WEST
♠ 8 7 6
♥ A

EAST
♠ J 10 9
♥ K

SOUTH
♠ Q 5 4
♥ 2

Q: Starting in the North hand, how would you play this combination of cards to get the most out of your four-card spade suit?

A: Visualize what happens if North plays the ♠A first and then the ♠K. Which cards remain? Is this what you visualized?

Example 3A.

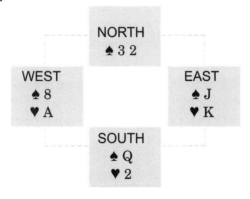

NORTH
♠ 3 2

WEST
♠ 8
♥ A

EAST
♠ J
♥ K

SOUTH
♠ Q
♥ 2

The lead is still in the North hand. But it wouldn't matter which hand you were in. You've already blocked the suit. At trick three North will play the ♠2 over to South's ♠Q, stranding the good ♠3 in the North hand. You will be stuck in the South hand and will have abandoned your winning long spade.

Had the name of the game been abandonment, you would be playing just fine. But the game is called *bridge*. A good player learns to keep an imaginary bridge open between his hand and his partner's. Keeping the lines of communication open between partners is one of the central concerns on any hand.

Try Example 3 again. With North on lead, this time try cashing just one of the honors, say the ♠A. At trick two, instead of cashing another honor, play a low spade from the North hand and, using the ♠Q, **bridge across** to the South hand. Then, at trick three bridge back to the North hand. This way North–South win four tricks in a row. Note the opponents never have a chance to cash their quick tricks because they never got a chance to lead. In this example you can also accomplish the same thing by *not* cashing either the ♠A or ♠K immediately. At trick one simply lead a low spade toward the ♠Q in the South hand. Then bridge back to North at trick two.

In Example 3A you remained stuck in the South hand after your ♠Q won the third trick. Your ♥2 lost the fourth trick. You won three tricks.

In the second example you used your carefully preserved little ♠5 as a reentry to North's hand. This spot card allowed you to bridge back to North's ♠K and once there you were in the correct hand at trick four to make good use of your long spade. You won four tricks.

You are learning to keep the lines of communication open between you and your partner. Notice how you *transport* yourself between hands with the help of a little visualization.

Example 4.

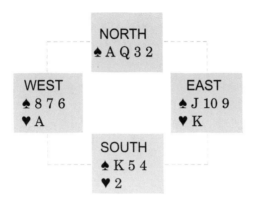

NORTH
♠ A Q 3 2

WEST
♠ 8 7 6
♥ A

EAST
♠ J 10 9
♥ K

SOUTH
♠ K 5 4
♥ 2

Q: North or South is on lead. If played correctly, which card will win the last trick?

A: North's ♠2 or ♠3.

Q: In order for the ♠2 or ♠3 to win the last trick what card must have won the next to last trick?

A: North's ace or queen of spades. In order to win the fourth trick with North's ♠2 or ♠3 we must plan to be leading from the North hand at the start of that trick. To be in the North hand, North must win at trick three. It takes the ace or the queen to do that. As with Example 3 the order in which you play the first two tricks can vary: (a) You might have started by first cashing North's ♠Q. At trick two, you'd play a small spade over to South's king. The third trick would have you bridging back to North with the ♠A, in order to be in the correct hand at trick four to enjoy the long spade. Or (b) You might have started by first bridging over to South's ♠K and then jumping back across to North's ♠Q. This time you would wind up in the North hand a trick early, but it comes to the same thing.

Here's another way of putting it: **When playing suits with different lengths, always save an honor card, an entry, in the longer hand for as long as possible.**

▪ EXERCISES

1.

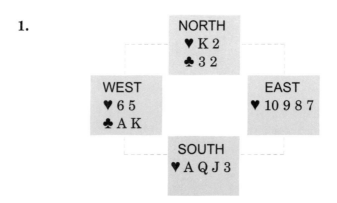

NORTH
♥ K 2
♣ 3 2

WEST
♥ 6 5
♣ A K

EAST
♥ 10 9 8 7

SOUTH
♥ A Q J 3

Q: You are South and you're on lead. Can you make four tricks? (Hint: be careful not to block your suit.)

A: Yes. Unblock your honor from the short hand first. You do this by playing your spot card (♥3) to North's ♥K. Then use North's ♥2 to bridge back to your hand.

If you played your ace, queen or jack first, then bridged over to North's ♥K, how were you planning on getting back to South's high (winning) hearts? You would have abandoned them, and you would make two tricks rather than the four you are entitled to.

2.

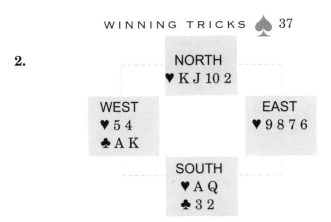

NORTH
♥ K J 10 2

WEST
♥ 5 4
♣ A K

EAST
♥ 9 8 7 6

SOUTH
♥ A Q
♣ 3 2

Q: Again, you are South. Can you make four tricks?

A: Yes. Notice North and East both have four heart cards. Three of North's cards are higher ranking than any of East's. Only North's ♥2 would lose to any of East's hearts. South's ace covers North's only losers. Your ♥Q will provide the transportation between the two hands. At trick one unblock your ♥A, carefully playing North's losing ♥2 under it. Play your ♥Q next, **overtaking** it with North's king. Now that you are in the North hand, your ♥J and ♥10 can win the remaining two tricks.

It may feel funny to play an honor from one hand and overtake it with an honor from your partner's hand, but in this case it's the only way that access can be provided between the two hands.

3.

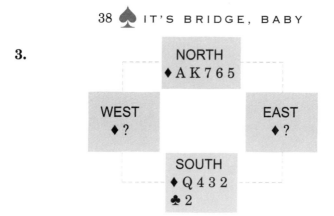

NORTH
♦ A K 7 6 5

WEST
♦ ?

EAST
♦ ?

SOUTH
♦ Q 4 3 2
♣ 2

Q: You are North. How must West's and East's diamonds be divided in order for you and your partner *not* to make five diamond tricks?

A: Between you and your partner you have nine diamonds. That leaves the opponents with four. Unless one of your opponents has all four of the remaining diamonds, ♦J 10 9 8, you will make all five diamond tricks.

Lay out the cards and try it for yourself:

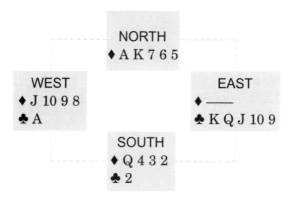

NORTH
♦ A K 7 6 5

WEST
♦ J 10 9 8
♣ A

EAST
♦ ——
♣ K Q J 10 9

SOUTH
♦ Q 4 3 2
♣ 2

In this scenario, West has all of the remaining diamonds. Once North–South cash the ♦A, K,Q, West can step in, win the next diamond trick, and cash his good club.

What if the cards were more evenly distributed, say like this:

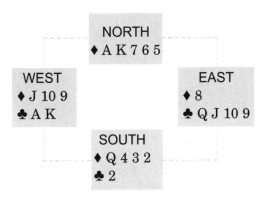

NORTH
♦ A K 7 6 5

WEST
♦ J 10 9
♣ A K

EAST
♦ 8
♣ Q J 10 9

SOUTH
♦ Q 4 3 2
♣ 2

After playing three rounds (three tricks) North–South's ♦A, K, Q will wipe out all of East–West's diamonds. They will then be in position to win two more diamond tricks with their five-card suit.

4.

Q: Which of these diamond suits do you think has the distribution with the most potential?

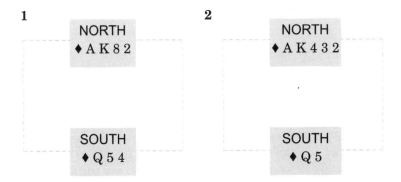

1

NORTH
♦ A K 8 2

SOUTH
♦ Q 5 4

2

NORTH
♦ A K 4 3 2

SOUTH
♦ Q 5

A: Number two. Both suits contain seven cards. Both have the top three honors. But number one has only four cards in its long suit. Even if the opponents' diamonds divide evenly (three each), that would leave you with only one extra trick (the fourth diamond).

If the opponents' six diamonds were divided evenly for number two as they are in the diagram below, North–South would be able to make two extra tricks (the fourth and fifth diamond).

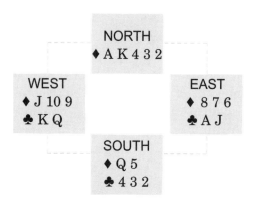

NORTH
♦ A K 4 3 2

WEST
♦ J 10 9
♣ K Q

EAST
♦ 8 7 6
♣ A J

SOUTH
♦ Q 5
♣ 4 3 2

If you are North, you will have to be careful to unblock the ♦Q in the short hand (South) by leading a low diamond at trick one. Playing the ace first, then a diamond, locks you in the short hand at trick two, and you'll be forced to let the opponents win two tricks with their high clubs.

5.

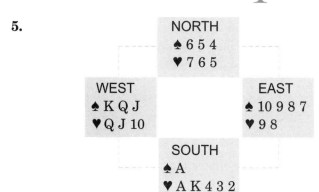

NORTH
♠ 6 5 4
♥ 7 6 5

WEST
♠ K Q J
♥ Q J 10

EAST
♠ 10 9 8 7
♥ 9 8

SOUTH
♠ A
♥ A K 4 3 2

Q: You are South and you're on lead. How many tricks at most can North–South win?

A: Five. First assess the N–S potential in spades. There is none. You do, however, have one quick trick there, the ♠A. How about hearts? There are two quick tricks in hearts (the ace and the king), plus South has length (potential). Between North and South, you have eight hearts. This is how you plan to make use of them.

First you start with hearts, the suit that offers your side potential. You start by cashing the ace and king, then letting West win a heart trick. Why? Well, West started with the ♥Q J 10. He must make a heart trick. You let West have his due, but in so doing, you give up the lead.

Now, I know what you're thinking. You won't want to give up the lead, you don't want to give up *control*. You want to win all your tricks right away. But are you really giving up control? What can West do with his precious lead? With only spades left in his hand he's got to come back to you— after all, you have the ace of spades. What if you had cashed that ♠A stopper before you embarked on trying to set up **(establish)** long-suit heart tricks for your side? When West won his heart trick, you really would have given up control. With no spade stopper, West could not be prevented from cashing every one of his spade tricks. Your side would take a grand total of three tricks—two hearts and one spade. But you foresaw that. You carefully preserved that ♠A for just this purpose. Once you have regained the lead, go ahead and cash the two long-suit heart tricks that you worked so hard to establish. Your trick total is no longer three, but five . . . one spade and four hearts. Sometimes you have to give a little to get a lot in return.

Remember the story of the tortoise and the hare? It's the same story in bridge: it's not who wins the most tricks right away; it's who wins the most tricks by the very end of the game.

▪ HANDS ON: PLAYING BRIDGE

The most exciting part of the game now awaits you. It's time for you to play your first bridge hand. You will be the declarer. You will be able to see twenty-six cards: your own hand of thirteen and the dummy's thirteen. The opponents' cards will be hidden from your view. Unlike the opponents, who work together, you alone will be doing the thinking for your partnership. Your partner says and does nothing to influence your play. He's the dummy. Your play is guided first by rules and logic, but ultimately by the bounds of your imagination.

▪ A NOTE ON THE MECHANICS

Once the very first card is played, the dummy is placed faceup or **faced,** on the table. This is how a bridge hand looks when it's placed on the table.

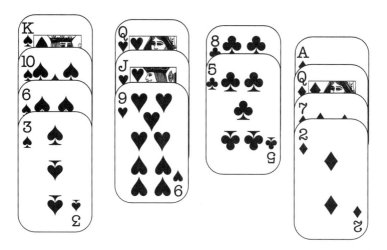

The cards are arranged by suit in four columns, and the columns alternate black-red-black-red in order to make it easier to distinguish between like-colored suits. The highest card in each suit is laid down first, then all the rest of the cards in descending order.

In a home game of Bridge, each player would play his card by placing it in the center of the table. Whoever won the trick would grab the four cards, place them facedown in front of him and begin the next trick. (Usually one defender keeps all the tricks for her side, and the declarer keeps all the tricks for his side.) For learning purposes, there is a better way of playing the cards, a method that allows you to backtrack and see what happened after a hand was played. Instead of placing the played cards in the middle of the table, each player faces the card he intends to play to a particular trick and places it right in front of him near the edge of the table. When the trick is over, the side that won the trick would place their card facedown vertically in front of them; the side that lost the trick would place their card facedown horizontally in front of them. In this way, you and your partner should have precisely the same pattern of used cards in front of you, and you will easily be able to keep track of how many tricks

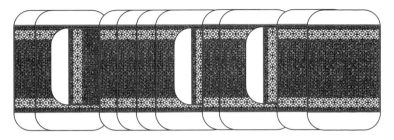

you've won and lost. Even in a social, nonlesson format, most players now prefer this method as it greatly reduces the number of problems that can arise.

At the end of the hand the tricks will be laid out something like this:

Using this method, the players can pick up their cards at the end of a hand and replay it in its entirety if they want to.

Practice Hand 1

You need twelve tricks.

You, South, are the declarer, which puts West on lead.

The ♠J is led:

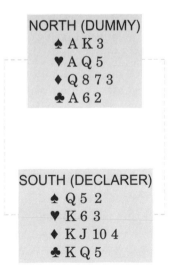

NORTH (DUMMY)
♠ A K 3
♥ A Q 5
♦ Q 8 7 3
♣ A 6 2

SOUTH (DECLARER)
♠ Q 5 2
♥ K 6 3
♦ K J 10 4
♣ K Q 5

West leads the ♠J. The dummy comes down. (The dummy comes down only after the first card is led.) Your job is to take twelve of the thirteen tricks. The stakes are high: if the defenders take more than one trick they will defeat you. How do you start? One way to look at it is that you must win twelve tricks. The other way to look at it is that you can lose only one trick. With four suits, you have four different places where you can win or lose tricks. You must look at each suit separately and then view the hand as a whole.

Where do we start? Bridge is tricks. Start there. First, count how many quick tricks you have. If you have twelve tricks off the top (quick tricks), there is no problem. All you would need to do then is cash them. But things usually aren't so straightforward. Let's count our winners. We'll start at the top, with our spade holdings.

DUMMY   DECLARER
♠ A K 3   ♠ Q 5 2

Here you have three top winners, the ♠AKQ. You are going to make three tricks, no more and no less. There is no potential, no possibility of a fourth trick in this suit. But what about the opponents? They have seven cards in the suit. (There are thirteen cards in each suit and you have six of them. 13 − 6 = 7) Here they have some length potential. One of them must have at least four spades. If you went ahead and played your A K Q, you would make three tricks, but you would be setting up (establishing) a long-suit trick for the opponents. Your A K Q are quick tricks; you can take them whenever you want. Quick tricks in suits that have no potential are referrered to as "stoppers"—they stop the opponent's potential from being realized. A suit that has potential only for the opponents is their suit.

The heart and clubs suits on this hand are basically carbon copies of the spade suit; the honor cards are just spread out (configured) differently. In each of these suits you have three tricks and no potential. In these three suits you already have the ability to win nine of the twelve tricks you need. Where are you going to get the remaining three tricks? They'd better come from the diamonds. Let's take a look at your diamond holdings:

DUMMY	DECLARER
♦ Q 8 7 3	♦ K J 10 4

In this suit you do not have the master card. In order to start taking tricks with your high honors, you must knock out the opponents' ♦A. You can't take that trick, but you can get it out of the way. Between the dummy and the declarer you have the next four highest cards. Any one of them can be used to force out the opponents' ♦A, leaving you with three promoted tricks. These three tricks are called **slow winners**, since they take a little time to set up. If you add these three slow tricks to our nine quick tricks, that gives you twelve tricks.

Now that you've gone over each suit separately, you can view the hand in its entirety and try to come up with a plan that will allow you to take these twelve tricks. So what is the plan? **Go after your potential first**. Before cashing your nine quick tricks, which aren't going anywhere, you must plan on building those extra three tricks first.

West led the ♣J. The dummy came down and you, the declarer, went through the thinking process described above. Your plan is to win the first trick and then drive out the opponents' ♦A in the next trick. Only then will you be able to cash all your twelve winners without danger.

Let's see what would happen if you took a different approach. Say you were impatient to start taking winners. You might win the ♣J with your ♠A and immediately cash your ♠K and ♠Q winners. Then you turn your attention to the work that must be done eventually, namely, creating three more diamond tricks. So you play your ♦K, driving out West's ♦A. Good. You've now established the three diamond winners you needed, and that brings you to your goal of twelve tricks.

West, however, has other plans for you. He is on lead. Now I'll show you West's original thirteen cards:

♠ J 10 9 6 4   ♥ 7 4 2   ♦ A 5   ♣ J 8 7

West led the ♠ J, a card from a suit that offered his side potential. Yes, his ♦A is a sure trick, but he needs two tricks to defeat you. With his ♠J lead, he is hoping to build a second winner for his side.

You, the declarer, as we saw, won the ♠A and excitedly cashed the ♠K and ♠Q. On these two cards, West followed with small spades. With the playing of the ♠A, K, Q, and J, his ♠10 and ♠9 were promoted to master cards. Now, to West's surprise and delight, you produce the ♦K. He plays his ♦A and . . . bang, bang, down come his two established spades, sending you to a quick two-trick defeat. What went wrong?

Instead of immediately going about the business of establishing tricks for your side, you went ahead and established tricks for the defense. Your ♠K and ♠Q were supposed to act as shields, protecting you from attack by all the opponents' little spades. It was their job to knock them out, not yours.

The moral of the story is this: Don't put off until tomorrow what must be done today. **Go after your potential first. Quick tricks and stoppers must be played last.**

Practice Hand 2

We know that a declarer goes about making tricks basically by using high cards and length. With the defenders, it's the same. The techniques for making and creating tricks for the defense are the same as for the declarer.

Let's see how defenders work together to defeat declarer's goal of nine tricks on the following hand:

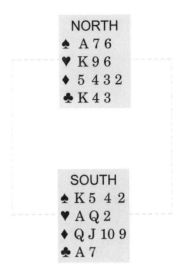

NORTH
♠ A 7 6
♥ K 9 6
♦ 5 4 3 2
♣ K 4 3

SOUTH
♠ K 5 4 2
♥ A Q 2
♦ Q J 10 9
♣ A 7

West leads with a ♣J. Let's begin by analyzing the hand from declarer's point of view. Where are the nine tricks coming from? Declarer counts the quick tricks:

♠ 2 tricks (A,K)
♥ 3 tricks (A,K,Q)
♦ 0 tricks
♣ 2 tricks (A,K)

Total: 7 quick tricks

Declarer needs two more tricks. One might come in spades. Declarer and his partner have seven spades, which means the opponents have six. If those spades are divided evenly, three to an opponent, declarer may have a long-suit trick. That would bring the total to eight. He still needs to look elsewhere. The diamond suit has potential, even though it had no quick tricks. All the declarer need do is promote two winners for himself.

The only cards the opponents have that are higher than his ♦Q J 10 9 sequence are the ♦A and ♦K. If declarer plays on diamonds until he drives out both cards, he will develop two tricks in the suit.

The declarer goes straight for diamonds, since both tricks he needs can be found there. It's a good plan.

Now how do the defenders go about thwarting it? The answer is timing. True, the declarer has nine tricks, but if the defenders can make five tricks before the declarer sets up his potential tricks, then he may not make it. (13 total tricks – 5 tricks by the defense = 8 tricks left for declarer—not enough.)

Suddenly it's a race. The defenders have the immediate advantage in that they are on lead. Take a look at West's hand:

♠ Q 8
♥ J 7 5
♦ K 8 7
♣ J 10 9 6 5

On opening lead, West has to make what we call a **blind lead**—meaning, the dummy hasn't come down yet. As the defender, West has no visible help. She has to rely on experience and logic. The declarer's advantage is that he will see his own cards and his partner's (the dummy's) throughout the play of a hand. Defender's partner's cards will never be visible; therefore the advantage the defense is given is the opening lead, playing the suit that they hope will win them the most tricks.

Just as declarer goes about establishing his potential first, so does the defender. West's side needs five tricks to beat this hand. Maybe her ♦K and ♠Q will take two tricks, and maybe her partner will take one or two tricks, but chances are West will have to develop a few tricks of her own. Which suit offers the most potential? Clubs. It is five cards long and contains a sequence that is missing the A, K, and Q. West considers where those three cards might be. There are two opponents and one partner. If each person has one of the honors, then the opponents have only two. With her opening club lead, she will drive out one of those honors. When she or her partner gets on lead again, they will lead another club and drive out another club honor. If they get on lead one more time, they will be able to defeat the declarer by cashing their three promoted clubs. The defenders hope to win those three club tricks and the two tricks that enabled them to get the lead each time:

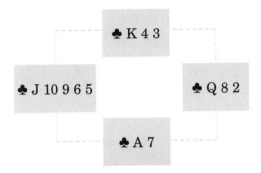

We've established that West is going to lead her longest suit. Now she must decide which card to lead. Does it matter? Let's take a time out on this hand for a general discussion on opening leads.

■ OPENING LEADS

Say you're on opening lead. You decide to lead clubs. With the holding below, which club should you lead?

Let's set up one possible layout:

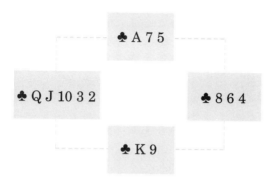

You are West and it's your opening lead. Visualize what would happen if you lead a low card, say the ♣3 or ♣2:

Trick one: [W] ♣3, ♣7, ♣8, ♣9

South would win a cheap trick with the ♣9 and still retain the ♣A and ♣K. You are no closer to promoting your ♣Q J 10. North–South will now win 3 tricks: the ♣A, K, 9.

Replay this situation, this time taking care to lead a card of one of West's three card sequence (♣Q J 10). Because we've insisted so far that when leading from a sequence we lead from the top of the sequence, let's continue that policy and lead with the ♣Q. This time the first trick looks like this:

Trick one: [W] ♣Q, ♣7, ♣8, ♣K

Notice this time South could not win a cheap trick. Visualize tricks two and three. West's ♣J would drive out North–South's remaining stopper (♣A), promoting West's ♣10 to the master card. Should E–W regain the lead, they would be ready to cash that card along with the ♣3 and ♣2, which became tricks through sheer force of length.

The point is, when you have a sequence, lead it. That

way no little card can sneak in at random and win a cheap trick. The only cards that can beat the ♣Q, J or 10 are the ♣A and K. Force the declarer to use them to win a trick.

What if you don't have a nice sequence? Say you have ♣Q 6 4 2. Which card do you lead? In the previous example you had a reason to lead the queen and let it lose. You knew you were moving toward the promotion of the other cards in the sequence. But with ♣Q 6 4 2, what purpose would the loss of the Queen serve? The answer is none: it wouldn't get the ♣6 much closer to becoming a master card. On opening lead, when you do not have a sequence, test the waters with a low card, in this case the ♣2. If it loses, it doesn't matter. It probably wasn't going to take a trick anyway. Save your unsupported honors (that is, honors that are not in a sequence) for later.

Now let's get back to the actual hand. West, on lead with the ♣J 10 9 6 5, now knows to lead the ♣ J from her holding. The dummy comes down. Let's turn our attention to West's partner, East, and see what information is available to him at this moment.

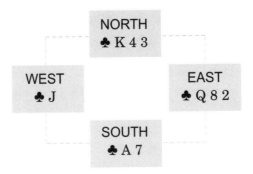

NORTH
♣ K 4 3

WEST
♣ J

EAST
♣ Q 8 2

SOUTH
♣ A 7

East sees seven club cards: his own three, the dummy's three, and his partner's lead card. From this he knows the following:

1. West, his partner, selected clubs as the suit with the most potential from her point of view.

2. West therefore has to have at least four or more clubs. Potential is length. West's longest suit must be at least four cards long.

3. West led the ♣J, an honor. It must be backed up by at least two other honors in sequence. Otherwise she would have led low.

Putting all this information together, East can form a picture of his partner's club suit and then use that picture to figure out the declarer's holding. Here is what he comes up with:

- Partner could have led from ♣ J 10 9 x (with x being any spot card) . . . or . . .

- ♣J 10 9 x x . . . or . . .

- even ♣A J 10 9 x. This is called leading from an interior sequence. In this case, when West led the J, East knows he's not holding the ♣Q, but he might be holding the ♣A or K—cards that are not in sequence with the J.

The weakest of these holdings is ♣J 10 9 x. Even if her partner led from that, declarer would have no better than ♣A x x. East–West have at least two tricks potential in the club suit.

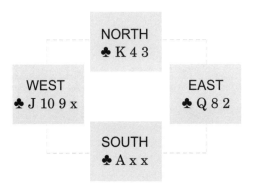

NORTH
♣ K 4 3

WEST
♣ J 10 9 x

EAST
♣ Q 8 2

SOUTH
♣ A x x

Between them, East and West have the ♣Q J 10 9 8 x 2. The opponents have only the ♣A and K to stop them. This is clearly the defender's suit. With West's opening lead, East and West are well on the road to establishing two long-suit winners. They expect the ♣J to drive out the ♣A, leaving only the dummy's ♣K to stop the suit.

Notice how East was able to use West's ♣J to see all thirteen cards in that suit: the defenders do this all the time. They can't look at the declarer's hand, so they rely on each other for information that allows them to visualize the hand.

Now comes my favorite part of defense. East, having formed a picture in his mind of what's going on in the club suit, must now transmit what he knows to West. Remember, West made a blind opening lead of ♣J, the top of a sequence. It turns out she has hit on a great opening lead. East isn't allowed to give a big thumbs-up signal. He can't even smile. The only way he can legally show approval of this lead is by the choice of card he plays to this trick.

East is holding the ♣Q 8 2. Between an 8 and a 2, which do you think shows encouragement? The 8. East signals West to continue this suit by playing the ♣8—a high spot card. Had East instead played the ♣2, he would have signaled displeasure with his partner's choice of leads.

High card = I like your lead, partner.
Low card = I don't like your lead.

After your partner has led, a card played by you that is not involved in the winning or losing of the trick can be used to signal information to your partner. Here West's ♣J is going to be involved in the winning or losing of the trick. East's card should be used as a signal.

Now both defenders are on the right path to defeating the declarer's goal of nine tricks. The race has begun. Will the declarer establish nine tricks before the defenders grab five? We've seen that the declarer has seven quick tricks: two spades, three hearts and two clubs. In order to make the extra two tricks, he must go after diamonds. Let's now follow the play with the complete hand:

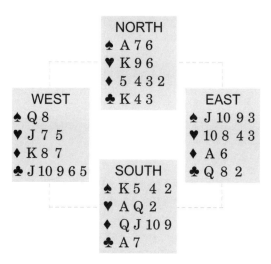

trick one: [W] ♣J, 3, 8, A
trick two: [S] ♦Q, 7, 2, A
trick three: [E] ♣Q, 7, 5, K
trick four: [N] ♦3, 6, 9, K
tricks five–seven: West cashes her good ♣10 9 6 to go along with the ♦A and ♦K, taking a total of five tricks and defeating declarer.

Let's go back to trick three for a second. Why did East lead the Queen?

Remember, when playing a suit of different lengths, play the honor from the *short* hand first. Visualize what would happen if East had played the ♣2 instead of unblocking the ♣Q:

The next club trick would look like this:

East would win the next trick, but how will West's clubs, poised to win two tricks, be reached?

Now try replaying this hand with the defenders doing anything but leading their long-club suit and continuing to pound away until they are established and cashed. If West chooses another suit, or if East doesn't unblock and continue, then the declarer will get to nine tricks before East–West get their five.

All of life is timing. A lot of bridge is, too.

2 MORE TRICK-WINNING STRATEGIES

▪ FINESSES WIN TRICKS

We've learned that high cards and length can take tricks. Now I'll show you a third way—how to win with finesse—which is a way of winning tricks that wouldn't otherwise be ours.

Set up your cards so that each player has two diamond cards, as below:

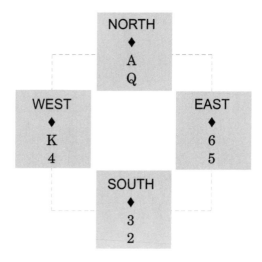

In this example, as has been the case up to this point, we're assuming that each player can see the other players' cards.

Q: With South on lead, how many tricks can North–South make?

A: Two. South leads a spot card, say the ♦2. West, seeing the ♦A on his left, decides not to use his ♦K at this time and follows instead with the ♦4.

Now North has a choice. He can certainly win the trick by playing his ace—in effect, bludgeoning the lowest cards on the table with his omnipotent ♦A. His other choice is to use a little **finesse.** If he wins the trick more cheaply with the queen, he will still win this trick, and he will also win the next trick with the ♦A that he reserved for the next trick. In order to win two tricks he should take the finesse by playing the queen.

To take a finesse is to try to win a trick with a card lower-ranking than one the opponents hold. Notice the word *try*. In the previous example, if East (not West) held the king and the queen was finessed, it would lose the trick.

Here's what that would look like:

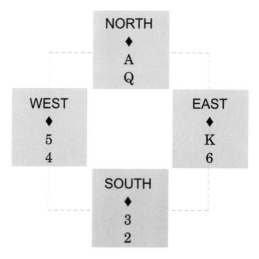

South is on lead and plays the 2. West follows with the 4. North finesses the queen and East wins the trick with his king.

Why would North play the Queen? Because when bridge is actually played, two of the four hands are always hidden: in certain situations a player has to guess what to do. In this case, we could see all the cards, so we knew ahead of time that the finesse would fail.

I'll show you how different things get when cards are hidden:

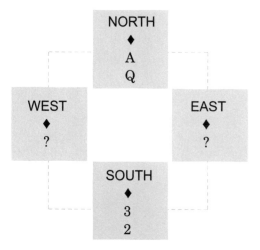

You are North. With two tricks remaining, let's say you know that everyone has two diamonds. You also know that either East or West has the king. South, your partner, leads the ♦2. West contributes the ♦4. Should you finesse the ♦Q? Here are the two possible scenarios:

A.   **B.**

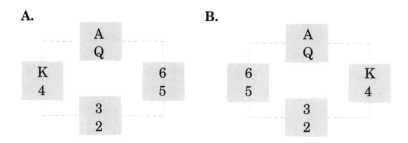

In A, if you finesse the queen and West has the king, you'll win two tricks. If you don't finesse the queen, you'll limit yourself to one trick.

In B, when East has the king, if you finesse the queen you'll only win one trick. If you don't finesse the queen, you'll also only win one trick. So when East has the king, you can't gain (or lose) by finessing the queen.

How often do finesses work? About half the time. As we just saw, taking a finesse wins whenever West has the king and loses whenever East has the king. It's a fifty-fifty proposition.

▪ TENACE ANYONE?

Let's take a look at just the West and North positions from example A.

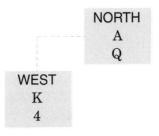

Notice that North's A Q surrounds West's king. North is holding one card immediately higher-ranking than West's king and one card immediately lower-ranking. This surrounding formation is called a **tenace position** (pronounced "tennis"). North's tenace position has the power to capture the king every time, as long as West plays a card before North. If West plays the king, North plays the ace. If West plays the 4, North finesses the queen, saving the ace to capture West's king the next time around.

▪ PRACTICE IN TENACE POSITIONS

Can you pick out the tenace positions below? Which card are you trying to capture?

A.

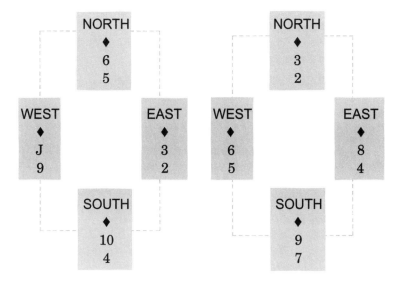

B.

C.

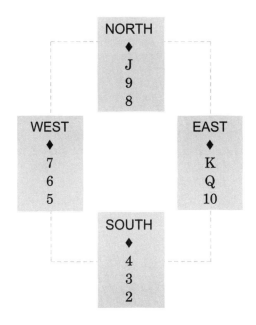

A. The J–9 is the tenace. The 10 is the card you're hoping to capture.

B. The 9–7 is the tenace. The 8 is the card you're hoping to capture.

C. The Q–10 is the tenace. The J is the card you are trying to capture.

Simply having a tenace position is not enough to guarantee success. Two conditions must be met:

1. The card that you are attempting to surround must be in the correct hand.

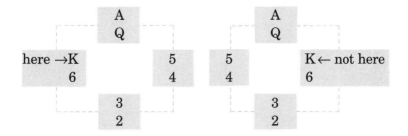

2. You must force the hand with the card you are trying to surround to act *first*.

Let's look more closely at condition one.

Take out your deck and set up the following cards (all of the same suit):

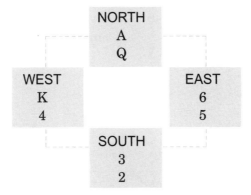

Humor me. Place South's 3 in the middle of the table. He's on lead. West follows next. Place West's king on top of the 3. North follows by playing the ace. Put it on top of the pile and *stop*.

Where is the king? Is it *over* or *under* the ace? It's under the ace. That's how we refer to the position of important cards that we hold. Are they over or under other important cards that the opponents hold? In this case if we were West, we would say our king lay under the opponent's A. Our king is *un*favorably placed. For a tenace position to be effective the card you are trying to surround must lie *under* your tenace.

Moving on to condition two:

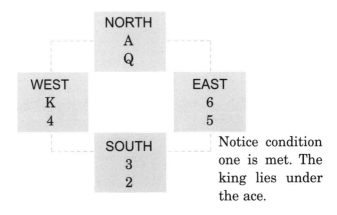

Notice condition one is met. The king lies under the ace.

Q: West sees that his king is unfavorably placed. If you are North and you are on lead, can you capture it? Try it.

A: The answer is no. If you play your ace, West will give you the 6 and save his king for your queen.

Q: In bridge terms, why can't you capture West's king?

A: a. He's not stupid.
  b. West commits after you. He sees your ace on the table and *reacts* accordingly.

So in order for you to take a successful finesse through your tenace position, you've got to force your opponent to commit the card you are attempting to surround first. To do that, you must lead from the hand *opposite* the tenace position—which in this case would be South.

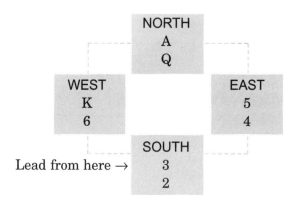

NORTH
A
Q

WEST
K
6

EAST
5
4

Lead from here →

SOUTH
3
2

If you lead from the South hand, then West must commit, or not commit, his king. Whichever he chooses, North is now favorably placed to react accordingly.

That said, a finesse does not always require the presence of a tenace position. But it always requires that conditions one and two be met. Consider this example:

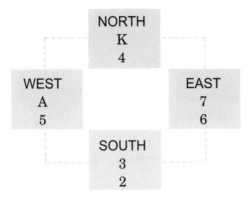

Say you are South, and it's your lead. You and your partner want to make one trick. Will you be successful? The answer is yes. When you lead a card, West has two choices. He can either play the 5 and let North win the first trick by finessing the king or commit the ace right away and have North take the king on the next trick. In either case North is in the catbird's seat. He simply has to sit back and wait to see what West will do.

▪ LOCATION, LOCATION, LOCATION

To fully appreciate the importance of being favorably (over) or unfavorably (under) placed, observe the relative strength of North's queen in these two examples:

A.

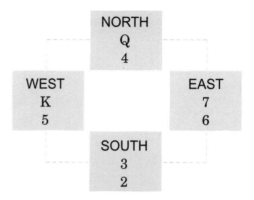

NORTH
Q
4

WEST
K
5

EAST
7
6

SOUTH
3
2

1. If East is on lead, will North's queen win a trick?

2. If South is on lead, will North's queen win a trick?

3. If West is on lead, will North's queen win a trick?

4. If North is on lead, will North's queen win a trick?

The answer to 1, 2 and 3 is yes. North's queen wins a trick because in each case West's king must commit first. Sitting over the king, North's queen is favorably placed. Only in 4 when North is on lead and must commit the queen before West has taken action will the queen not score a trick.

Results: North's favorably placed queen takes a trick three out of four times.

Switch the East and West cards . . .

B.

NORTH
Q
4

WEST
7
6

EAST
K
5

SOUTH
3
2

1. If South is on lead, will North's Queen win a trick?

2. If West is on lead, will North's Queen win a trick?

3. If North is on lead, will North's Queen win a trick?

4. If East is on lead, will North's Queen win a trick?

The answer to 1, 2 and 3 is no. North's queen, lying under East's king, is unfavorably placed. Only when North is on lead and must commit first will North make a trick.

Results: North's unfavorably placed queen takes a trick only in one out of four times.

In each example on the following pages, place ♦Q ♦7 ♦6 ♦5, two to a hand, so that the required number of tricks can be made. Indicate whether you or your partner has to be on lead.

A.
You are West.
You need two tricks.

```
            NORTH
WEST                  EAST
♦K J                  ♦3 2
            SOUTH
```

B.
You are West.
You need one trick.

```
            NORTH
WEST                  EAST
♦3 2                  ♦J 4
            SOUTH
```

C.
You are North.
You need two tricks.

```
            NORTH
            ♦K 10
WEST                  EAST

            SOUTH
            ♦3 2
```

D.
You are North.
You need one trick.

```
            NORTH
            ♦4 3
WEST                  EAST

            SOUTH
            ♦10 2
```

Answers:

A.   **B.**

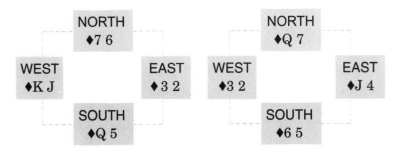

A. Place the queen under the K J. Your partner, East, must be on lead to force the queen to commit. It doesn't matter where the spot cards go.
B. Place the queen under the J 4. West must be on lead to force the queen to commit first.

C.   **D.**

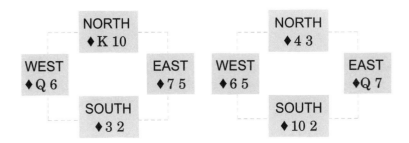

C. Place the queen under the K 10. South must lead through West's queen.

D. Place the queen under the 10 2. North must be on lead.

In examples B and D your opponents' queen is the master card. This card *must win a trick.* You are hoping to make a trick with your lesser card.

In examples A and C you have a tenace position. You have the master card, your opponent has the second-highest card, and you have the third-highest card. What you are trying to do is surround your opponent's card and *deny him a trick.*

Test Your Understanding of Finessing

1.
You are South.
See if you can make
four tricks.

2.
You are North or South.
Can you make five tricks?

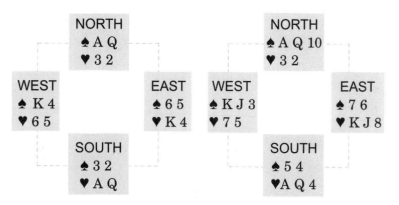

	NORTH			NORTH	
	♠ A Q			♠ A Q 10	
	♥ 3 2			♥ 3 2	
WEST		EAST	WEST		EAST
♠ K 4		♠ 6 5	♠ K J 3		♠ 7 6
♥ 6 5		♥ K 4	♥ 7 5		♥ K J 8
	SOUTH			SOUTH	
	♠ 3 2			♠ 5 4	
	♥ A Q			♥ A Q 4	

3A.
You are North. See if you
can make two tricks.

3B.
You are North.
Again, make two tricks.

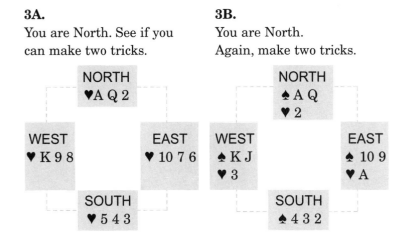

3C.
You are North. Make one trick.

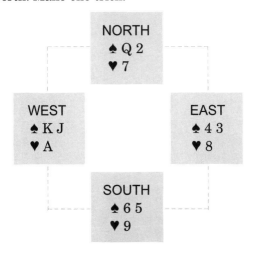

4A.
South on lead
Can you make three tricks?

4B.
You are South.
Can you make three tricks?

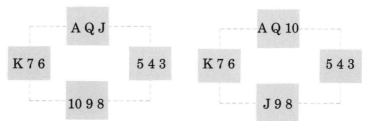

5.
North on lead.
Can you make three tricks?

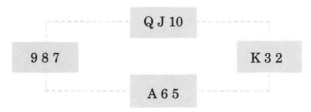

Answers:

1. This is a transportation issue. Lead a spade toward the ♠AQ tenace in North, finessing if West plays low. At trick two you have two options, both of which are fine. Either cash your other high spade and then lead a heart with a plan to finesse, or vice versa.

2. This is a fun hand. Lead a low spade, planning to *double finesse* if West plays low. This is how the tricks would go: (1) ♠4 to the ♠10; (2) ♥2 to the ♥Q; (3) ♠5 to the ♠Q; (4) Now remember to cash the ♠A, and discard the losing ♥4; and finally (5) ♥3 back to your ♥A. That's five tricks. Notice how the lead keeps moving back and forth between North

and South. It's the concept of *communication* in action.

3A. Your ♥Q is the key here. It *must* take a trick. Remember, to take a finesse you must position yourself so that you do not lead the card you are trying to finesse. You must lead toward that card, getting the person with the higher card to commit first. Lead the ♥2; it's a certain loser anyway. West or East wins this trick and will have to lead up to your ♥A Q tenace.

3B. Different look, same idea, same results. You can't break your tenace position, so lead your ♥2. Make them come to you.

3C. Different look again. In this case you don't have a tenace position, but you still need someone other than yourself to be leading spades. Get out of your hand by leading the ♥7.

4A. You can't make three tricks unless West is very helpful. While it is true that West's king is finessable, it is unfavorably placed under North's ace–queen tenace, watch what happens when the finesse is taken and West doesn't play the king. Who wins the trick? North *has to* because his three cards are all higher than South's. He then has to lead away from his AQ and West's king takes a trick.

4B. You can make three tricks only if South leads with the jack. If South leads with the 9, he'll transfer the lead to the North hand, and then North will have to lead away from his A–Q tenace position, thereby permitting

West to win a trick with his K. If South leads with the jack and North plays the ten, he'll keep the lead in the South hand. In the second trick, West is trapped in a simple tenace position and the next two tricks go to N–S. (It would have done West no good to cover South's jack with his king to the first trick, because once it's played, North's Q and 10 would be promoted to master cards and N–S would win all three tricks.)

5. Lead the queen, trapping the king between a rock—your Q J 10 sequence—and a hard place—South's ace. Notice here you can lead the card you are planning to finesse because East gains nothing by covering it with his king. Your sequential cards (Q J 10) become promoted to the master cards in the suit.

▪ HANDS-ON PLAY

Practice Hand 1

You need 12 tricks.
You, South, are the declarer; West is on lead.
The ♠Q is led.

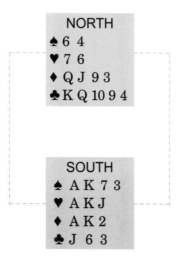

NORTH
♠ 6 4
♥ 7 6
♦ Q J 9 3
♣ K Q 10 9 4

SOUTH
♠ A K 7 3
♥ A K J
♦ A K 2
♣ J 6 3

You, declarer, need twelve tricks. Your first step is to count how many quick tricks you have. If the number comes to less than twelve, you'll have to look around for possible ways to develop those extra tricks.

On the lead of the ♠Q you have: two quick tricks in spades, two in hearts, four in diamonds, and none in clubs. That comes to eight, four short of what you need. There's work to be done.

Look at each suit's potential and try to find places where you might win those four tricks.

♠ 6 4

♠ A K 7 3

Q: Any potential here?

A: No. You have six cards between you, the opponents have seven.

♥ 7 6

♥ A K J

Your ♥A and ♥K are quick trick winners.

Q: How often will the ♥J be able to win a trick?

A: About fifty percent of the time. This ♥K J tenace position surrounds the ♥Q and captures it only if the ♥Q is
in the East hand, under the ♥A K J. The possibility of a
successful finesse is the only potential in this suit. This
suit will provide one extra trick at most. You still need
to find at least three more.

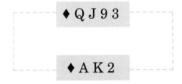

♦ Q J 9 3

♦ A K 2

This is your suit. You have the four master diamonds, the
♦A K Q J, between you. The longer of the two hands contains four diamonds. This suit will provide you with four
tricks. But care must be taken as to how best to play this
suit so that you don't strand that fourth diamond by acci-
dent. Remember to cash your honors (♦ A K) from the short
hand first. Then play your ♦2 over to dummy's ♦Q J. You
will make four tricks in this suit, but you've already counted
these in your quick trick total of eight. Unfortunately for
you, this beautiful suit offers no potential for any more than
those four tricks.

You're still looking for at least three more tricks and
we're fast running out of suits.

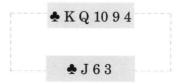

This is where you will strike gold. See how South's ♣J solidifies North's holding (♣K Q J 10 9)? After you drive out the opponent's ♣A stopper, you will have promoted the four tricks you needed to reach your total of twelve. Again, be careful to cash the ♣J from your three-card suit before crossing over to the long hand.

You have eight winners, plus potential from two places. You need four more tricks. All four of them can come from one source: clubs. Why take a heart finesse when, even if it won, you would still need three more tricks and have to play on clubs? Bridge players like to call this type of a finesse a **practice** finesse. It can't gain anything for you, and it may lose you that second trick. So turn your interest from hearts and go after clubs for your four potential tricks.

Now that you've analyzed the four suits and found where your tricks are going to be coming from, you need to make a plan that will allow you to take these tricks. As you saw in the first practice hand, you must go after your potential tricks as soon as possible. You must also be aware of the order in which you play your club and diamond suits, taking care to cash the honors from the short sides first.

Here is the hand in its entirety:

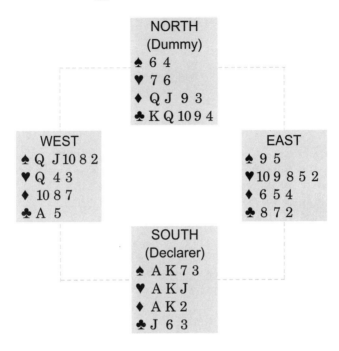

NORTH
(Dummy)
♠ 6 4
♥ 7 6
♦ Q J 9 3
♣ K Q 10 9 4

WEST
♠ Q J 10 8 2
♥ Q 4 3
♦ 10 8 7
♣ A 5

EAST
♠ 9 5
♥ 10 9 8 5 2
♦ 6 5 4
♣ 8 7 2

SOUTH
(Declarer)
♠ A K 7 3
♥ A K J
♦ A K 2
♣ J 6 3

The play might go like this (the lead is indicated in parenthesis):

Trick one: (W) ♠Q ♠ 4 ♠ 5 ♠ A

Trick two: (S) ♣ J ♣ A ♣ 4 ♣ 2

Trick three: (W) ♠ J ♠ 6 ♠ 9 ♠ K

Trick four: (S) ♦ A ♦ 7 ♦ 3 ♦ 4

Trick five: (S) ♦ K ♦ 8 ♦ 9 ♦ 5

Trick six: (S) ♦ 2 ♦ 10 ♦ J ♦ 6

Trick seven: (N) ♦ J ♣ 7 ♦ 3 ♣ 5

Tricks eight–eleven: Four winning club tricks

Tricks twelve–thirteen: Ace and king of hearts.

You wind up with two spades, two hearts, four diamonds, and four clubs for a total of twelve tricks!

Practice Hand 2

Let's look at a hand from the defender's perspective first. You are that defender and on this hand you are East. Here's your hand:

♠A 7 2   ♥J 10 3 2   ♦Q 4   ♣6 5 4 3

The declarer is trying to make at least seven tricks. Your partner leads the ♠K.

The dummy is tabled:

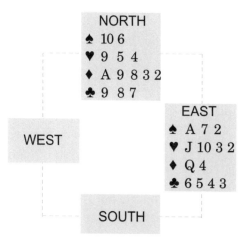

After admiring your hand, you turn your attention to the dummy. It is rather weak. The ♦A is the only card worth mentioning, but it is part of a five-card suit. There is some length potential there. Now look more closely at your partner's opening lead.

Q: From this ♠K lead, what can you deduce about declarer's holding in this suit?

A: To figure out what declarer has, you must first try to figure out what your partner has. His ♠K lead must indicate that he also possesses both the ♠Q and ♠J, along with at least one other spade. Why? Because . . . (a) the lead of an honor is made only from the top of a sequence (K Q J) and (b) partner leads his longest suit in an attempt to establish long-suit tricks. The shortest a long suit can be is four cards. Therefore, partner must have led from K Q J x or longer.

That's at least four spades accounted for. You see dummy's two and your three. That leaves South with at most four tiny spades.

Do you like partner's lead? Yes. You have the ♠A and know that between the two of you, you can take at least the first four tricks on this hand.

Q: What card should be played to this trick?

A: The ♠7 to show pleasure and to urge partner to continue the suit.

He does! He continues with ♠Q.

Q: Now what card do you play?

A: You must overtake the ♠Q with your ♠A to avoid blocking the suit. Here is everybody's holdings in spades:

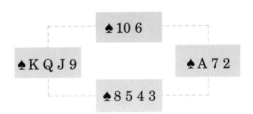

$$
\begin{array}{c}
♠\,10\;6 \\
♠\,K\,Q\,J\,9 \qquad\qquad ♠\,A\,7\,2 \\
♠\,8\,5\,4\,3
\end{array}
$$

If you fail to play your ♠A by trick three, this will be the situation:

You will have two tricks to cash, but on winning with the ♠A, you will be stuck in the wrong hand. So foreseeing (visualizing) this, you overtake with your ♠A and continue the suit with your ♠2. Sure enough, partner wins two more tricks with his ♠J and ♠9. On the ♠9 you must find a discard. (The dummy has had to find two discards already and declarer discarded, or **pitched** from the dummy the ♥4 and the ♣7, while being careful to keep all five diamonds.)

You now have three different suits from which to select and a total of ten different cards. This is your hand and the dummy just before you must discard:

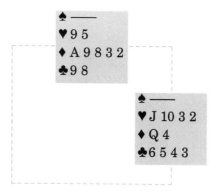

First, you must keep the ♦Q and ♦4. This is declarer's long and potentially dangerous suit. This is where he hopes to score some serious tricks.

So it comes down to hearts and clubs. Of these two suits, which offers less of a chance to make tricks? The clubs. They appear almost worthless. While the ♥J may eventually take a trick, it's hard to imagine the ♣6 capturing anything. You therefore decide to discard a club and to show your partner your displeasure with the suit, you discard a low one—the ♣3.

Let's leave the defenders now and see what's been occupying declarer all this time.

Here's the same hand, four tricks deep, after the defenders have won those first four spades.

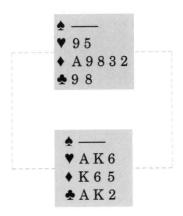

At trick five, West leads the ♣Q. The declarer needs to make at least seven of the remaining nine tricks. Declarer sees:

- Two heart tricks—no potential

- Two club tricks—no potential

- Two diamond tricks—length potential

When you have suits with no potential, just quick tricks, leave them be. You might use them for transportation but otherwise go after suits with possibilities.

Declarer wins West's ♣Q with his ♣K and then sets his sights on diamonds. He needs to develop at least one long-suit trick from this holding:

♦ A 9 8 3 2

♦ K 6 5

Declarer must visualize how the remaining diamonds may be divided between the two opponents. If the five missing diamonds were divided three-to-two (the natural way for five to divide), then it may be possible to create two extra tricks in this suit—dummy's fourth and fifth diamonds— because after three rounds of the suit have been played, North will be the only one left with diamonds. Between them, the opponents have three big cards, the ♦Q J 10. Declarer has only two cards that can beat these three, his ♦K and the dummy's ♦A; therefore he can't win all the tricks in this suit. The opponents have a trick coming to them.

Q: Which diamond trick should he give them?

A: This is one of the toughest answers for new players to visualize. Before we continue, I want to make you aware of how weak the dummy is. The only possible entry to dummy's long diamonds is the ♦A itself. This is the key to playing the suit properly. Once declarer establishes those long diamonds and they become winners, he will still have to get to them. Otherwise, they will serve no useful purpose. When we have an honor in a long suit and an honor in a short suit, you'll remember, we must play the honor from the short suit first. Let's do that— let's play the ♦K. Here is one possible complete layout of the suit:

♦ A 9 8 3 2

♦ J 10 7   ♦ Q 4

♦ K 6 5

Trick one: [S] ♦K, ♦7, ♦2, ♦4
Trick two: [S] ♦5, ♦10—STOP!
Do not play your inclination. Resist the temptation to play
the ♦A! If declarer cannot resist this temptation, after two
tricks the situation will look like this:

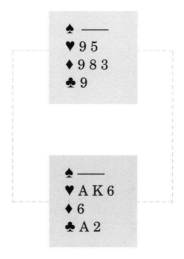

♠ ⸺
♥ 9 5
♦ 9 8 3
♣ 9

♠ ⸺
♥ A K 6
♦ 6
♣ A 2

The dummy would be on lead. The opponents would still
have the ♦J, stopping the suit. Dummy could play a diamond now, giving them the trick, but how would you get
back to dummy? It is entryless.

Now look at the situation if, instead of playing your ♦A
at trick two, you gave the opponents that trick by playing
your ♦3:

Now the ♦J is the only diamond left in the opponents' hand when you win the return. Notice you still have stoppers in hearts and clubs because you did not play these suits, which had no potential early. You now can reach those established diamonds through that carefully preserved ♦6. You, declarer, will now come to two hearts, two clubs, and four diamonds, for a total of eight tricks.

Here's the entire hand:

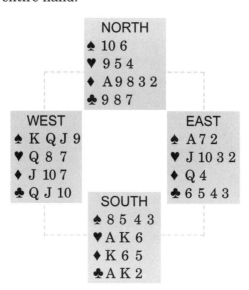

The moral of this hand: **When you must lose a trick in a suit, lose it early.**

3 TRUMPS

***Let's** take this opportunity, having spent a* couple of chapters on the nuts and bolts of the game, to present a bridge fantasy. Imagine you were in the West position and you happened to be dealt the following hand:

WEST

♥ A K Q J 10 9 8 7 6 5 4 3 2

If you are on lead, does it matter which card you play first?

If you played three hours of bridge a day, every day, in about 170,000 years you will get a one-suited hand like this. People *are* living longer these days.

It doesn't matter which card you lead. You will win thirteen tricks in a row, and North–South will be unable to take even one little trick. Your ♥2 is as strong as your ♥A. You will hold onto the lead, and North, East and South will discard and discard until you have won every trick.

Now here's a bridge nightmare. Say you pick up that same hand but you are not on lead. How many tricks will you make? None. Zero. Zip. Nada. What you'll be doing is making thirteen discards. Your one-in-a-zillion hand will be absolutely useless.

Now imagine there's a wild-card suit out here. Say that, on this particular hand, the heart suit is wild, meaning that it has special powers: if a card of a different suit is led and you can't follow suit (which in this case will be at the very first trick) instead of *discarding* a heart, you can play any of your hearts and it will win the trick!

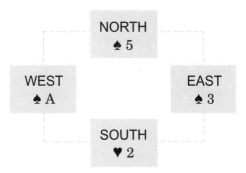

With no wild-card suit, if West leads the ♠A, it will win the trick. North and East will follow with small spades and South will discard her losing heart.

Now let's make hearts wild and see the dramatic effect this has on the outcome of this trick. Again, West leads his ♠A, fully expecting it to win the trick. North and East follow suit. This time, however, when South plays her ♥2, West is in for a surprise. Now that hearts are wild, the lowly ♥2 automatically outranks a card of any other suit, including West's ace, and takes the trick.

A wild-card suit in bridge is called a **trump suit**. Playing a card of the trump suit on a card of another suit is called **trumping** or **ruffing**.

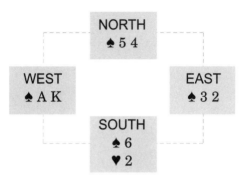

Once again, hearts are trump and West leads the ♠A. This time, South cannot trump the ♠A with his ♥2 because she is bound by the first rule in bridge: You must follow suit if you can. South must wait until she no longer has any spades (until she is **void** in spades) before she can use her ♥2. On the next lead of a spade (♠K), South is now void in spades and can trump (or ruff) the ♠K with her ♥2, winning the trick.

Fully half of all bridge hands are played with one suit wild, or trump. How and why this comes about we'll learn in a later chapter. Cards in a trump suit work exactly like cards in any other suit—an ace of trump beats a king of trump, a six of trump loses to a nine of trump, etc.

Having a trump suit affects the play of the cards in three key ways.

▪ 1. A TRUMP SUIT LETS YOU TURN LOSERS INTO WINNERS!

Example 1A.

South on lead
Spades trump

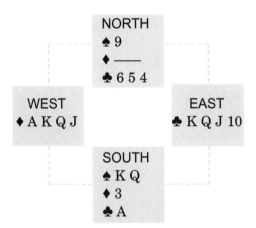

NORTH
♠ 9
♦ ——
♣ 6 5 4

WEST
♦ A K Q J

EAST
♣ K Q J 10

SOUTH
♠ K Q
♦ 3
♣ A

Playing as we have up until now with nothing trump, or **no trump,** how many tricks will South win if he is on lead? How many will he lose? If he plays the ♣A first, then the two spade honors, South will win three tricks and lose only the ♦3.

Now let's imagine that spades are trump. South's hand is high (all his cards are winners) except for the little ♦3. But North is void in diamonds and has a trump. This combination allows South to trump his losing ♦3 with North's ♠9, turning the losing ♦3 into a winner. Trumping a card is optional; in this case, it makes sense because it allows N–S to win a trick they would otherwise lose.

Trick one: [S] ♦3, ♦J, ♠9, ♣10
In bridge language South leads the ♦3, West covers with his ♦J, North trumps the ♦J with the ♠9 and West dis-

cards the ♣10. Trick one is won by North. She (N) is on lead for the next trick.

Trick two: [N] ♣4, ♣J, ♣A, ♦Q
South's ace of clubs wins trick two, with West discarding the queen of diamonds.

Tricks three and four are won with South's ♠K and ♠Q. Being the only wild cards left, they are automatically winners.

As a result, South makes four tricks, turning his diamond loser into a winner. When spades are trump, he makes one more trick than he would have if nothing was trump.

Example 1B.
South on lead
Spades trump

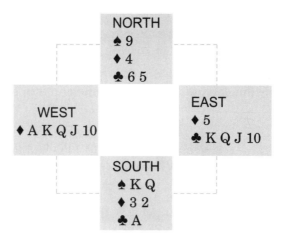

NORTH
♠ 9
♦ 4
♣ 6 5

WEST
♦ A K Q J 10

EAST
♦ 5
♣ K Q J 10

SOUTH
♠ K Q
♦ 3 2
♣ A

This is the same hand we started with except everyone has one more diamond.

Q: What must South do in order to be able to trump one of his losing diamonds?

A: South must create a void in the North hand. He plays a diamond at trick one, allowing the opponents to win the trick. What's theirs is theirs. (Don't be afraid of letting go of the lead if it will help you later.) After one trick, the cards look like the previous example, only this time West is on lead at trick two.

Trick one: [S] ♦2, ♦10, ♦4, ♦5 (South was on lead; West won the trick.)

Trick two: [W] ♦A, ♠9, ♣10, ♦3 (West was on lead; North won the trick.)

Tricks three–five: [N] South wins all three with his spade and club winners. South takes four tricks and loses one.

Remember, **in order to trump a card you must first create a void in the suit that's being led.**

Example 1C.

South on lead

Spades trumps

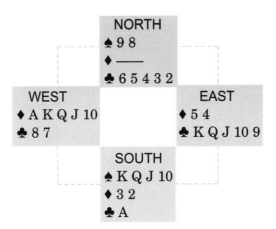

NORTH
♠ 9 8
♦ —
♣ 6 5 4 3 2

WEST
♦ A K Q J 10
♣ 8 7

EAST
♦ 5 4
♣ K Q J 10 9

SOUTH
♠ K Q J 10
♦ 3 2
♣ A

Q: If this hand were being played in no trump and South was on lead, how many tricks would he have to lose?

A: Two. After cashing his spade and club winners, he'd have to give West two diamond tricks.

Q: If Spades were trump, does South lose any diamond tricks at all?

A: Visualize: South has two losing diamonds. North has a void in diamonds and two trump cards, a winning combination. South's plan is to trump a diamond right away in the North hand, then get the lead back to the South hand and trump another one. This is how the play would unfold:

Trick one: [S] ♦2, ♦10, ♠8, ♦4

Trick two: [N] ♣2, ♣9, ♣A, ♣7

Trick three: [S] ♦3, ♦J, ♠9, ♠5

Tricks four through seven are won by South's K Q J 10 of trump. Note that it would be wrong to play trump (spades) before South went about the business of trumping his two diamond losers. This idea of having the right number of trumps and using them at the right time is called **trump management.**

■ 2. HAVING TRUMP PREVENTS OPPONENTS FROM RUNNING A LONG SUIT!

Example 2A.
East or West on lead

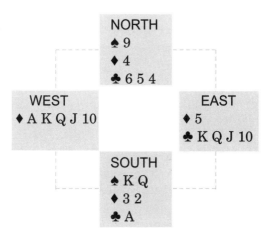

NORTH
♠ 9
♦ 4
♣ 6 5 4

WEST
♦ A K Q J 10

EAST
♦ 5
♣ K Q J 10

SOUTH
♠ K Q
♦ 3 2
♣ A

Q: Playing in no trump with East or West on lead, how many tricks will N–S win?

A. They cannot win a trick. If West leads, he'll take five diamond tricks. If East hits on her singleton ♦5, her partner will again win five tricks. In either case, N–S are powerless to prevent it, since as we know from previous discussions, length takes tricks.

Q: What happens when spades become trump?

A: After West wins the first trick with a high diamond, he is powerless to prevent North from trumping his second diamond and gaining control of the play by taking over the lead.

▪ 3. A TRUMP SUIT ALLOWS YOU TO DISCARD LOSERS!

Example 3A.

West on lead
Hearts trump

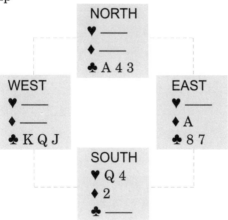

NORTH
♥ ——
♦ ——
♣ A 4 3

WEST
♥ ——
♦ ——
♣ K Q J

EAST
♥ ——
♦ A
♣ 8 7

SOUTH
♥ Q 4
♦ 2
♣ ——

Q: With hearts trump and West leading the king, how many losers do you think North–South will have?

A: They will not lose a trick. At trick one, North covers West's ♣K with his ♣A, winning the trick. Now South need not use any trump since North has already won the trick. Instead he discards his losing ♦2. He wins the next two tricks with his Q 4 of trump.

Notice, had South been on lead, he would have lost a diamond to East's ♦A. The dummy's ace of clubs would have had to have been discarded.

When both hands of a partnership have trump cards, things get really interesting. Here's one of my favorite examples:

Example 3B.

Hearts trump

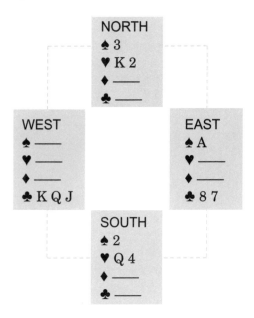

With North, East or South on lead, N–S will lose a spade trick. But if West is on lead, they won't. Here's why:

> Trick one: West leads the ♣K, North *discards* his losing spade. East follows with the ♣7 and South ruffs it—trumps it—with the ♥4.
>
> Tricks two and three: South's ♥Q and North's ♥K win the next two tricks.
>
> Or
>
> Trick one: Again West leads the ♣K, North trumps it with the ♥2 while his partner discards his losing spade.

Exercises

1.
South on lead
Clubs trump

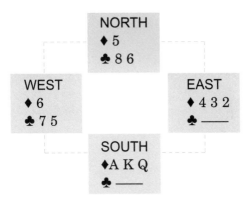

NORTH
♦ 5
♣ 8 6

WEST
♦ 6
♣ 7 5

EAST
♦ 4 3 2
♣ ——

SOUTH
♦ A K Q
♣ ——

Q:With South on lead and clubs trump, how many tricks do you think North–South will win?

A: All three. North holds a tenace position over West.
Trick one: [S] ♦A, 6, 5, 4
Tricks two and three: [S] ♦K led by South. West is caught. Whichever card he uses to trump, North will be able to overruff him and win the third trick with the higher remaining club.

Q: How many tricks will N–S win with North on lead?

A: All three if North first uses his ♦5 to bridge back to South's hand so that South will be on lead at trick two and again catch West in a tenace position. If instead at trick one North plays his ♣8, he will eventually lose a trick to West's ♣7.

2.
South on lead
Hearts trump

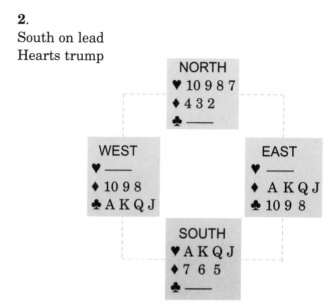

NORTH
♥ 10 9 8 7
♦ 4 3 2
♣ ——

WEST
♥ ——
♦ 10 9 8
♣ A K Q J

EAST
♥ ——
♦ A K Q J
♣ 10 9 8

SOUTH
♥ A K Q J
♦ 7 6 5
♣ ——

Q: How many tricks will N–S win?

A: Four. They will have to lose three diamonds. **Both hands have to follow suit, even in trump.**

3.

South on lead
Hearts trump

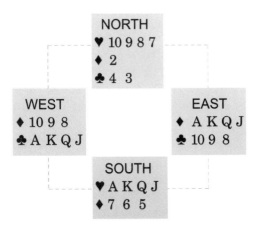

NORTH
♥ 10 9 8 7
♦ 2
♣ 4 3

WEST
♦ 10 9 8
♣ A K Q J

EAST
♦ A K Q J
♣ 10 9 8

SOUTH
♥ A K Q J
♦ 7 6 5

Q: Try to visualize—should you play all your trumps right away?

A: No. At least not more than two of them. Why? Because they have work to do. If you play four rounds (four tricks) of hearts, you'll be left with three losing diamonds. You want to trump your losers first.

What are your losers? The diamonds in the South hand. In order to trump those diamonds, you must create a void in the dummy. So lead a diamond. You will lose the first trick. That can't be helped. You've now created a diamond void in one hand. You already had a natural club void in the other hand. At this point whatever your opponents return can be trumped.

Say the first trick goes like this: [S] ♦5, ♦8, ♦2, ♦J. Now the N–S hands will look like this:

NORTH
♥ 10 9 8 7
♦ ——
♣ 4 3

SOUTH
♥ A K Q J
♦ 7 6
♣ ——

This is how the hand plays out.

Trick two: If East returns a diamond, it gets ruffed in the North hand.

Trick three: North leads a club, which gets trumped in the South hand.

Trick four: South leads a diamond, which gets trumped in the North hand.

Tricks five and six are won by South's trumps.

This technique of trumping back and forth is called **cross ruffing.**

■ TRUMP MANAGEMENT

4.

South on lead
Spades trump

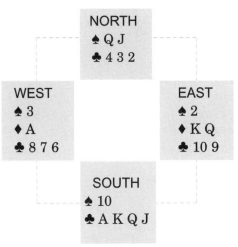

NORTH
♠ Q J
♣ 4 3 2

WEST
♠ 3
♦ A
♣ 8 7 6

EAST
♠ 2
♦ K Q
♣ 10 9

SOUTH
♠ 10
♣ A K Q J

Q: Can North–South make all five tricks?

A: Yes. But care must be taken. Their cards outside the trump suit (the ♣A K Q J) are all winners, but if they aren't careful, East–West might trump them. In order to avoid this, South must **draw** the opponents' trump. To draw trump means simply to play trumps until you've exhausted all the opponents' trump.

At trick one, South plays the ♠10, West plays the ♠3, north plays the ♠J and East plays the ♠2. Only now, when the opponents are out of trump, it is safe for South to play his winning clubs.

When do you draw trump? While there is no easy answer, my rule of thumb is to ask yourself two questions:

Do I have any losers that need to be trumped?

Do I need to discard any losers?

If the answer to these questions is no, it's probably right to draw trump.

Here's an example of a hand where the question of when to draw trump comes into play:

5.
South on lead
Spades trump

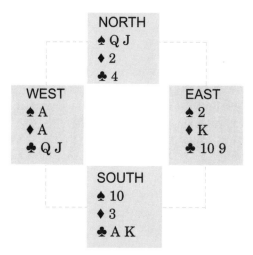

Q: Should South draw trump immediately?

A: Does South have any losers that need to be trumped? Yes. The ♦3 is a loser, but it can't be trumped until a void is created in the dummy. Does she need to discard any losers? Yes. She needs to discard the ♦2 from dummy. If she leads her ♠10, West will win the trick and then be in position to cash a high diamond. South will therefore lose two tricks. But South can avoid losing this diamond trick by not trying to draw trumps immediately. Instead she can plan on discarding her losing diamond on the ♣A and ♣K. The play would go like this:

Trick one: [S] ♣A, ♣J, ♣4, ♣9
Trick two: [S] ♣K, ♣Q, ♦2, ♣10
Trick three: [S] ♦3, ♦A, ♠J, ♦K
Trick four: [N] ♠Q, ♠2, ♠10, ♠A

The ♠A wins the only trick for East–West.

Remember, if you ask yourself the two questions and the answer to both is no, you should draw trump immediately. Don't give the opponents a chance to trump your outside winners (that is, winners in the other three suits).

▪ PLAY AND DEFENSE WITH TRUMP

Play and defense in no trump are based mainly on one idea: establishing long suits in the hope of taking tricks with the low cards of those suits. On defense, for example, it is often enough for the opening leader simply to close her eyes and lead her longest suit.

But the existence of a trump suit changes all that.

Because of the controlling nature of trumps, defenders rarely get to promote and cash their long-suit winners. For instance, look at this partial hand:

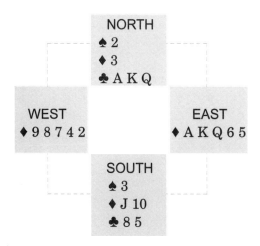

NORTH
♠ 2
♦ 3
♣ A K Q

WEST
♦ 9 8 7 4 2

EAST
♦ A K Q 6 5

SOUTH
♠ 3
♦ J 10
♣ 8 5

South is the declarer. Now, in no trump (**NT**) play, high cards (**HC**) and length (**L**) control the play. In the previous example, playing in no trump with five tricks remaining, East finds himself on lead. His ♦A and ♦K wipe out North–South's diamonds; and East–West, between them, can claim the remaining tricks.

But with spades trump, this cannot happen. With spades trump, East's ♦A lead creates a useful diamond void in the dummy (North) hand. When East tries cashing a second high diamond, the declarer (South) uses the dummy's trump, the ♠2 , to block East's plan. The ♠2 not only wins the trick, but takes control of the play away from East–West and hands it over to the declarer, who is then able to go about trying to implement his plan for the hand.

This knowledge is vital to defenders when planning an opening lead.

Let's look at another example. Say you're on lead in no trump play. Here's your hand:

♠ Q 3
♥ 8 7 4
♦ Q J 10
♣ J 10 9 4 2

What suit do you lead? You lead length: that's clubs. So the ♣J is the correct card to lead. Now let's say you're on lead, holding the same hand, with spades trump. Does this change your thinking? Yes. The club suit is no longer as attractive as before. Your length actually works *against* you. The more clubs you have, the fewer the declaring side has. When you have five cards in a suit, someone else must have two or less—putting that player a few steps ahead of you in the race to be able to trump. Look at the odds:

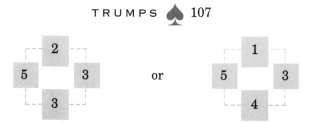

Most of the time it is one of the opponents who is short in the suit you are leading. That is because (a) they are long in the suit they named trump and therefore have fewer cards remaining in the other three suits, or (b) they decided to play in NT for a reason; perhaps they knew of their short-suit weakness.

Therefore, when playing against a trump suit, you should worry only about the first *two* rounds of the suit. Someone will probably be trumping the third round anyway. Here's your hand again:

♠ Q 3
♥ 8 7 4
♦ Q J 10
♣ J 10 9 4 2

Your diamond suit is a more attractive lead when the opponents have named a suit trump. It is only three cards long, and if your partner should have either the ♦A or ♦K, there is a good chance of taking two or three fast tricks in this suit. Let's see how this could happen:

a.

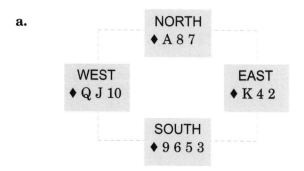

After your ♦Q knocks out the N–S stopper and your side regains the lead, you will be in position to cash two tricks.

b. Now let's switch the ♦A and the ♦K.

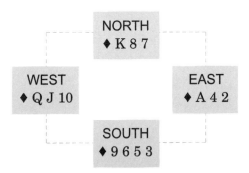

NORTH
♦ K 8 7

WEST
♦ Q J 10

EAST
♦ A 4 2

SOUTH
♦ 9 6 5 3

This is the situation every defender hopes for. Dummy's ♦K is sandwiched between your ♦Q J 10 sequence and partner's ♦A. In this case your side will make three quick tricks.

Another reason for leading a diamond in the original hand rather than a club is because your diamonds are also stronger than your clubs. The fact that your high card in the club suit is the jack means that it could take two rounds to build a trick in this suit. That is often more than enough time for declarer to discard a potential club loser on another suit.

Here's another lead problem. Say this is your hand:

♠ Q 9 7 3
♥ 5
♦ 8 6 4
♣ K Q 8 6 2

Q: How is your choice of leads affected by whether you're playing with nothing trump or with diamonds trump?

A: Let's first consider leading when nothing is trump. This is easy: just close your eyes and lead a club. Lacking a three-card sequence as you do, lead a low club to scout around. Experienced players lead the fourth-highest card from four or more of a suit. In this case, the ♣K is the highest, and the ♣6 is the fourth highest. Your lead should be the ♣6.

Now let's consider the other situation, leading against opponents who've named diamonds trump. With diamonds trump, it may take too long to build a trick in clubs or spades. But if your partner has a quick entry in hearts, something wonderful will happen for your side. Say that these are the players' holdings:

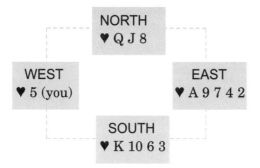

You lead your singleton ♥5. Partner steps up with his ♥A and plays one right back, allowing you to ruff, creating a trick for your side. Remember, defense is just the flip side of declarer play. Whatever methods are available to declarer are available to defenders too. Just as declarer uses his shortness to create winners from losers, so can defenders.

Benito Garazzo, one of the veterans of the famous Italian Blue Team—a bridge squad that held the World Championship for a record ten straight years—is credited with saying, "If my partner is on opening lead and doesn't lead a singleton, then he didn't have one to begin with." That's how basic the lead of a singleton is to defense play.

This last example focuses our attention on the strength defenders have when they hold outstanding small trump cards. These trumps are pesky little devils that can often prove dangerous—even fatal—to careless declarers. Remember that, as declarer, if you have no good reason not to draw the opponents' trump, then draw them. When playing with a trump suit, this should be your number-one priority.

With that general rule firmly in mind, let's look at a couple of hands that illustrate the exception—that is, when *not* to draw trumps first.

■ HANDS-ON PLAY

Practice Hand 1

You are South. You must make at least ten tricks.
Spades are trump.
West leads the ♦K.

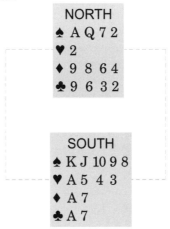

NORTH
♠ A Q 7 2
♥ 2
♦ 9 8 6 4
♣ 9 6 3 2

SOUTH
♠ K J 10 9 8
♥ A 5 4 3
♦ A 7
♣ A 7

When you first look at a trump hand, it's often a good idea to try and see how many tricks you might be able to make if this hand were being played in no trump. Here you'd make five spade tricks and three aces, for a total of eight tricks. One reason to do this is to help you envision how many shortness tricks—tricks made by trumping losers—you're going to need to create. Having eight, needing ten, you must create at least two shortness tricks.

The next helpful step, as you continue to examine your hand, is to count your losers. Look at the hand with the longer trump suit first, since it will have fewer cards in other suits that will demand your attention. In this case, the South hand has the greater number of trumps, so attempt to estimate South's losers. The trump suit, spades, is solid: you have no losers there. The heart suit looks to have three possible losers: that 5, the 4, and the 3. Diamonds and clubs each have one possible loser: the ♦7 and the ♣7. This brings us to a total of five possible losers.

Therefore, if you're to make ten or more tricks, clearly you have to eliminate some of the losers.

Now, can we do anything about the diamond and club losers? No. We can't trump them (dummy has more diamonds and clubs than we do) and we can't discard them on any other winners. We're essentially stuck with these two losers.

How about those three possible heart losers? Is there anything we can do there? Yes, there is. We can plan on trumping them with the spades in the dummy. Here's the plan. We will win the first trick, right off the bat, with the ♦A. We will delay drawing trumps because we need them for an important purpose. At trick two, we play our ♥A, voiding dummy's hearts. We are then in position at trick three to trump our first heart. We play the ♥3, trumping it with dummy's ♠2. We return to our hand with the ♣A to trump another heart. Finally, we return to our hand a third time, playing the ♠Q and **overtaking** it with the ♠K, to be in position to trump our third heart.

In this way, we win five spades, three aces, and three trump tricks: eleven tricks total, one more than the ten tricks I asked you to make. We lose only the ♦7 and the ♣7 and manage to turn three losers into three winners. This is a powerful demonstration of the ability of a trump suit to create tricks.

Notice that we started with eight tricks: five spades and three aces. When we trumped our first heart, we created a ninth trick because we trumped in the **short hand**—the four-card spade hand. We could have done things differently. Say we decided to trump a diamond in the declarer's hand. Would this have created a trick? Let's try it and see. Say we win the opening lead with the ♦A as before and immediately play back a diamond. Let's have the opponents win this trick and continue diamonds. Here's how our holdings look just before we follow to the third round of diamonds:

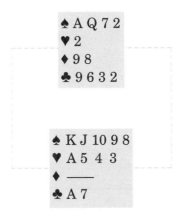

♠ A Q 7 2
♥ 2
♦ 9 8
♣ 9 6 3 2

♠ K J 10 9 8
♥ A 5 4 3
♦ ——
♣ A 7

Thus far we have won one trick and we still expect to win five more spades and two aces for our original total of eight.

Now we get to trump that diamond in South's hand. Let's trump it with our ♠8. Do you think we have created a trick? Have we reached nine tricks? Let's count: four spades, two aces, and the two winners we have now earned only comes to eight. How's that? Why didn't we create a trick when we trumped a diamond with one of our five spades? Because we were trumping with a trick we had already counted as a winner. We were already counting on five spade tricks. After we trumped a diamond with one of these five spades, we only had four spades left. Sure, we created a trick by trumping; but it was at the expense of the long-suit trick, so in effect we simply substituted one for the other.

The moral of the story: to create tricks, it's important when dealing with trump suits of unequal length to trump in the shorter hand.

Practice Hand 2

Let's look at another deal. Here, once again, you are South. You need to make ten tricks to be successful.

Hearts are trump.
The ♠K is led.

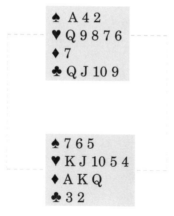

♠ A 4 2
♥ Q 9 8 7 6
♦ 7
♣ Q J 10 9

♠ 7 6 5
♥ K J 10 5 4
♦ A K Q
♣ 3 2

Playing in no trump after the ♠ K lead, we would have a hard time making very many tricks. The opponents would win the ♥A at trick two and cash three or four spades plus the ♣A and ♣K. Playing with a suit trump affords us plays that thwart the opponents' goals.

Let's first count our losses. Since the trump suits are equal in length, let's look at our hand (the declarer's hand)

and see how many potential losers we have. Two spades, one heart, no diamonds, and two clubs, for a total of five. However, needing ten tricks to be successful, we can only lose three. How do we eliminate two losers from our hand?

If you are able to recognize the problem on a hand, as you just have, then you are usually halfway to solving it. Now, is this a situation where we should draw trumps immediately so the opponents can't ruff our winners? No. If we try to draw trump, one of the opponents will win the ♥A and cash two spades and two clubs to beat us. We must therefore postpone drawing trumps and see how we might first go about eliminating losers. Playing in trump, there are basically two ways to do this: trumping them or discarding them.

We can't trump our two spade losers because both hands have at least two spades each. Nor can we trump clubs, for the same reason. Therefore the first option won't help us. Now let's look at the second option. Can we discard losers? Look at your diamond holding:

At trick one, win West's opening lead, the ♠K, with dummy's ♠A. At trick two, play ♦A, creating a diamond void in the dummy. Your ♦K and Q are now master cards. On the winning ♦K, you can now discard one of your losing spades. The ♦Q will provide a second losing spade discard. You've now created a void in spades, the suit you had two losers in. At trick four, play one of your losing spades and trump it in the dummy, turning a loser into a winner. You can **draw the opponent's trump**—that is, remove trump from their hands—by leading hearts until no trumps remain in their hands. You will lose only the ♥A and the ♣3 and ♣2. You will win one spade, four hearts, three diamonds and two ruffs (trumping declarer's two losing spades with two of dummy's trump) for ten tricks.

Success.

The complete hand, as it turns out, was:

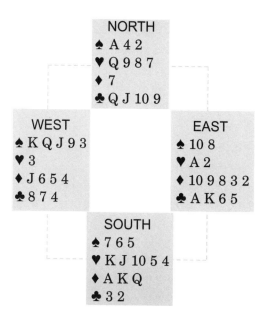

NORTH
♠ A 4 2
♥ Q 9 8 7
♦ 7
♣ Q J 10 9

WEST
♠ K Q J 9 3
♥ 3
♦ J 6 5 4
♣ 8 7 4

EAST
♠ 10 8
♥ A 2
♦ 10 9 8 3 2
♣ A K 6 5

SOUTH
♠ 7 6 5
♥ K J 10 5 4
♦ A K Q
♣ 3 2

Conclusion: By discarding dummy's two small spades on your ♦A and ♦K, you created a spade void. You were then able to trump your two losing spades in the dummy, eliminating two losers while creating two winners at the same time.

UCTIONS AND BIDDING

How do you know when hearts are going to be trump? How do you know if you're going to be the declarer or the dummy? As a defender, do you have any clue at all what your partner's hand looks like?

So far we've been working on the play of the hand; but before the play even begins, all four players get a chance to talk about their respective hands during a period known as the **auction**. It is during this period that declarer, dummy, and opening leader are determined, as well as, things like how many tricks each side is trying to make.

■ THE AUCTION

Let's say you pick up the following hand:

Hand 1

♠ A K 5   ♥ A K 4   ♦ K Q J 10 9 3   ♣ 2

If you could name diamonds trump, you would be pretty excited about this hand. After all, your trick-taking potential would be around nine. (2 spade tricks + 2 heart tricks + 5 diamond tricks + no club tricks = 9.)

Now suppose you picked up this hand:

Hand 2

♠ 8 3 2 ♥ 9 5 3 ♦ 5 4 2 ♣ 10 7 6 5

What's the trick-taking potential here? Right around zero. You wouldn't be sure which suit to name trump, because even if it were clubs, where you have length, your cards aren't high enough to guarantee much trick-taking ability.

So which hand do you think would be more valuable to a bridge player? Hand 1, of course, because it could be worth nine tricks, as opposed to hand 2's zero tricks.

In the complete deal below we'll give West hand 1 and South hand 2.

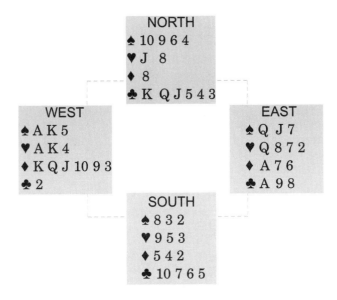

Let's look at how each player might view his cards. This is West's hand:

♠ A K 5 ♥ A K 4 ♦ K Q J 10 9 3 ♣ 2

West quickly realizes, as we did, that if he can name diamonds as a trump suit, he (and consequently his partner) should be able to make *at least* nine tricks.

This is North's hand:

♠ 10 9 6 4   ♥ J 8   ♦ 8   ♣ K Q J 5 4 3

North decides that if clubs were trump, she would be one happy bridge player. She sees the potential for several tricks with clubs trump.

East's hand:

♠ Q J 7   ♥ Q 8 7 2   ♦ A 7 6   ♣ A 9 8

East is holding five honor cards. He likes this hand. But no suit readily suggests itself as a trump suit. He decides he might like to play the hand in no trump—meaning without any suit trump.

Now South takes a look at her cards:

♠ 8 3 2   ♥ 9 5 3   ♦ 5 4 2   ♣ 10 7 6 5

And after a moment she says to herself, "Maybe I ought to take up bingo."

Look at West and East's hands together. Between the two of them, can they make all thirteen tricks? Put them side by side:

WEST
♠ A K 5
♥ A K 4
♦ K Q J 10 9 3
♣ 2

EAST
♠ Q J 7
♥ Q 8 7 2
♦ A 7 6
♣ A 9 8

East–West should make three spades, three hearts, six diamonds, and one club. That's thirteen tricks. East–West could make thirteen tricks with no trump suit.

Taking thirteen tricks is a very big deal in bridge. When we get to scoring you will see that the value of making thirteen tricks, a **grand slam** (2,220 points) dwarfs all other contracts. All you and your partner have to do is look at your cards, count your tricks, and go for it. But there's a catch. You have to commit yourself to going for the grand slam without seeing each other's cards! In other words, East and West have to state that they intend to make all thirteen tricks *before* the dummy comes down and they can actually see what's going on.

What if East and West don't commit to taking all thirteen tricks? Well, their score may end up being less. A lot less. In the extreme, they may misjudge their combined strength so badly that they wind up with a score of only 140 points, about 6 percent of the value of the grand slam.

Here's a riddle for you: How do East and West predict how many tricks they will make if they can't see each other's cards? The answer, if you haven't guessed it already, is by talking to each other and telling each other what is in their respective hands. We call this talk the **auction** and the way they do it, the **bidding.**

In the above example, West can say, "Partner, I have the ace, king third of both spades and hearts, six solid diamonds missing the ace, and a stiff club." East can reply, "Well, I have the queen, jack third of spades, the queen fourth of hearts and the ace third of both diamonds and clubs."

Simple! So where's the problem?

Unfortunately bridge rules forbid some of the aforementioned words from being spoken during the auction. Words such as *ace, king, queen, jack* are on that list of disallowed words. Words such as *third, fourth, solid, stiff*—also prohibited. In fact, only about a dozen words make up your entire vocabulary during a bridge auction. Here then is your collection of twelve permissible terms:

> *one, two, three, four, five, six, seven;*
> *clubs, diamonds, hearts, spades;*
> and *no trump.*

Now try describing those two hands.

Oh, there's one other small problem. You can't use just any combination of these words—you must choose both one number and one suit (also called a **strain**). *One spade*, or *two diamonds*, or *four no trump*—you get the picture. A number, from one to seven, paired with a strain: that's the language of bridge bidding.

Now, using these few words, this new language, you and your partner will learn to describe every imaginable combination of twenty-six cards. Of course, as with any new foreign language, this may take some time; but the fluency and powers of communication you will achieve will surprise you.

If both sides were dealt an equal number of aces, kings, queens, and so on, all the way down to the tiny deuce, then both sides would be expected to make the same number of tricks. But as we have noted, thirteen, the total number of tricks contained in a deck of cards, is a number that cannot be divided equally. One side may make six tricks, the other seven—but that's as even as we get. Who makes that pivotal seventh trick? Clearly that's the one to focus on. When talking about a bridge contract, we discount the first six tricks (after all, anyone can make six); the fight is over that seventh trick. We call the first six tricks **book,** as if it's a standard completion of duties: having won your first six tricks, you are said to have **made book**. The next trick after that is the first truly crucial one. For bridge players it is the first **level** of importance. A **level-one** contract requires seven tricks be made. (If book is six tricks, then book plus one trick is seven.) A **level-two** contract requires eight tricks. (Six tricks, book, plus two tricks.) A **level-three** contract requires that nine tricks be won. (Book plus three is nine.)

Q: How many possible levels are there in the game of bridge?

A: Seven. There are thirteen possible tricks in a deck of cards, and counting up from six, or book, leaves us with seven levels, $13 - 6 = 7$.

Let's pretend we're at an auction. Let's auction off something pertinent—say, a deck of brightly colored playing cards. We'll put some constraints on the bidding: the opening bid has to be at least one dollar, and all subsequent bids must be in increments of twenty cents. Only four people will be involved in the auction—their names happen to be South, West, North, and East—and they can bid only when it's their turn to do so.

Now let's hear how the auction for those playing cards might sound when, say, South starts the bidding, and bids proceed clockwise.

South:	*"I don't want to bid at this point. I'll pass."*
West:	*"I'll open the bidding with $1."*
North:	*"I'll bid $1.20."*
East:	*"Okay, then I'll offer $1.40."*
South:	*"Even though I passed at first, what I've heard here has changed my mind about the merchandise. I'll step in now with a bid of $2."*
West:	*"I bid $1.80."*
Auctioneer:	*"Um . . . our last bid is $2. You can't call out $1.80. Your bid is insufficient."*

West:	*"Whoops, sorry. Guess I wasn't paying attention. I'll change that to $2.20."*
North:	*"$2.40."*
East:	*"I pass."*
South:	*"I pass too."*
West:	*"Too high for me: pass."*
Auctioneer:	*"Three passes end the auction. North, with the highest bid, buys this gorgeous deck of cards for $2.40."*

Of course, following the bidding in a game of bridge, you don't walk away with any brand-new merchandise. So what are you bidding on or buying in a bridge auction?

Remember, from chapters 1 and 2, that there are a declarer, a dummy, and two defenders. The declarer is trying to make some predetermined number of tricks in one of the five strains: spades, hearts, diamonds, clubs or no trump. Should he or she be successful, as we will see in our section on scoring, then that player will be rewarded accordingly. Basically, the more tricks the declarer contracts for and makes, the greater will be the reward. So one of the things you're bidding on in bridge is simply the right to play the hand; another is the right to determine how many tricks to try to contract for; and yet another is the right to decide what strain to play the hand in—meaning, playing the hand with one suit trump or nothing trump. (This ability to name the strain can be crucial, as the number of tricks available to your side is greatly determined by the amount of trump your side happens to hold, and getting to name the trump suit is a huge advantage.)

A bridge auction has many of the similarities and constraints shown in the fictitious auction above. At least four distinct guidelines govern the bidding.

1. To open the auction, first of all, a predetermined **minimum bid** or higher must be entered.

2. You have to bid in a certain order—clockwise around the table.

3. Each bid must be higher than the previous one and must be made in predetermined increments.

4. The auction ends when there are three consecutive passes.

The lowest level contract in bridge (level one) requires that seven tricks be made, book plus one. In order to enter a bid, you must understand that what you're doing is announcing to the table that—if you're the declarer—you intend to take more tricks (seven or more) than the opponents and you are going to try to take them in one particular strain.

Your bid, therefore, has two parts to it. First, it states how many tricks you are contracting for; and second, it tells what strain you would like to play in. A typical bid might sound like this: *one heart*. This would mean: "With hearts trump, I think our side can make seven tricks." That doesn't mean, however, that you have to be looking at seven tricks in your own hand. Bridge is a partnership game; and when you bid, you are actually seeking to communicate with your partner. What you're saying, in fact, with a bid of one heart is, "Partner, if you have your share of the remaining hearts and high cards, then, combined with the hearts and high cards in my hand, together we should be able to make at least seven tricks." Your hand might look like this:

♠ A 7 2   ♥ K Q J 10 5   ♦ K 9   ♣ 4 3 2

With hearts trump, you can't guarantee that you'll make seven tricks; but if your partner has his or her share of the remaining eight hearts (two or three of them) and his or her share of the remaining fourteen honor cards (four or five of them) then, together, that goal should be reached.

Let's now assign you a direction—North, for argument's sake—and make you the dealer. As dealer, you get to bid first. If you want to bid, and in this case you do, then you can in effect **open** the auction with a call of one heart (simply written, from here on in, as 1H). From this point on, throughout the life of the auction, you will be referred to as the opening bidder. Here's an update on the auction thus far:

N	E	S	W
1H			

As we progress in clockwise fashion, East gets to speak next. Let's give East the following hand:

♠ J 5 4   ♥ 9 4   ♦ J 8 7 4   ♣ Q 8 6 5

East, as you can see, has no long suit, no aces, no kings, and only one queen. East should have no expectation, then, of his side being able to take more tricks than the opponents, no matter what strain they might play in. Therefore, he should not get involved at this point. He says, "I pass" or "Pass" (written as **p** from now on). So:

N	E	S	W
1H	p		

South's hand, let's say, is:

♠ K Q 9 6 3   ♥ 3 2   ♦ A 10 6 5   ♣ 7 3

South, as it turns out, has his share of the honors (four) and a lot of spades. His partner, North, has already announced that, all things being equal, he thinks his side can take more than half the tricks. But although South's partner likes hearts, he has only two little ones; maybe together, as a partnership, they'd like spades better. South would like to offer that possibility to his partner and see what North thinks. How can he do it?

Let's refer again to our make-believe auction. The bidding started at $1 and rose in increments of 20 cents. There were five possible bids, then, below $2: $1, $1.20, $1.40, $1.60, and $1.80. Bridge allows for five possible bids between the level one and the level two. Remember when we learned to say a bridge hand? It was important to order the suits correctly: spades first, then hearts, then diamonds, and finally clubs. If you'll notice, every time we present a bridge hand for you to bid, we keep that same order. Spades are highest in value, clubs lowest. Your familiarity with this order will now pay off. Bridge's equivalent to the $1 bid— that is, the lowest possible bid—is **one club**, the lowest level (one) and the lowest-ranking suit (clubs). Next up the scale comes **one diamond**, then **one heart**, and then **one spade**. But spades, while the highest-ranking suit, are not the highest strain you can bid on a contract level: there are *five* strains, not four. **No trump** is the highest strain that can be bid. So:

MONEY BIDS		BRIDGE BIDS
$1.00	=	1C
$1.20	=	1D
$1.40	=	1H
$1.60	=	1S
$1.80	=	1NT

During the auction, from the opening bid on, you must always bid in order of rank: first clubs, then diamonds, then hearts, then spades. This is called bidding **up the**

line. You don't have to bid each and every suit; you just have to bid a higher suit or level, each turn, than the previous bidder.

> one no trump (highest)
> one spade
> one heart
> one diamond
> one club (lowest)

Q: Which bid is higher, one spade or two clubs?

A: Any level-two bid must be higher than any level-one bid. (Two dollars is higher than one dollar and any amount of change.)

Q: Which is a higher bid, four hearts or four diamonds?

A: Four hearts. On any level, one to seven, the hearts suit outranks the diamonds suit.

Our auction has so far proceeded like this:

N	E	S	W
1H	p		

Now, let's take another look at how South can enter the auction. South's hand, once again, is:

♠ K Q 9 6 3   ♥ 3 2   ♦ A 10 6 5   ♣ 7 3

Q: How can South tell you, his partner, that he likes spades and has his share of the remaining honors?

A: He can bid one spade. That is a higher-ranking bid than one heart, and so is a valid and progressive bid; it also

conveys a specific message to North: "I am long in spades and have some valuable cards."
Therefore:

N	E	S	W
1H	p	1S	

And the auction proceeds from there.

Bridge auctions can come in many shapes and sizes, from astoundingly complex to ridiculously simple. Here are a few examples to give you a clearer sense of the dynamics and outcomes of auctions.

1.

W	N	E	S
p	p	1H	p
2H	p	p	p

The contract for this auction is for 2H. West and East have contracted for eight tricks (book plus two) with hearts trump. Notice that the auction ended after three players said pass.

Q: Who, in this auction, is the declarer (i.e., who plays the hand)?

A: **The declarer is the first person to introduce the strain that the hand is ultimately played in.** Here East introduced the heart suit; therefore, no matter how many times or how high West bids hearts, if the contract winds up with hearts trump—as it has—then West will be the dummy and East, as declarer, plays the hand.

2.

W	N	E	S
1C	1S	1NT	2S
p	p	p	

In this example North–South bought the contract for 2S.

Q: Who is the declarer?

A: North. After all, it was North who bid spades first.

Q: How many tricks do East and West need to make in order to beat this contract?

A: Six. North–South need to make eight tricks. Therefore, to defeat that effort—that is, to keep North–South from fulfilling their contract—East–West would have to make six. If East–West make six tricks before North–South get to eight, there will not be enough tricks left for North–South to make eight. (13 − 6 = 7, one less than the eight tricks N–S contracted for.)

3.

S	W	N	E
p	p	1D	1S
3D	p	3NT	p
p	p		

Here North–South contracted for nine tricks with nothing trump.

Q: Who plays the hand?

A: North: North was the only one to bid no trump.

4.

W	N	E	S
1NT	p	2H	p
2S	p	3C	p
4C	p	4NT	p
5D	p	5NT	p
6D	p	7S	p
p	p		

East–West have contracted for all thirteen tricks. If successful, they will have bid and made a grand slam.

Q: Who plays the hand?

A: Look back to see who first introduced spades. It was West, with his second bid. West is the declarer.

Example 4 was a complex auction, with five rounds of bidding.
Now let's look at two of the simplest auctions.

5.

S	W	N	E
1NT	p	p	p

A one-bid auction: North–South contract for seven tricks with no suit trump.

6.

S̲	W̲	N̲	E̲
p	p	p	p

No one bids. Nobody opens the auction. In this case, the hands get reshuffled and dealt again.

Now, let's formalize the elements of the auction and give you the bridge terms that you'll be using. Here's an auction written out, and what follows is a step-by-step description of the process:

N̲	E̲	S̲	W̲
p	1S	p	2S
p	3D	p	4S
p	p	p	

a. North, the dealer, starts the auction with a **call** of pass.

b. East **opens** the auction with a **bid** of 1 spade. (Bids name a number and a strain. Bids and passes are both calls; a call, the more general term, is any action taken during the auction.) For the life of the auction East will be referred to as the **opening bidder**.

c. After South passes, West makes a bid of two spades in response to his partner's opening bid. He is the **responder** and will be referred to as such for the rest of the auction.

d. East's bid of three diamonds, after a pass by North, is called a **rebid.** In fact, after each player made their first bid, every subsequent bid by that player is a rebid.

e. After another pass by South, West rebids 4 spades.

Notice the skipping of a level. After East bid 3D, West could have bid spades at the level three (three spades); but West chose to raise the stakes. We call this a **jump bid,** or a **skip bid.**

f. The third pass ends the auction.

East, then, is the declarer—he introduced spades in the first place. West is the dummy. South makes the opening lead, as South is to the left of the declarer.

Let's review the auction as a seasoned player would:

"North/South passed throughout. East opened one spade, West raised to two. East rebid three diamonds, West then jumped to four spades ending the auction."

EVALUATING BRIDGE HANDS: THE POINT-COUNT SYSTEM

By looking at some sample hands, you can get a sense of the **value** of your holdings and begin to learn how to bid accordingly.

A.	♠ J 8 7 2	♥ Q 4 3	♦ J 5	♣ 9 8 7 6
B.	♠ A K 8 7	♥ K Q	♦ A 5	♣ Q J 10 9

Q: Between A and B, which hand would you rather be dealt? Which "feels" stronger to you? Which, in other words, has more trick-taking potential?

A: B. The higher honor cards should make this a no-brainer.

But it's not always that clear-cut. Imagine being dealt each of these three hands:

C.	♠ Q J 9 5	♥ K J 9 8	♦ Q 10 4	♣ K 9
D.	♠ A 8 7 5	♥ A 9 8 3	♦ A 7 4	♣ 9 2
E.	♠ K Q J 5	♥ K Q J 3	♦ 10 7 4	♣ 9 2

Which of these hands feels strongest to you?

Hand C contains the most honor cards (seven: two kings, two queens, three jacks), but if I asked you how many tricks you would expect to make from this collection, you'd be hard-pressed to name even one sure one. After all, there are a lot of honor cards that C *doesn't* hold that can beat even C's highest-ranking cards.

Hand D contains the fewest number of honors (three), but they're all aces. That means D will take three sure tricks.

Hand E has six honor cards, and they're in two KQJ sequences. You have no sure tricks; but potentially, if you could drive out both the spade and heart aces in your opponents' hands, then you'd be able to promote four tricks for yourself: two in spades, two in hearts. *If . . .*

So which hand feels strongest?

From bridge's inception in the 1840s through the early part of the twentieth century, the bidding—that is, the predicting of how many tricks your hand, and ultimately your partner's hand, could take—was extremely difficult. You did it mainly by feel. ("I *feel* like, together, we can take eight tricks.") Feel comes from experience, of course. You can't teach experience, and therefore you can't teach feel. This is frustrating for new players, and a real turn-off. And inaccurate, at best, even for old-timers.

In the late teens and early 1920s, a man named Milton Work revolutionized the bidding by making it simpler and more logical than ever before. He did it by popularizing the now universally accepted point-count method for evaluating bridge hands. (Twenty years later, Charles Goren would add the finishing touches to this system.) The point-count system, combined with the showmanship of Eli and Josephine Culbertson and the exciting new refinements in scoring introduced by Harold Vanderbilt, turned bridge in a mere ten years from a stuffy, egghead-intellectual pursuit practiced by only a few into the second most popular indoor sport in the United States, with over 40 million devotees. The essentials of this system are so simple that they seem almost laughable.

Bidding systems had always focused attention on the four highest-ranking cards, the ace, king, queen, and jack. It was common knowledge that these sixteen cards were responsible for winning the preponderance of tricks on any given hand (eight or nine out of the thirteen available). These systems, as we've discussed, were cumbersome, inaccurate, and relied heavily—and unfortunately—on feel.

What Work (and his colleague Bryant McCampbell) tried to do was to discover whether a simple relationship might exist between these four honor cards: one that would make it easy to evaluate hands that contained random amounts of each of them. They decided to assign different weights to these four cards. They started with the simplest numbers first: one, two, three and four, with the jack, the weakest, given the weight (or value) of one, the queen two, the king three, and the ace four.

Ace	=	4 points
King	=	3 points
Queen	=	2 points
Jack	=	1 point

1 + 2 + 3 + 4 = 10. Each suit's points added up to the nice, easy, familiar, workable number of ten. Four suits in the deck, ten points per suit, forty points in all.

I'm sure at this point old Work and McCampbell didn't think much would come of these simple and random designations. But they had to start somewhere, and these numbers were really the easiest to work with. If they felt like they were on the right track, I'm sure they assumed there'd be some serious fine-tuning needed later.

So imagine their shock and delight when they realized that their baby system enabled them to evaluate even extremely complex hands with startling precision.

It couldn't be easier. One, two, three, four: add up the combined high card points that each partnership held, and—*eureka!*—out came a number that determined how many tricks each partnership could make! It didn't matter what combination of aces, kings, queens, and jacks went into the mix; the only thing that was important was the total itself. The point-count system determined the outcome perfectly. It worked early in the century, and it works today. It's the system we've used ever since!

Before I explain any more, let's try out the point-count system in the following hands. Here's the first hand:

1. North	♠	♥	♦	♣	
	A	10	K	Q	
	K	9	3	9	
	7	5		8	
	4	2			
	7	0	3	2	= 12

South	♠	♥	♦	♣	
	Q	K	J	A	
	J	8	10	K	
	9	7	4	5	
			2		
	3	3	1	7	= 14

Q: How many combined high card points (**HCP**) are there in these two hands?

A: If you count, you'll see that there are twenty-six. Here are the subtotals and totals, suit by suit:

North:	7 HCP (in spades) + 0 (hearts) + 3 (diamonds) + 2 (clubs) = 12 HCP
South:	3 + 3+ 1 + 7 = 14 HCP
North + South =	12 + 14 = 26 total high card points

Now try these:
Here's the second hand:

		♠	♥	♦	♣
2.	North	K	A	K	K
		7	Q	J	7
		5	J	4	
		2		2	
					=
	South	♠	♥	♦	♣
		A	6	Q	Q
		8	5	10	J
			3	7	4
			2		2
					=

Q: How many high card points are there between North and South?

A: Counting them up will reveal that, as with the first hand, there are once again 26 HCP. Here it is, step by step:

North:	3 + 7 + 4 + 3 = 17
South:	4 + 0 + 2 + 3 = 9
North + South =	17 + 9 = 26

Based on this data, even though hands A and B look nothing alike, what Work's point-count system is able to predict is that since both North–South pairs have, between them, the same number of high card points (HCP), both pairs would take the same number of tricks.

Let's go back now and look at the three hands that we asked your opinion of at the start of this section.

Using your newly acquired skills of evaluation, we can now ask which of the following hands is strongest, rather than simply which feels strongest?

1. ♠Q J 9 5   ♥K J 9 5   ♦Q 10 4   ♣K 9

2. ♠A 8 7 5   ♥A 9 8 3   ♦A 7 4   ♣9 2

3. ♠K Q J 5   ♥K Q J 3   ♦10 7 4   ♣9 2

Our new point-count method finds that each hand contains the same HCP total of twelve. Surprise ! They are all of equal strength!

One, two, three, four . . . I told you it was ridiculously simple. In its simplicity lies its beauty and appeal. Any second grader worth his salt can add to ten. What clarity this system afforded. And what fun! Imagine being able to communicate with your partner in a language that was now so easy to learn and understand.

Bridge had always been acknowledged as the most exciting card game to play. When Work and McCampbell came along with the new point-count system, it also became the most exciting card game to bid. Bridge's one-two punch (bid it–play it) quickly knocked out the competition. Converts from every other card game rushed to embrace bridge.

Understanding the Point-Count System

If we take the forty high card points in the deck, then randomly count out any combination of honors totaling twenty HCP and give it to one partnership—say N–S—and give the other partnership the remaining 20 HCP, *with nothing trump*, which partnership do you think would make more tricks?

According to Work's point-count system, knowing the number of HCP each partnership has is enough, in itself, to know how many tricks each side would make. If both sides have the same number of HCP, that would mean that both sides should take the same number of tricks.

13 tricks in a hand, divided by 2 teams = 6½ tricks per team.

Each side *should* take six and a half tricks, but of course you can't divide thirteen by two, because you can't split a trick in two. We know that each side should have no trouble making six tricks (making book). The fight would be over the seventh trick. We could expect it to be a toss-up as to who would win it. Perhaps it would depend on the lead, or a favorable tenace position. But with an equal number of HCP we wouldn't be able to predict who would make the seventh trick.

What would we have to do, according to the point-count system, to insure that one side, rather than the other, makes that seventh trick? The answer is that we'd have to give that side the equivalent of one trick more in HCP. And what is the equivalent of a trick? In the simplest terms, an ace. In a no trump contract, an ace, being the master card, will always win a trick. An ace has a 4-point value. Therefore in order to ensure that East–West makes that seventh trick, we have to divide the HCP so that they have four points more than their opponents.

Algebra Quiz 1 (and don't worry, there isn't a 2!):

If both sides have a combined total of 40 HCP, and one side has 4 points more than the other, how many points does each side have?

The answer is that one side has 22, the other 18. 22 − 18 = 4, there's your 4-point difference.

So to see if you and your partner can make seven tricks with *nothing trump*, add up your combined high cards. If the total comes to twenty-two, then you'll succeed. If it comes to less, you'll probably fail. It's that simple.

Summary: **To make seven tricks, one trick more than book, your side needs 4 points more than the opponents.**

Let's take it up a level.

Q: With nothing trump, what if you wanted to make eight tricks, or two tricks more than book. How many HCP would you need?

A: You would need the equivalent of *two* aces, or two tricks more than the opponents. 2 aces = 8 HCP. You'd need 24 points. That would leave your opponents with 16: 24 −16 = an 8-point difference.

Q: And finally, not only to see if you are digesting all this, but also to introduce you to the single most important number in bridge: With nothing trump, what if you wanted to make nine tricks, or three tricks more than book? How many HCP do you think you would need?

A: 26 HCP. To make three tricks more than book you would need the equivalent of three tricks more in ammunition than the opponents. 3 aces = 3 tricks = 12 HCP. You would have 26 HCP, and your opponents would have 14 HCP. *Twenty-six,* there it is. The most important number in bridge. We'll be back to it shortly.

THE NO TRUMP BIDDING BOX			
Numbers of tricks in no trump you and your partner want to make	HCP you and your partner need	HCP your opponents will have	Points needed over opponents
seven tricks (the one level— 1 NT)	22 points	18 points	4 (one trick)
eight tricks (the two level—2 NT)	24 points	16 points	8 (two tricks)
nine tricks (the three level—3NT)	26 points	14 points	12 (three tricks)

If bidding no trump hands simply requires that we know the combined point count of the two hands, all we need to do is figure out how to tell each other how many points we each have and then, using simple arithmetic, add the two together and come up with the right bid to fit the total.

For example, count your points in the hand below:

♠A 7 6 3   ♥A 5 2   ♦Q J 9   ♣K J 10

Did you get 15?

Q: Now, if you have 15 HCP, how many HCP does your partner need to make a one level no trump contract (1NT)?

A: The one level requires your side to make one trick over book. You need, in total, four points more than the opponents, so between you and your partner you need 22. If you bring 15 points to the table, your partner needs to bring 7.

His hand might be:

♠K 8   ♥Q 10 3   ♦10 8 7 2   ♣Q 8 5 2

Q: What if you wanted to attempt a two level contract?

A: You and your partner need two tricks more than book. Two tricks is 8 HCP.

Your side needs 8 HCP more than their side. That translates to your side needing 24 combined HCP to their 16 HCP. So if you bring 15 points to the table, in order for your partnership to total 24 HCP, your partner needs to bring 9 HCP.

His hand might be:

♠K 8 2   ♥J 10 3   ♦K 8 7 2   ♣Q 8 5

▪ NO TRUMP BIDDING

You'll need your deck of cards for this section. I'd like you to make up a bridge hand that meets the following two requirements:

1. The hand must contain a total of 15, 16 or 17 HCP.

2. The hand cannot contain a void (a suit with no cards), nor can it have any singletons (a suit with only one card) nor more than one doubleton (a suit with only two cards).

Q: Which of the following hands meet these requirements?

1.	2.	3.
♠ A K 5	♠ 9 8 7 6	♠ A K J 7 5 4 2
♥ A 7 2	♥ A K 5	♥ A K 5
♦ K J 5 4	♦ A 10 7 2	♦ 9 6
♣ J 10 6	♣ K J	♣ 7

4.	5.	6.	7.
♠ Q J 9	♠ K 9	♠ A K 9	♠ A J 7 4 2
♥ K 10 7 2	♥ A Q 3	♥ A Q 5 4	♥ A K
♦ A 6 3	♦ J 9 8 4 2	♦ K J 6 2	♦ 9 5
♣ K 10 5	♣ K Q 7	♣ K 9	♣ A J 8 6

Answers:

1: Yes.	16 HCP	no void no singleton no doubleton
2: Yes.	15 HCP	no void no singleton only one doubleton
3: No.	15 HCP	one singleton
4: No.	13 HCP	
5: Yes.	15 HCP	no void no singleton no doubleton
6: No.	20 HCP	
7: No.	17 HCP	two doubletons

Look carefully at hand 1:

♠ A K 5
♥ A 7 2
♦ K J 5 4
♣ J 10 6

See how evenly the cards are distributed? No suit contains fewer than three cards or more than four. We call this
type of even hand a **flat hand.** If we wanted to discuss the

shape of this hand, we would say it was a "4–3–3–3" or "4 triple 3." We start by saying the number of cards in the longest suit, followed by the next longest, down to the shortest suit.

Look at hand 2:

♠ 9 8 7 6
♥ A K 5
♦ A 10 7 2
♣ K J

The distribution of this hand is 4–4–3–2. We can turn it into a 4–3–3–3 hand by simply turning the 6♠ into the 6♣:

♠ 9 8 7 6		♠ 9 8 7
♥ A K 5		♥ A K 5
♦ A 10 7 2		♦ A 10 7 2
♣ K J		♣ K J 6
a 4–4–3–2 hand	turns into	a 4–3–3–3 hand

(Alternatively you could have changed the 2♦ to a 2♣— either way it would have changed the distribution to a 4–3–3–3 hand.)

Hand 5 is a 5–3–3–2 hand. What card can we move in order to make this a flat hand, or a 4–3–3–3? The answer is to change any diamond into a spade.

♠ K 9		♠ K 9 2
♥ A Q 3		♥ A Q 3
♦ J 9 8 4 2		♦ J 9 8 4
♣ K Q 7		♣ K Q 7
a 5–3–3–2 hand	turns into	a 4–3–3–3 hand

All of this is just to give an idea of what **distribution** is all about. The flattest hand possible in bridge has a

4–3–3–3 shape. The next two flattest hands, 4–4–3–2 and 5–3–3–2 are only one card removed from being perfectly flat.

Now let's put this into a bridge context. Look at the first hand we discussed:

♠ A K 5
♥ A 7 2
♦ K J 5 4
♣ J 10 6

Which suit stands out among these as special? If you could name one of them trump, which would you choose? You might guess the four-card suit, but wouldn't it depend to a large degree on how many cards of that suit your partner had? If your partner had zero, one, or two, the opponents would actually have more of this suit than your side.

Let's say for a moment that we went ahead and named our four-card diamond suit trump. What remaining suit would we be likely to trump? Remember, to trump a suit you must first void yourself of that suit. All your other suits have three cards in them. That's a lot of work to do to create a void. When you have one of three flat shapes, by definition you have no short suit (void or singleton)—no suit to ruff.

Q: What strain comes to mind when you have no obvious trump suit and nothing to trump in your hand?

A: You should think in terms of playing this hand in no trump.[1]

_____

1. Different countries developed different bidding systems over the years. In the United States, our system is called—what else?—Standard American. The ACOL system used in England has a 13–15–point range for

All over the world, if your distribution is 4–3–3–3, 4–4–3–2, or 5–3–3–2 your shape is considered no trumpish. In the United States if your no-trumpish hand also contains 15–17 HCP, then you have met the requirements for an opening bid of one no trump. Here's an example. Say you are West and this is your hand:

♠ 9 8 7 6
♥ A K 5
♦ A 10 7 2
♣ K J

Provided no one before you has bid, when it's your turn to speak you can open the auction with a bid of 1NT. (You have 15 HCP, 4–4–3–2 distribution.)

This is how the auction would go:

Say East, your partner, deals the cards and says "pass." North also says "pass." You, West, say "one no trump."

South	East	North	West
——	p	p	1NT

With this one bid, one no trump, look at all the information you've conveyed to your partner (and to the opponents, who are listening as well):

---

an opening one no trump bid. In Italy, no trumps in their Precision system are from 12–14 points. Recently 17–19–point no trumps are finding favor among experts.

What defines most bidding systems is their no trump range. Like an axiom in mathematics, certain assumptions must be made (the fewer the better). Standard American's axiom is that no trump is defined as 15–17 HCP. (Even this has changed over the years. As recently as the early 1970s Standard American's range was 16–18 HCP. Fortunately, this one-point change has made little difference in the overall strategy of bridge play.)

- You have narrowed the number of HCP in your hand from anywhere from one to forty down to only a three point range . . . fifteen, sixteen or seventeen.

- You have also narrowed the distribution of your hand from thirty-six possible shapes, down to only three . . . 4–3–3–3, 4–4–3–2, 5–3–3–2.

Now that you've communicated to your partner what you're holding in your hand, what does he do with that information? That brings us to chapter 5.

5 NO-TRUMP SCORING AND MORE BIDDING PRACTICE

Playing **bridge without keeping score is** like going to a baseball game and not caring who wins. The score is so closely linked to the strategy and the play of a bridge game that not to keep score would take away half the fun of the game.

In fact, scoring in bridge is a lot like scoring in baseball. Any hit in baseball, be it a single, a double or a triple is good. But in order to turn them into runs, you have to put a couple of them together and bring the runners home. That's what counts and what defeats your opponents.

Bridge's equivalent to base hits are called **part scores** (or **partials**). Getting the runner home in bridge is called completing the **game.**

Imagine that you and your partner contracted to make seven tricks with nothing trump—a 1NT bid— and you pulled it off. How do you figure out the score?

Bridge scoring works off the metric system, with 100 points being the goal (getting the man home). Making a 1NT contract is worth 40 of those points. If 1NT is what you predicted you would make before play began, and then you made it, you and your partner would receive 40 points. Now where and how do you record them?

This is what a bridge score sheet looks like:

We	They

The "We" column, of course, is for our score, and the "They" column is for our opponents' score. There is a horizontal line across the middle of the pad. This is known as **the line.** The scores for making contracts go below the line. Everything else goes above the line.

The 40-point value for our 1NT *contract* therefore goes below the line like this:

We	They
40	

Had we been in this 1NT contract and made an extra trick (eight tricks rather than the seven we contracted for) we would have:

a: made our contract

b: made an **overtrick,** or an extra trick.

In no trump scoring, the first level, or the first seven tricks you make, are worth 40 points. All subsequent tricks are worth 30 points apiece. So if our contract was 1NT, and we made an overtrick, we would record the overtrick above the line like this:

We	They
30	
40	

Note that overtricks go above the line as they are not part of what you contracted for.

Now try a few scoring exercises on your own:

Q: What if we contracted for 2NT and made eight tricks. What would that be worth and how would we write it on our score pad?

A: A two-level contract requires eight tricks (book + 2). Since we made eight tricks, we fulfilled our contract. We would get 40 points for the first seven tricks plus 30 points for the subsequent trick. In this case they would both be part of the contract (the eighth trick was not an overtrick); therefore they would get added together, 40 + 30, and all 70 points would go below the line.

We	They
70	

▪ CONTINUOUS SCORING

Now that you are familiar with how to record part scores, let's take a look at how to keep score during the course of a bridge game. Suppose we actually played those two example hands one after the other.

Our score pad after the first hand looked like this:

We	They
30	
40	

After the second hand, we would add the 70 points for bidding and making 2NT. The 70 would join the 40 below the line, bringing the total to 110 points below the line.

We	They
30	
40 **70** **110**	

In baseball when you put two or more base hits together and bring a base runner home, you are credited with a run. That's your bonus.

In bridge once you've put two or more contracts together that total 100 points or more, you've completed a game. Your bonus is an additional 500 points.

Five hundred points! Every other score we're familiar with so far pales in comparison.

After the game is made, the scores are added up and a new sheet is started.

500 (bonus) + 40 + 70 (from below the line) + 30 (from above the line) = 640

We'd start the new score sheet off like this:

We	They
640	

This total is called the **carryover.**

Here comes the big one, bridge's equivalent to a home run.

Let's say you and your partner contract for 3NT and make nine tricks. What's this worth, and how do we enter it on our score pad?

Nine tricks are required to make a three-level contract. You've made nine, so you have fulfilled your contract.

The value of a 3NT contract is: 40 (for the first level) + 30 + 30 (for each of the two additional tricks). Altogether that comes to 100 points. And all 100 points go below the line.

Bonus time! Not only do you get the 100 points for the value of the contract, but you also get the 500 additional points for making game. And it is all in one hand. Our new carryover (we've completed another game) is the 600 points from this game + the 640 points we already amassed, for a total of 1,240 points.

Three no trump is an awesome contract as it carries a value of 100 points all by itself. It is our first **game contract.** Bidding and making 3NT should continue to give you a rush for as long as you play this game.

▪ UNDERTRICKS

We are now going to look at what happens if you *fail* to make a contract. Say your contract is again 3NT, but this time you only make eight tricks. We know that 3NT requires nine tricks. You are about to suffer your first penalty.

Penalty: For each **undertrick** (trick contracted for and not made) you lose 100 points. Undertrick points are not contract points, so they are recorded above the line. Rather than using pluses and minuses, you simply give the 100 points to your opponents:

We	They
	100

Going plus means that a score will be entered on your side of the ledger. You go plus by making a contract or by defeating your opponents and collecting a penalty.

Going minus means that a score will be entered on your opponents' side of the ledger. You go minus when the opponents make a contract or when they extract a penalty from you.

■ DOUBLING

You are West. South opened the bidding 1NT, you passed. North bid 6NT, and East and South passed. Now it's your bid. This is your hand:

♠ A K 7 2
♥ 5 4 3
♦ 9 5 2
♣ 8 7 6

Ask yourself these questions:

Q: How many tricks do the opponents need to fulfill a six-level contract?

A: Book (6 tricks) + 6 = 12 tricks total.

Q: How many tricks can your opponents afford to lose?

A: There are thirteen total tricks, and they have contracted for twelve, so they can only afford to lose one trick.

Q: How many tricks are they *definitely* going to lose?

A: You have the ♠A K. You know that these two cards will win two tricks. South, having introduced NT as the strain that this hand would be played in, will be the declarer. You, West, with your two sure tricks, will therefore be on opening lead.

You know that your opponents are not going to make their contract, so after North makes his 6NT bid, when next it is your turn to call, you can say, "Double." **Doubling** increases the penalty if your opponents fail to make their contract. A double of a high-level contract (usually nine tricks or more) is called a **penalty double.**

Remember, undertricks are 100 points each. Even if you had just passed rather than saying double, your side would have still collected the 100-point penalty from the opponents for defeating the contract by one trick. Doubling doubles the profit, giving you 200 points in this case.

The first doubled undertrick doubles the penalty. All subsequent doubled undertricks *triple* the penalty.

PENALTIES: UNDOUBLED AND DOUBLED		
Undertricks	Undoubled	Doubled Undertricks
1st	100	200
2nd	200	500
3rd	300	800
4th	400	1,100*
5th	500	1,500*
*These last two numbers are euphemistically referred to as telephone numbers because of their four-digit size.		

The penalty double is like a traffic cop. It prevents the players from going too fast. Without it, almost every hand would be played in 3NT—the bonus is so big that it would always be worth going for. The threat of a double, which greatly increases the penalties involved and says, "I'm willing to bet you *can't* make that contract," is real enough to discourage frivolous attempts.

▪ PRACTICE

Let's put it all together.

First hand: Your side bids up to 2NT. The opponents defend badly and let you make ten tricks.

How it gets scored: You get 70 points for bidding and making 2NT. Since this was part of your contract, the score goes below the line. You get 60 points for two overtricks (30 + 30). These are recorded above the line. Your score sheet would look like this:

We	They
60	
70	

Second hand: The opponents bid 3NT. Your partner doubles them. They take only six tricks.

How it gets scored: The opponents contracted for nine tricks but took only six. You defeated them by three tricks. Had your partner not doubled them, your side would have collected a 300-point profit. Look at the penalty chart. The double increases your profit to 800 points! Since they are not the result of a contract, these

800 points go above the line and are added to the score from the previous hand.

We	They
800	
60	
70	

Third hand: Your opponents bid 1NT and make exactly seven tricks.

How it gets scored: They get a straightforward 40 points below the line. This is how the score sheet looks now:

We	They
800	
60	
70	40

Here's where the scoring gets interesting. Both sides have partials (parts of 100 points; parts of a game). If we want to make game, all we need to do is make a contract of 1NT, which will get us past 100 points under the line.

The opponents' 40-point partial requires them to make at least a 2NT contract to complete the partial.

Neither one of us need bid higher than that.

Fourth hand: They bid 2NT and make ten tricks.

How it gets scored: They made their contract with two overtricks. They get 70 points below the line and 60 points above the line. They also completed their part score (40 + 70), so they also get the bonus of 500 points, for making game.

We	They
800	500
60	60
70	40
	70

At the end of the game we have 930 points total, and they have 670 points. To move on to the next game, subtract the lower score from the higher; the difference gets **carried** onto the next score sheet. This is how it would look:

We	They
260	

▪ NO TRUMP BIDDING

Now that we have some ideas of the equities involved, let's see if we can appreciate what goes into your partner's thinking when he hears you open one no trump.

One no trump says to him that you have only one of three possible suit distributions (4–3–3–3, 4–4–3–2, or 5–3–3–2) and one of only three possible numbers of high card points (15, 16, or 17). Remember the no-trump bidding box? The number 26 was the number of HCP your partnership needed in order to be able to make nine tricks. Let's review how we got to that number.

With the forty HCP divided equally, no side was assured more than six tricks (book): 20-20.

When one side had the equivalent of an ace (4 points) more than the other, that side would be able to make one trick more than book: 22–18.

When one side had the equivalent of two aces (8 points) more than the other, that side would be able to make two tricks more than book: 24–16.

When one side had the equivalent of three aces (12 points) more than the other, that side would be able to make three tricks more than book: 26–14.

22 HCP = 7 tricks
24 HCP = 8 tricks
26 HCP = 9 tricks

These numbers refer to the number of HCP needed to make the corresponding number of tricks when playing with nothing trump.

Here's some practice:

Q: How do we say a seven-trick contract with nothing trump?

A: 1NT

Q: How do we say a nine-trick contract with nothing trump?

A: 3NT

Q: What about an eight-trick contract with nothing trump?

A: 2NT

You get the picture. When we learned to keep score, we saw that if we bid and made a 3NT contract we received a huge bonus. There are no bonuses for bidding and making 1NT or 2NT. This huge bonus is what bridge bidding is all about. If you and your partner think that between your two hands you have the material to make nine tricks, then you'll want to go ahead and bid up to that level. In order to get the bonus you have to contract for it. If you contract for 1NT but end up making nine tricks, you don't get the huge bonus. To get the bonus for making nine tricks, you must contract for it.

Q: How many HCP does it take to make 3NT?

A: Twenty-six. (1NT = 22, 2NT = 24.) That is why the number twenty-six is so significant. It is the total amount of high cards—aces, kings, queens, and jacks—needed to produce nine tricks.

You'll recall that in Standard American bidding, an opening bid of 1NT means that the player has 15, 16, or 17 HCP. If he holds less than that, he cannot open 1NT.

Q: When your partner opens 1NT, what is the minimum number of HCP you need to be holding in order to

guarantee your partnership will have that magic total of 26, which will allow you to shoot for the bonus?

A: Your partner could be holding as few as 15 HCP. In order to reach 26 you must have at least 11 HCP. 11 + 15 = 26.

Example:
Here's your hand:

> ♠ K 9 6 3
> ♥ K 10 5
> ♦ A 8 4 2
> ♣ J 7

If your partner, North, opens the bidding with 1NT, and East on your right says pass, what do you think your bid would be? You have 11 HCP, and since your partner bid 1NT, you know he has at least 15 HCP. Between the two of you, you have enough HCP to make nine tricks. So you bid 3NT.

Why the eagerness to jump to 3NT? Well, if you're successful you'll get the 500-point bonus. This is good strategy and good bidding. If you don't raise your partner's 1NT bid, and he subsequently makes nine tricks, you and he will not get the bonus.

▪THE HARSH REALITY

Having sung the praises of a combined HCP total of 26, let me inform you that 26 points do not insure that you will make nine tricks. If they did, there would be no need to play out any hands. You would simply inform the opponents that, from the bidding, you determined that you had 26 HCP and would they be so kind as to credit your side of the ledger with an extra 500 points. Their benevolence probably wouldn't extend that far. They probably will want you to play the hand out and prove it to them.

In reality what 26 points does give you is a fifty–fifty shot at nine tricks. Every additional HCP increases your chances significantly. So why take a chance with only 26 points and a fifty–fifty proposition? Why not wait until we have 28 or even 30 HCP when the percentages for success are in the high 90s? Let's take a lesson from the casinos of Las Vegas.

You know the game roulette, right? A wheel that contains an equal number of red and black spaces is spun in one direction, and a little ball is spun in the other direction. When the ball slows down, it lands in either a red or a black square. You bet either red or black—it's a fifty–fifty proposition.

The casino pays you accordingly. Let's say you bet $10 on black. If it stops on black, you win. The house matches your bet, and you come away with $20. If it comes up red, you lose, and they take your money.

What would happen if the odds changed? Imagine if when you won, instead of paying you an extra $10, they paid you an extra $30. Trust me. If that were the case, you wouldn't be reading this book right now. You'd be lined up around the block waiting to take the house's money.

Won't happen.

In bridge it happens all the time!

That's the significance of the 500-point bonus. It's well worth the risk because the payoff is so high.

Let's take a look at the difference between two partnerships who are bidding on their 26-point hands. Pair A is comprised of two timid souls who just can't stand to lose. They hate to take any risk at all, preferring to go plus whenever they can. Pair B are two players who always play the odds. If the odds say bid, they bid. Let's follow their strategies over the following two hands, played at different times over the course of an evening, and see how they fare.

Both hands contain exactly 26 HCP. On both hands Pair A, the timid couple, stays out of danger. Rather than bid

3NT and risk defeat, they stop at 2NT; they know they're a shoo-in to make it because 2NT only requires 24 HCP to make. And since making nine tricks with only 26 HCP is only a fifty–fifty proposition, true to form, the first time around they make eight tricks; the second time they make nine tricks. They are happy: they went plus both times. This is what their score looks like:

Hand 1: bidding 2NT, making 8 tricks: 40 + 30 = 70 points

Hand 2: bidding 2NT, making 9 tricks: 40 + 30 (contract) +30 (overtrick) = 100 points

TOTAL: 170 points

Under the exact same circumstances Team B bids 3NT both times. On both hands they make the same number of tricks as Team A:

Hand 1: bidding 3NT, making 8 tricks: one undertrick = −100 points

Hand 2: bidding 3NT, making 9 tricks: 100 for the game + 500 bonus . . . + 600 points

TOTAL: 500 points

Pair B did almost three times better than Pair A! On a fifty–fifty shot they got three-to-one odds. It wasn't much of a gamble after all. Because of the bonus, every time your side has 26 HCP you must look for game.

You may be wondering why some 3NT contracts make and some fail. There are many reasons. If you need to take one or two finesses and they fail, chances are you'll go down. If the opponents lead a long suit and they're able to knock out your stoppers quickly, chances are you'll go down. If you need a key suit to split evenly in order to establish long-suit winners, and it does, chances are you'll make. And of course if you play poorly, chances are you'll go down.

▪RESPONDING TO YOUR PARTNER'S BID OF 1NT

Say your partner opens the bidding 1NT. You know that he has 15–17 HCP.

Q: What is the *least* number of points you need so that between you, you and your partner have enough points to possibly make game?

A: Between you, you need 26. The very most he can have is 17. So the least you can have to reach 26 together is 9.

$$9 + 17 = 26$$

When your partner opens 1NT, 9 is the minimum number of points you need to start thinking about bidding a game. If you have fewer than 9 points, 26 combined points is out of reach and you will have to pass.

If you had any of the following hands, and your partner bid 1NT, what would you say?

♠ K 9 5 2	♠ K 5 4	♠ 10 9 8 2
♥ Q J 3	♥ K 4 3 2	♥ 8 7 6
♦ 10 7 5 4	♦ Q 9 5 4	♦ J 4 3 2
♣ 9 8 2	♣ 7 6	♣ J 10

You would have to pass. None of these hands contain even the minimum 9 points you need to have any chance at reaching the 26 combined HCP needed to try for game.

What if you have exactly 9 points? If your partner has 17, you want to be in game. If your partner has only 15 or 16 points, then you don't.

$$15 + 9 = 24 \text{ (no)} \qquad 16 + 9 = 25 \text{ (no)} \qquad 17 + 9 = 26 \text{ (yes)}$$

When you have exactly 9 HCP and need to know if partner has 17, how do you express "Partner, do you have 17 points?" in bridge terms?

What bid do you think might say, "Partner, if you like your hand, bid 3NT"? Did you guess 2NT? That's right. A bid of 2NT says, "Partner, I'd like to bid 3NT, but I'm just not strong enough. I'm close but I need your help."

I suspect there are some of you wondering right now, if you were the opening 1NT bidder, and your partner raised you to 2NT, how were you supposed to know your partner is asking you to bid 3NT and not just telling you that you, as a partnership, can make 2NT? Let's break it down:

Think about the scoring we just did. How many total points do you receive for bidding and making 2NT, or eight tricks? The answer is 70.

How many points do you get for bidding 1NT and making it with one overtrick? Again, the answer is 70.

It's the same total.[1] In neither case are you eligible for the 500-point game bonus, so it doesn't make sense to bid 2NT over 1NT unless there's something else going on. When you raise your partner's 1NT bid to the two level, you're doing it for a different purpose. When you respond 2NT, you've got your sights set on something greater—the 500-point bonus. When you raise to 2NT you're not hoping to play there. You're hoping your partner will come back with a 3NT bid.

Say your partner bids 1NT and you have 9 points. You bid 2NT. If your partner *doesn't* have 17 points, he'll pass the next time around, and you will play in 2NT. (Remember,

---

[1]Observant readers might see that all 70 points go below the line in a 2NT contract, while only 40 go below the line in a 1NT contract. After playing and keeping score for a while, you will see that this difference is of little significance.

it takes 24 points to make 2NT. If your partner has only 15 or 16 added to your 9 points, you'll still have the 24 or 25 points needed to make 2NT.)

So, to review, when your partner bids 1NT:

... if you have 11 or more points, **go for the game** (bid 3NT)

... if you have exactly 9 points, **invite the game** (bid 2NT)

... if you have fewer than 9 points, **let your partner play in 1NT** (pass)

There's a number missing from this equation. What do you do if your partner bids 1NT and you have 10 points? Because of the equities involved, gamble and bid 3NT. If you have 10 points and your partner has 15, 16, or 17, here are the totals you might have:

$$15 + 10 = 25 \qquad 16 + 10 = 26 \qquad 17 + 10 = 27$$

Remember, 26 is the magic number. If you have 10 points, then two out of three times you will have enough ammunition to make a game. One of three times you'll have 25 points, and you would be a distinct underdog. There would be only a 40 percent chance of success, but the bonus just about covers that.

Summing up:

when partner opens 1NT ...

... with less than 9, you should pass,

... with 9 points, invite a game (bid 2NT), and

... with 10 or more points, go for a game (bid 3NT).

The association of *N*ine and *N*o trump might help you remember this; however, the real way to remember is to understand the logic behind the bids. Even someone with an above-average memory will have trouble memorizing all the different auctions possible.

So far we've explored four bridge auctions. In total there are more possible bridge auctions than moves in a chess game—about 5^{47}, that's a 5 with 47 zeroes after it. As creative as I am, I'm going to run out of memory tricks long before that. For that reason, I want you to memorize as little as possible and understand as much as possible.

For no trump bidding, this is what I want you to memorize:

1. 15–17 . . . the number of HCP needed to open 1NT.

2. 26 . . . the number of points needed in a partnership to try for game.

That's it! Haven't you done that already?

In the rest of the book you will be asked to memorize numbers less than half a dozen times.

Before we go any farther, though, please make sure you understand why when your partner opens a 1NT, you pass with 0–8 points, invite a game with 9, and bid 3NT with 10 or more. If you have to reread this section, do it before continuing. Try to own these bids.

▪ THE POINT-COUNT SYSTEM AND LENGTH

The point-count method we've used so far, devised around 1915 by Work and McCampbell, got a fine-tuning some thirty years later. Charles Goren, pehaps the most famous name in bridge history, brought **distribution** into the equation. This completed the picture. It has changed little since then.

In addition to HCP, Goren added points for suits longer than four cards. These are called **length points (LP).**

Which of these hands do you think offers more potential?

1. ♠ 9 8 7
   ♥ 9 8 7
   ♦ 9 8 7
   ♣ A K 9 7

2. ♠ 9 8 7
   ♥ 9 8
   ♦ 9 8
   ♣ A K 9 7 5 3

If you're holding hand 1 with 7 HCP, and your partner opens 1NT, you should pass. But hand 2 has a good long six-card club suit to go along with 7 HCP. Visualize your partner's hand. Since he opened in 1NT, you know he has at least two clubs. (He can't have a singleton or void; remember the three possible shapes to open in no trump? 4–3–3–3; 4–4–3–2; 5–3–3–2.) He might even have three or four clubs. There is a strong possibility that your club suit will produce five or six tricks.

This layout will produce 6 tricks:

This one will also produce 6 tricks if the opponents' suit splits 2–2, like this, and 5 tricks if the split is 3–1:

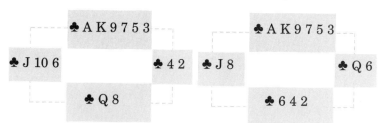

Remember, bridge is a game of tricks. Points were devised to make it easier for you to evaluate your hand, but don't lose sight of the forest for the trees. In the end it's all about tricks! When your partner opens 1NT and you know you can provide five or six tricks for him, his 15, 16 or 17 HCP may provide the three or four tricks you need to make game.

Goren added points for length to take the trick-taking power of length into account. All you have to do is **add one point for each card in a suit after the first four.** With just four cards, chances are overwhelming that another player also has four or more cards in a suit.

▪ DISTRIBUTION

Let's go back, for a moment, to the random laws of probability. When you shuffle a deck of cards and deal thirteen to each player, you never know how those cards will divide. But thanks to the laws of statistics, we can tell you how the cards are *likely* to fall:

If you have a four-card suit, chances are very good that someone else also has at least a four-card suit:

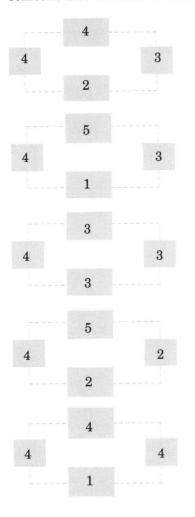

4–4–3–2: This is far and away the most likely distribution. If you deal millions of hands, the suit will divide this way 45 percent of the time.

5–4–3–1: The suit will divide this way 13 percent of the time.

4–3–3–3: The suit will divide this way 11 percent of the time.

5–4–2–2: The suit will divide this way 11 percent of the time.

4–4–4–1: If you deal millions of hands, the suit will divide this way 10 percent of the time.

The other possibilities account for less than 10 percent of all hands.

If you have a five-card suit, it is highly unlikely that someone else will also have a five-card or longer suit. That is why length points (LP) are counted from the fifth card and on.

13 percent of the time   1.5 percent of the time

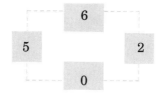

1.5 percent of the time

The remaining possibilities add up to about 1 percent of all hands dealt.

▪ PRACTICE COUNTING TRICKS

In the following examples, you are North–South. How many tricks will you make? How about your opponents?

A.

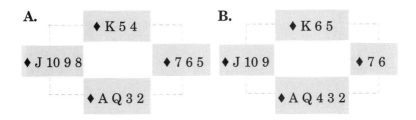

B.

C.

♦ 7 6 5

♦ 9 8   ♦ Q J 10

♦ A K 4 3 2

A. You will make three tricks; the opponents will take one.

B. You will make five tricks; the opponents will take none.

C. You will make four tricks; they will take one.

Counting HCP *and* LP (length points) in the hands below, how would you respond to your partner's opening bid of 1NT? Your choices are pass, 2NT or 3NT.

a. K x x
     x x x
     K Q 10 x x
     x x

b. Q x x
     K x
     x x
     K J x x x x

c. Q J
     K x x
     x x x
     J 10 9 x x

(Note: The x's stand for random spot cards.)

Answers:

a. Invite with 2NT. You have 8 HCP + 1 LP = 9 total points. Your partner could have 17 points. If he does, your total will come to 26. By bidding 2NT, you ask your partner to bid 3NT only if he has 17 points.

b. Jump to 3NT. You have 9 HCP + 2 LP = 11 total points. Even if your partner has 15 HCP, the fewest he can have to open 1NT, you still have enough to reach 26.

c. Pass. You have 7 HCP + 1 LP = 8 total points. Even if your partner has 17 points, 17 + 8 = 25, you won't be able to reach 26.

■ NO TRUMP REVIEW: OPENING AND RESPONDING

The following six hands may or may not be 1NT hands. Remember the two criteria: a 3-point HCP range and only three possible distributions. In the following examples, count the HCP first. If they come to 15,16 or 17, then *say* the distribution. If you hear yourself saying "four triple three" (4–3–3–3), "four four three two" (4–4–3–2), or "five three three two" (5–3–3–2), you know you've got a no trump opening.

Are the following 1NT hands?

1. ♠ A K 6 3	2. ♠ A 6 3 2	3. ♠ A K 9
♥ Q J	♥ K 9	♥ K J 6 3
♦ K Q 7 4	♦ A K 8 4 3	♦ Q 8 7
♣ K 5 4	♣ Q 5	♣ J 7 6

4. ♠ A Q 6 3	5. ♠ K Q 9 4	6. ♠ A K 7 4
♥ Q J 7 4	♥ A J 9 2	♥ K J 6 4
♦ 7	♦ A K 4	♦ Q J 2
♣ K Q J 9	♣ 3 2	♣ Q 7 6

Answers:

1. No. Right distribution (4–4–3–2), but too many HCP (18) for 1NT.

2. No. Right number of HCP (16), but wrong distribution (two doubletons).

3. No. Right distribution (4–3–3–3), but too few HCP (14).

4. No. Wrong distribution: a singleton is not allowed. 15 HCP.

5. Yes. Right HCP (17); right distribution (4–4–3–2).

6. No. Are you paying attention? There are fourteen cards! This is a misdeal. You would be surprised at how often hands get played with one person having fourteen points and another having twelve! This embarrassing moment would never happen to you if you took the time to sound out the distribution, what I call "sounding the shape." Like a method for learning a foreign language, this kind of repetition works to ingrain the patterns of card distribution in your mind. Being able to summon these patterns will be critical to you in the play of the game. So start repeating yourself!

Now imagine that *your partner* opens 1NT. If each of the following hands were yours, how would you respond? Again your choices for the time being are limited to pass, 2NT and 3NT.

7. ♠ Q J 9 4	**8.** ♠ Q 8 7 6	**9.** ♠ Q J 9
♥ 7 5	♥ Q 7 4 2	♥ 7 5
♦ A K 8 7	♦ Q 10 3	♦ A 10 9 8 4
♣ A 9 4	♣ Q 7	♣ J 9 3
10. ♠ K Q 7 6	**11.** ♠ Q 7	**12.** ♠ 7 3
♥ A K Q	♥ Q 6	♥ 8 4
♦ 8 7 6	♦ J 7 6 5	♦ 9 5
♣ 5 4 3	♣ 10 8 7 4 2	♣ A K 9 8 7 6 2

7. 3NT. Your partner has 15–17 HCP, you have 14. Together you have between 29–31 points, which should produce an easy game.

8. Pass. You only have 8 points. Even if your partner has 17, you cannot reach 26.

9. 2NT. Your 8 HCP + 1 LP = 9 points. Invite your partner to bid 3NT, because if he has 17, you want to be in game.

10. 3NT. Even though you have no stoppers in diamonds or clubs, you'll make game with this hand on sheer power. Partner has 15–17 HCP, which are clearly not in spades and hearts. Where do you think they are? They'd have to be in diamonds and clubs, no?

11. Pass. With 5 HCP and 1 LP, you'll be lucky to make even 1NT.

12. At first glance this looks like a pass, but with this

length strength in clubs, you should bid 3NT. Partner has at least two or three clubs with you (you know this because he has a NT distribution). Between the two of you, your clubs might produce seven tricks. His 15–17 HCP should produce at least the other two tricks.

For those of you who have already fallen under the spell of counting points (though, let's hope, not to the exclusion of everything else), in points this would add up to 7 HCP and 3 LP. With 10 points the correct response happens to be 3NT. Isn't it nice and consistent?

▪ PRACTICE IN BIDDING AND PLAYING THE HAND

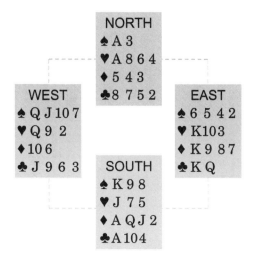

The Auction: South deals and notes (to herself) her shape, 4–3–3–3, a no-trump shape. Then she counts her HCP, which add up to 15—a 1NT number.

When you are dealt a no trump hand, you have to find a reason *not* to open 1NT. Here there is none. Not only does

South have a perfect no trump shape, but she has stoppers in every suit (which is not essential, but it can't hurt).

South opens 1NT. West says pass. (We will get to the opponents' bidding in a later chapter.)

North hears his partner open 1NT and his right-hand opponent (RHO) pass. He has two aces, or 8 HCP. Even if South has 17, he won't make it (17 + 8 = 25). Close, but no cigar. Unable to reach 26, North does not want to give South the green light with a bid of 2NT. North will have to pass and let his partner play in 1NT.

East also passes. This ends the auction.

The person who *first* named the strain in which the hand will be played becomes the declarer. That was South. She opened 1NT. She will be the declarer. The dummy will be South's partner, North. The person sitting to the *left* of the declarer makes the opening lead; in this case it is West. With his opening lead, West starts the defense for his side. He must choose his lead carefully.

Q: How does one take tricks in a no trump contract?

A: Basically there are two ways, with high cards and with long suits.

The defenders need at least seven tricks to defeat declarer's objective of making 1NT. High cards alone are almost never enough. Through fairly accurate bidding most declarers have about the right number of HCP to come mighty close to making what they bid. To defeat them usually takes a combination of high cards and length. The high cards can take care of themselves. The defense's strategy should be to try to set up long-suit tricks for themselves. Against a no trump contract, the opening leader usually chooses to play a card from his longest and strongest suit. In this case, West has two four-card suits. His spade suit is stronger, plus it contains a three-card honor sequence. If the

♠Q and ♠J can eliminate the opponents' ♠A and ♠K, then his ♠10 will be promoted to master card and his ♠7 may even take a long-suit trick. The spade suit offers West two tricks in potential—an excellent choice for an attacking opening lead. He leads the ♠Q, the top of the sequence.

The dummy comes down.

South now studies the situation. She might first look at the card that was led. She knows that it must be from the opponent's longest and strongest suit. The bad news for South is that she and her partner only have five spades between them. The good news is that she has two stoppers, the ♠A and the ♠K in the suit. South reasons that West's lead must be from at least a four-card suit (after all it is probably his longest) and since he led an honor, the ♠Q, he must have a sequence of at least three cards, the Q J 10. She visualizes West's spade holding as Q J 10 x or Q J 10 x x.

South knows she has two quick tricks in the spade suit. Can she take a third trick? No, because of West's sequence, South's spot cards in this suit will never get promoted to master cards. She looks at her heart suit. She has one quick trick this time, but she has a total of seven hearts. That means the opponents have six. Though she is missing the ♥K Q 10 9, the suit has some potential if the missing six cards are divided evenly, three each, between East and West. She would, in that case, have one long-suit trick. But an even number of cards (in this case six) tends to break unevenly : 4–2 rather than 3–3. Developing a long-suit trick would be a long shot (about three to one).

South's club suit also contains seven cards divided 4–3 between her and North. She has the ♣A, a quick trick, but again only a one-in-three chance of establishing a long-suit trick. Finally she comes to diamonds, a girl's best friend! Again she has only a 4–3 fit, and again only a one-in-three chance of establishing a long-suit trick. Here she has only one quick trick, the ace, but she also has two other honors. There's good potential here for extra tricks.

Now we'll put it all together. First off, there are South's quick trick winners: two in spades + one in hearts + one in diamonds + one in clubs. That's five. South has contracted for 1NT, which requires seven tricks, so she needs two more. She plans to look to her diamond suit to make those additional tricks.

Let's look again at the North–South diamond holdings:

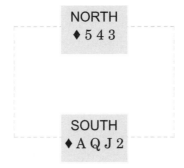

NORTH
♦ 5 4 3

SOUTH
♦ A Q J 2

Visualize where South would like to find the missing ♦K, over or under the ♦A Q J tenace? She would like to find East with the ♦K, under the tenace, because then it would be finessable. If West held the ♦K, North–South would not be able to make three diamond tricks (West's ♦K would capture South's ♦Q or ♦J). If the ♦K is indeed with East, South would need to be leading from the North hand (the hand opposite the tenace). Let's have declarer win the opening lead in dummy in order to start carrying out her plan.

Trick one: West leads the ♣Q and South wins the trick with the ♠A in the dummy. South now switches to a low diamond to start taking a finesse.

Trick two: South leads the ♦3 from the dummy, East plays the ♦7, and South finesses the ♦J successfully as West follows with the ♦6.

Trick three: South still has an A Q tenace. She still needs to take a second finesse. To bridge back to dummy she plays a low heart over to North's ♥A.

Trick 4: Now the lead is in the North hand. The ♦4 is led. East plays the ♦8, and South successfully repeats the finesse, this time using her ♦Q, as West follows with the ♦10.

South now has three diamond tricks to go along with her four outside winners and can fulfill her 1NT contract.

In order to carry out her plan South needed to take two successful finesses, each requiring that she start by leading a diamond from the dummy. To do that she needed to have two entries to the North hand. Before playing even one trick she needed to think through the whole sequence of plays and make sure her plan was not flawed. The more experienced the declarer, the easier it will be to visualize this whole series of plays.

▪ HANDS-ON PLAY

In each of the four hands below, attempt to do the following:

1. Bid the North–South cards

2. Look at West's opening lead, then plan your play.

The object is to make the number of tricks required to make your contract. Helpful tips and/or underlying principles will follow the hands. A complete layout of the cards, along with suggested bidding, will appear at the end of the section.

Hand 1:

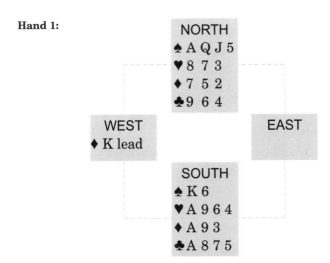

NORTH
♠ A Q J 5
♥ 8 7 3
♦ 7 5 2
♣ 9 6 4

WEST
♦ K lead

EAST

SOUTH
♠ K 6
♥ A 9 6 4
♦ A 9 3
♣ A 8 7 5

South deals. What is the number of HCP that South has? Is that within the range for an opening bid of 1NT? Say South's shape: 4–4–3–2. Is that a NT shape? The answer is yes to both questions. Therefore, South opens 1NT. West passes.

North has 7 HCP, no LP. Added to South's 15, 16, or 17, this total cannot reach the 26 needed to look for game. North should pass and hope to make a part score of 1NT. East's pass ends the auction.

South is the declarer; therefore West gets to make the opening lead. He leads the ♦K. As declarer, before the dummy comes down, what do you already know about West's hand? You know that he has at least four diamonds, three of which should be in a sequence, headed by the ♦K.

Okay, plan your play. (Always try counting your winners first.) Hint: be careful to unblock the ♠K. You should take three aces and four spade tricks for your required total of seven.

The complete hand was:

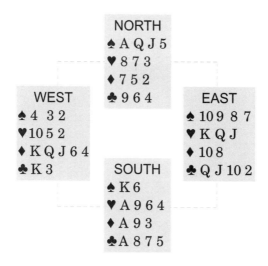

NORTH
♠ A Q J 5
♥ 8 7 3
♦ 7 5 2
♣ 9 6 4

WEST
♠ 4 3 2
♥ 10 5 2
♦ K Q J 6 4
♣ K 3

EAST
♠ 10 9 8 7
♥ K Q J
♦ 10 8
♣ Q J 10 2

SOUTH
♠ K 6
♥ A 9 6 4
♦ A 9 3
♣ A 8 7 5

Hand 2:

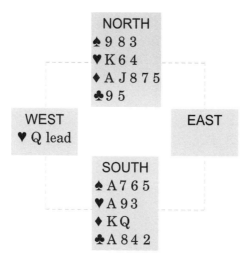

NORTH
♠ 9 8 3
♥ K 6 4
♦ A J 8 7 5
♣ 9 5

WEST
♥ Q lead

EAST

SOUTH
♠ A 7 6 5
♥ A 9 3
♦ K Q
♣ A 8 4 2

South deals. She has a 4–4–3–2 shape, 17 HCP and no LP. Therefore, she opens 1NT. North, meanwhile, has 8 HCP, 1 LP (that fifth diamond). With 9 points, there is a possibility of 26 combined points if South should have a maximum no trump holding of 17 points. North invites by bidding 2NT. South has 17 points and accepts by raising to game: 3NT.

West leads the ♥Q, showing a sequence and at least four-card length. Now plan the play. First, count your winners. Which card should win the first trick, dummy's ♥K or declarer's ♥A? Take your time and play out the hand in your head.

As with hand 1, it is crucial to unblock your honors. But this hand presents an additional problem. As declarer, your thinking should go something like this: "I have four tricks outside of diamonds. I need nine tricks total. I must make all five diamond tricks to fulfill my contract. I intend to unblock my ♦K and ♦Q, then play my ♦A and ♦J, and by then my little diamond should be a long-suit winner."

Did you notice a problem here? How will you get over to the dummy after you cash in your ♦K and ♦Q? Let's see, does the dummy have an **outside** (that is, outside of diamonds) **entry**? Yes: the ♥K, which you must be careful to preserve until it's needed for that purpose. Therefore, at trick one, you should plan on **ducking the ♥Q lead** around to your ♥A—that is, not winning with the first card that can win the trick.

The complete hand was:

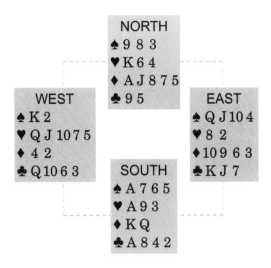

NORTH
♠ 9 8 3
♥ K 6 4
♦ A J 8 7 5
♣ 9 5

WEST
♠ K 2
♥ Q J 10 7 5
♦ 4 2
♣ Q 10 6 3

EAST
♠ Q J 10 4
♥ 8 2
♦ 10 9 6 3
♣ K J 7

SOUTH
♠ A 7 6 5
♥ A 9 3
♦ K Q
♣ A 8 4 2

You end up taking five diamond tricks, two heart tricks, one spade trick and one club trick, for a satisfying total of nine tricks.

Hand 3:

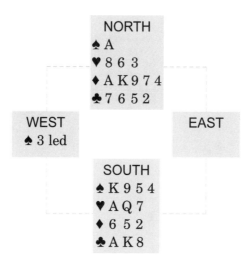

NORTH
♠ A
♥ 8 6 3
♦ A K 9 7 4
♣ 7 6 5 2

WEST
♠ 3 led

EAST

SOUTH
♠ K 9 5 4
♥ A Q 7
♦ 6 5 2
♣ A K 8

South deals. He has 4–3–3–3 shape and 16 HCP: a 1NT opening bid. North, meanwhile, has 11 HCP and 1 LP for a total of 12 points: 26 points are assured. Even with the singleton spade, North raises directly to 3NT, thus making sure that we do not miss game. (Remember, the responder is not under the same constraints as the opening bidder to have a no trump shape.)

West leads the ♣3, and the dummy comes down. What is West leading from? He's leading from length, at least four or five cards of it; but he doesn't have a sequence. He could have something like ♣Q 10 8 3, or ♣ Q 10 8 3 2. When leading from four or more cards of a suit, if we don't have a sequence, it is usually best to lead the fourth highest.

So plan the play. Start by counting your winners.

Again, we have an entry problem. In order to get to nine tricks, we must establish our long diamond suit. This is no surprise. In no trump contracts, it is often the central theme for declarer. It is almost always the central theme for the defenders too.

The lead of the ♠3 unfortunately deprives declarer of a vital entry to the North hand. After the first trick, the only cards that will permit the declarer to bridge across to the North hand are the ♦A and ♦K. The underlying principle is this: When faced with a hand that has no outside entries, you'll have to use the honor cards in the suit you are trying to establish as entries.

Hint: After winning with the ♠A, give the opponents what's already theirs. In other words, they are entitled to a diamond trick, no matter how the missing five diamonds are divided; so give it to them at once. At trick two, duck a diamond. If the outstanding diamonds divide 3–2, then your carefully preserved ♦A and ♦K will win the second and third rounds of this suit and will place you in the dummy, ready to cash your third and fourth long-suit winners.

All told, you'll make four diamond tricks, two spade tricks, one heart trick, and two club tricks. (If you get the chance, you might even be able to finesse that ♥Q. But be careful. Do it only if it cannot possibly cost you the contract.)

Here was the complete deal:

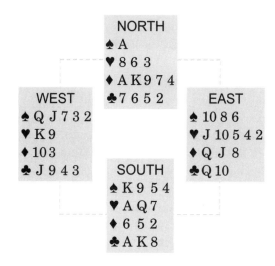

Hand 4:

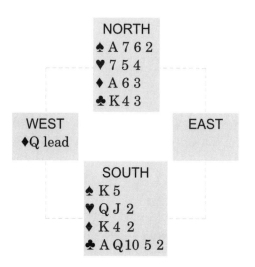

South deals. She has a 5–3–3–2 shape, 16 HCP, and 1 LP. South opens 1NT. With 11 HCP, North raises directly to game: he bids 3NT. The ♦Q is lead; dummy comes down. West, clearly, led from four or more diamonds headed by a sequence.

Plan your play. Count your winners.

With two spades and two diamond winners, it is clear we need as many clubs as we can make. Five would be nice. Otherwise, we would have to tackle the heart suit and try to build a slow winner there before the opponents are able to come to five tricks themselves. We have eight clubs; the opponents have five. If they split 3–2, our A K Q will wipe them all out.

Win the ♦Q lead with, say, the ♦A. When establishing a long suit (clubs), cash your winners from the short hand (North) first. At trick two, we play the ♣K; then at trick three we play a small club to our ♣A or our ♣Q. Surprisingly on this trick, West **shows out** (cannot follow suit), discarding the ♠3.

Time to regroup. Can we still make all five club tricks, even though it looks as though East started with four clubs, including the J—a 4–1 split, not the 3–2 we'd hoped for? This is where all our newly developed visual skills will pay off handsomely. Put them to use: visualize the layout at this point. Can you "see" East's holding the ♣J and one other club? If we now play the ♣Q, we will be establishing a trick for him. Here's the layout of remaining clubs:

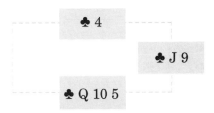

Hint: we have a tenace position with our ♣Q and ♣10—and it happens to be over East's ♣J. In order for the

tenace to be effective, we must force East to commit
before us. In other words, East must play a card before we
decide whether to play our ♣Q or ♣10. To force this, we
must position ourselves in the North hand. At trick four,
instead of cashing our ♣Q, use the ♠A as an entry to the
North hand so that at trick five, we can play the last
remaining club from the dummy and—literally—force
East's hand. With North on lead, then, South must make
both club tricks.

This was the complete hand:

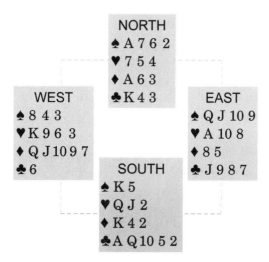

NORTH
♠ A 7 6 2
♥ 7 5 4
♦ A 6 3
♣ K 4 3

WEST
♠ 8 4 3
♥ K 9 6 3
♦ Q J 10 9 7
♣ 6

EAST
♠ Q J 10 9
♥ A 10 8
♦ 8 5
♣ J 9 8 7

SOUTH
♠ K 5
♥ Q J 2
♦ K 4 2
♣ A Q 10 5 2

You ended up making two spade tricks, two diamond tricks
and five club tricks, for a total of nine tricks.

6 TRUMPS: BIDDING AND SCORING

Here's *a classic example of the difference* between a trump and a no-trump contract.

Example 1.

Declarer: South

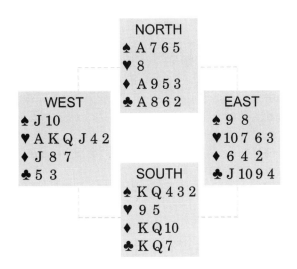

```
                    NORTH
                  ♠ A 7 6 5
                  ♥ 8
                  ♦ A 9 5 3
                  ♣ A 8 6 2
   WEST                             EAST
 ♠ J 10                           ♠ 9 8
 ♥ A K Q J 4 2                    ♥ 10 7 6 3
 ♦ J 8 7                          ♦ 6 4 2
 ♣ 5 3                            ♣ J 10 9 4
                    SOUTH
                  ♠ K Q 4 3 2
                  ♥ 9 5
                  ♦ K Q 10
                  ♣ K Q 7
```

North–South—with 27 HCP and 1 LP, 28 total points—find themselves in 3NT. West is happy to be on lead and quickly cashes his six heart winners in a row, thus defeating the 3NT contract by two tricks and going plus 200 points. N–S are left to bemoan the fact that without this lead, they could have made twelve tricks: five spades, four diamonds (the suit broke 3–3), and 3 clubs. Was there a better contract for North–South to play in?

Let's focus our attention on North–South's weakness, their heart holdings. Playing in no trump, they were powerless to prevent the opponents from "running" their six heart tricks. If they chose to play with one of their suits trump instead, the opponents would still be able to win the first heart trick, but when they tried to cash another one, North—at that point out of hearts—would ruff it with whatever suit North–South had chosen to be trump. That ruff would transfer the lead to North–South and, now in control, they would be able to direct the play.

If North–South could choose to name a suit trump on this hand, logic would dictate that they look to their longest combined suit holding. Between them, they have seven diamonds, seven clubs, and nine spades. A trump suit is more powerful than any of the other three suits. If your side had nine trumps, the opponents would have only four. Your side would have five more wild cards than they would. Therefore, if North–South could choose to name any suit trump, they would choose spades.

Now, let's take a look at the play of Example 1 again, this time with spades trump:

Example 2.

Declarer: South

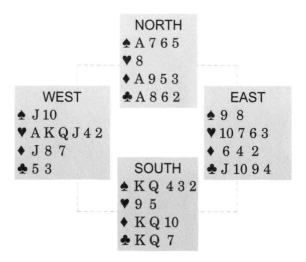

NORTH
♠ A 7 6 5
♥ 8
♦ A 9 5 3
♣ A 8 6 2

WEST
♠ J 10
♥ A K Q J 4 2
♦ J 8 7
♣ 5 3

EAST
♠ 9 8
♥ 10 7 6 3
♦ 6 4 2
♣ J 10 9 4

SOUTH
♠ K Q 4 3 2
♥ 9 5
♦ K Q 10
♣ K Q 7

Trick one: West leads the ♥A, North follows with the ♥8, East plays the ♥3, South throws the ♥5.

Trick two: West, having won the first trick with the ♥A, leads the ♥K; declarer (South) is able to trump this heart in the dummy (North) because North is now void in hearts; East, who still has hearts, plays one of them, the ♥6; and South follows with the ♥9.

Trick three: The lead is now in the North hand.

You, as the declarer, have one trick in the bank already. Pausing to count your tricks, you can count on at least three diamonds and three clubs to add to your total. That makes seven. With nothing more to trump and all your outside cards high (winners), it's time to draw trump. **Drawing trump** is our expression for exhausting, trick by trick, all the outstanding trump cards in opponents' hands. Thus:

Trick three: North leads any high trump—let's say the ♠A. East plays the ♠8, South the ♠2, and West the ♠10.

Trick four: North leads the ♠6, East plays the ♠9, South the ♠K, and West the ♠J.

All trump are now drawn. (The suit, as it turned out, broke 5–4–2–2.) As declarer, you can now **claim** the rest of the tricks saying, " I have three tricks already, and I will make three more spades, three diamonds, and three clubs, for a total of twelve tricks."

Now, twelve tricks is a level-six contract—that is, book plus six. A level-six contract in any strain is called a **slam.** The bonus value for a slam is 750 points. If you bid to the six level (here a six-spade contract) and make it, your side would be credited with 500 points for making game, plus 180 points (6 × 30) for making six spade tricks (we'll get to the value of major suits shortly) plus the added 750-point slam bonus for a whopping total of 1,430 points. In practice your side bid to 3NT and failed by two tricks (Example 1), losing in the process a total of 200 points—a difference, between the two outcomes, of 1,630 points.

It's high time we took a closer look at the suits and learned how to bid to a trump contract.

■ SUIT SCORING

You've already done the hard part. No trump scoring, with 40 points allotted for the first seven tricks and 30 points for each additional trick, is much more confusing than suit bidding. Let me illustrate.

The four suits are grouped into **minors,** diamonds and clubs, and **majors,** spades and hearts. If you look back, whenever we talked about a hand, we always mentioned spades and hearts first; the reason is simply that they are more important than the minors. Here's why.

Each trick in the minors is worth only twenty points. The score, then, progresses: 20, 40, 60, 80, 100. It takes book plus five (6 + 5), or eleven tricks, to get to that game bonus level of 100. Looking at it the other way, it leaves room for only two losers. Games in the minor suits are tough to make.

Each trick in the majors is worth thirty points; the score progresses 30, 60, 90, 120. Notice that, at 30 points a level, it is impossible to reach 100 on the nose. In order to get credit for the game bonus of 100, you must go past it, to 120. So it takes book plus four (6 + 4), or 10 tricks, to make a game in the majors. That leaves room for three losers, a full 50 percent more than are available in the minors!

Now, how do you write the score? Let's take an example: Say that our side, playing in a contract of two diamonds, succeeds in making ten tricks. Two diamonds requires eight tricks; having made ten, we are going plus—in other words, the score will appear on our side of the ledger. The contract, two diamonds at 20 points per diamond, goes under the line. We made two **overtricks,** extra tricks beyond what we contracted for, which are also worth 20 points apiece; those 40 points go above the line. So:

We	They
40	
40	

We'll make this a running score, as if we were playing a game.

In the second hand of the match, the opponents bid and make two spades, with no overtricks. How do we score this?

Spades is a major suit. Majors are added at 30 a trick. 2 × 30 = 60. So 60, the sum of contract points, goes below the line. With no overtricks, that's all that's entered on the ledger.

We	They
40	
40	60

In the third hand, we bid and made 2NT. The score is 40 for the first NT + 30 for the second for a total of 70 points. This gets added to our previous 40 points:

We	They
500 40	
40 70 —— 110	60

Note that our total below the line has now exceeded 100; therefore, we have earned the 500 points game bonus and enter it above the line.

When we talked about no trump bidding, we learned that what drove the auction was the search for the game bonus.

Let's compare game contracts:

3NT requires **9 tricks** and is worth **100 points** + 500 bonus = **600 points.**

4S or **4H** requires **10 tricks** and is worth **120 points** + 500 bonus = **620 points.**

5D or **5C** requires **11 tricks** and is worth **100 points** + 500 bonus = **600 points.**

From experience, I would guess that when a game contract is reached, 50 percent of the time that contract will be 3NT, 40 percent of the time it will be four of a major (4S or 4H), and 10 percent of the time it will be five of a minor. While we won't ignore minor suit bidding (part score bidding is important), the fact that we rarely search for the game bonus in a minor suit necessitates that we place a great deal more emphasis on no trump and major suit bidding. Those, after all, will be your tickets to fame and fortune at the bridge table.

Now let's compare the two most common game contracts: no trump games vs. major suit games.

First, a question. Given the option of playing in a contract of 3NT or a contract of four of a major, which should you choose?

Three no trump games require only nine tricks. That's their big advantage.

Four heart or four spade games require one additional trick, it is true. But it is actually easier to make ten tricks when playing in a trump suit containing eight or more trumps between you and your partner than to try to make nine tricks with nothing wild. There are several reasons why this is so:

1. When playing in a trump suit, you will always have the ability to stop an opponent's long-running suit. In Example 1, at the beginning of this chapter, the opponents rammed six tricks down our throat and we were powerless to stop it. Playing in a trump contract, when an opponent attempts to run to victory on the strength of a long series of cards of any par-

ticular suit, you can simply trump in once you run out of that suit, take the trick, and take control of the hand. This power alone often more than makes up for the one-trick difference. But there's more.

2. When your side has a clear advantage in the number of trumps, then your side has the ability to create at least one extra trick per hand. This can be accomplished by **trumping losers** in the dummy or sometimes even in the declarer's hand. There's still more.

3. In a trump contract, you can **discard losers,** an ability that you don't have in no trump. And lastly:

4. Back in chapter 4, I asked you to remember the number 26, saying that it was the most important number in the game of bridge. Now we'll begin to see why. Not only is it the number of points (HCP plus length points) needed to make 3NT; it is also the exact number of points (HCP plus length plus *something else*) that you need to make 4H or 4S. (That *something else*, which we'll reveal a bit later, is an addition that makes it **easier to reach 26 in a major suit than in no trump.** Three ingredients go into the mix, rather than just two.)

Therefore, given the choice between 3NT and four of a major, it is almost always preferable to play in the major suit.

But who's giving you that choice? And will you know when and how to take advantage of it? These are good questions—ones that bring us to our next "major" topic.

▪ MAJOR SUIT BIDDING

What happens when a hand gets **passed out**—that is, when all four players say "pass"? It gets reshuffled. I've never been at a table, after a hand got passed out, where the players didn't gab about how many points they each had. Let's listen in on one unfortunate pair.

> *North: "By the way, partner, just out of curiosity, how many points did you have on that last hand?"*
>
> *South: "Oh, I think it was 13. Yeah, 13—but I didn't like them. How about you? How many did you have?"*
>
> *North: "Aw, man! I had 13 points too! We had 26 together, so we would have had enough to contract for a game!"*

Yep, looks like North–South just threw away a chance at that 500 point bonus! And if that seems unfortunate, it is.

In a real bridge game, this can't happen. Any time you pick up half of the points (13) needed to produce game (26), you must open the bidding. **With 13 or more points in your hand, you must begin the auction by placing a bid.**

The only opening bid we've learned thus far is 1NT, and the minimum number of points necessary to make that bid is 15. So what do you do when you have only 13 or 14 points, or you have more than that but don't have the right shape to open 1NT? You open with something else! Usually that "something else" is one of a suit: either 1S, 1H, 1C, 1D. But how do you choose which?

Up until the mid-1950s, it was very simple: you looked at your hand and bid your longest and strongest suit. After all, it seemed the sensible thing to do. Let's say your hand was:

♠ A 7 6   ♥ Q 10 5   ♦ A K J 2   ♣ 9 8 7

With 14 points, you *had* to open the bidding; but you couldn't open 1NT (which requires 15–17 HCP). Therefore, you opened one diamond. All that said to your partner was, "Partner, I have 13 or more points, and so I'm opening the bidding; I have four or more diamonds, my longest suit; and there's a reason I can't open 1NT."

Or let's say you picked up:

♠ A 7 6   ♥ 3   ♦ K Q J 5   ♣ A Q 9 7 5

You had 16 HCP, plus 1 for length. You'd have liked to open 1NT, as the point-count fit, but you couldn't. Say the distribution out loud: 5–4–3–1. Sound familiar? Of course not: it's not one of the no trump distributions. The presence of a singleton, that ♥3, negated the chance of a no trump opening. Therefore open 1C, indicating your best suit. Prior to the 1950s this would have said, "Partner, I have 13 or more points; my best suit is clubs; and there's some reason I can't open 1NT."

Nonetheless, this nice, simple system changed somewhat in the 1950s, when bridge experts began to realize that it was fine to open one of a minor with a four-card or longer suit, but when opening one of a major suit, 1S or 1H, it was preferable to have at least *five* cards in the suit.

Let's see how this new wrinkle affects your choice of opening bids. Say you are dealt the following hand:

♠ A Q 7 5 2   ♥ K Q 2   ♦ A 3   ♣ K J 9

With 19 HCP and 1 length point, you're eager to start the auction. You bid one spade, in effect saying, "Partner, I have 13 or more points, and *at least a five-card spade suit.*"

But other hands may not prompt such obvious bids. Look over the following hands and carefully decide what opening bid you would choose.

Hand 1: ♠ K Q 10 5 ♥ A 10 ♦ Q J 4 2 ♣ Q 9 4

With a 4–4–3–2 distribution, you are allowed—and would like—to open with a NT bid; but you have only 14 HCP. Your spades are your strongest suit, and you'd like to open one of a major; but you have only four of them, not the five you now need. Therefore, open one diamond, your other four-card suit.

Hand 2: ♠ A Q 9 5 ♥ A Q 7 6 ♦ 8 4 ♣ Q 10 3

What do you do with this gem? You have 14 HCP, so you must open the bidding. You can't open 1NT; although you have the right 4–4–3–2 distribution, you have too few points. You can't open one of a major (1S or 1H) either since neither suit is five cards long or longer. Getting ugly, isn't it?

Look at your minors. They're called that for a reason. Since they are less important, we can and do take liberties with them. Your opening bid on this hand, believe it or not, is 1C! Here's what it now says to your partner: "I have 13 or more points, I couldn't open 1NT, I couldn't open 1S or 1H, but at least I have three or more clubs." As a general practice, **you should open 1C any time you have three cards in both minors and must choose between them,** for example:

Hand 3: ♠ A Q 9 ♥ Q J 7 4 ♦ K 10 4 ♣ Q 7 2

In this hand, even though your diamond suit is stronger than your clubs, it's better to open 1C. Your opening 1C bid will tip your partner off to the fact that you may have only three clubs, whereas your 1D opening will strongly suggest a four-card suit. When you open 1D, you will more likely have four or more diamonds, not three. (In rare instances you may be forced to open with only three diamonds . . .

♠A 6 4 2 ♥K 9 8 6 ♦A J 7 ♣Q 3. In almost thirty years of play I can count the number of times I was faced with this situation. It is so unlikely that for all intents and purposes when you open 1D, partner should play you for four or more diamonds and not worry about it.)

> **When you open 1C, you have three or more clubs.**
>
> **When you open 1D, you have four or more diamonds.**
>
> **When you open 1S or 1H, you have five or more of that major suit.**

Hand 4:   ♠ K 9 4   ♥ K Q 3   ♦ A 9 5 4 2   ♣ K 9

Were you lulled into a 1D bid? With a five-card suit, it's tempting. But look more closely, and remember the order of bids to consider. Count your points: 15 HCP. As soon as you say 15, a bell should go off: "Can I open 1NT?" With 15 points, and a 5–3–3–2 distribution, you can—and should open the bidding 1NT.

This almost fanatical insistence on checking first for 1NT is done for two reasons. The first is that, by bidding 1NT, you are able in one fell swoop to describe your hand to your partner very clearly: in terms of both HCP and shape. The second, and far more subtle reason is that if you neglect to open 1NT when you could, your partner will assume you don't have a 1NT opening bid. We'll see later the profound impact this has on the meaning of all your subsequent bids.

If it walks likes a duck and quacks like a duck, it's a duck. If you have 15 to 17 HCP and the right shape, it's a no trump.

Now, one last rule to complete your beginner's course in opening bids, and to further insure that you and your partner will read each other well:

When you have two five-card suits, bid the higher-ranking one first. For example, take the hand:

♠ A 7   ♥ Q J 9 4 2   ♦ A Q 10 7 5   ♣ 9

What should you open? You should bid 1H, your higher-ranking suit, even though your diamonds are slightly stronger.

Okay, let's imagine that, armed with your new education in opening bids, you sit down at the bridge table and are dealt the following hands. Looking over each of them, decide whether you have an opening bid and, if so, what that opening bid would be.

Hand 1: ♠ A K 10 7 4 ♥ A J 9 6 ♦ 8 7   ♣ 9 4

Hand 2: ♠ K 9   ♥ K Q 7 ♦ Q J 5 ♣ A J 9 7 3

Hand 3: ♠ 10 9 8 4 2 ♥ K 9 3 ♦ A K Q J ♣ 9

Hand 4: ♠ A 5   ♥ K Q 7 ♦ A Q 8 4 ♣ K J 10 3

Hand 5: ♠ A 2   ♥ 4 3   ♦ K 7   ♣ A Q 10 9 7 5 2

Opening Bids:

Hand 1: You have 12 HCP plus 1 for length. That's 13 points, so you have to bid; and seeing those five spades should make your decision easy. Open 1S.

Hand 2: You have 16 HCP plus 1 for length, and a 5–3–3–2 shape. Resist the urge to open 1C—remember your priorities—and open 1NT.

Hand 3: You have 13 HCP plus 1 for length; that's 14 points, so you have to bid. You have four bold and beautiful diamonds; but as you know, it's more important to look for five cards of a major suit. And you have them, crummy as they might look: five lousy spades. Length, not strength is the rule to follow when it comes to opening bids. Open 1S.

Hand 4: With 19 HCP, you're much too strong to open 1NT (15–17 HCP), even though your 4–4–3–2 shape is perfect and you'll only need your partner to have 7 HCP to make game. However, your partner knows to pass when he's holding 7 or 8 points when you open in no trump, so there's no way for you to get to 3NT. With two four-card minors of about equal strength, it's fine to open either one. Open 1D or 1C.

Hand 5: With 13 HCP plus 3 length points, open one of your beautiful 7-card club suit.Unfortunately, with this 1C bid, your partner must assume the worst until further notice—that is, that you may hold as few as three clubs.

If you look at all five hands on page 199, you'll quickly see that, unlike 1NT opening bids, suit opening bids come in all shapes and sizes. This prompts an obvious question. How is your partner supposed to tell what on earth your hand looks like? You could make an opening bid of 1C, and your hand could either look like this:

    ♠ K 7 6 5   ♥ A Q 10 2   ♦ 9 5   ♣ A 10 2

or like this:

    ♠ A 7 5 4   ♥ ——   ♦ K 4 2   ♣ A K Q 10 5 3.

An opening bid of 1H, for that matter, could be made with a hand like this:

    ♠ 9 3   ♥ K 8 7 6 5   ♦ A Q 4   ♣ K 10 4

or like this:

    ♠ 9   ♥ A Q J 7 6 5   ♦ A Q J 10 5   ♣ 7

The answer to the question goes to the heart of what bidding is all about. During the auction, the players try to describe their hands to each other *in a series of bids.* We like to say they try to "paint a picture" of their hands. The opening bid is important; but it's only the first sentence of a conversation between partners that will take place throughout the auction. On the basis of information exchanged during this conversation, they try to find the contract that will produce the greatest reward for their side.

Here, for instance, is our most descriptive auction to date:

<u>N</u>	<u>E</u>	<u>S</u>	<u>W</u>
1NT	pass	2NT	pass
3NT	pass	pass	pass

Here's the conversation that's taken place:

North (opening bid): "*My cards are evenly distributed, and I have 15, 16, or 17 HCP.*"

South (response): "*Well, I have 9 points. Do you have 17?*"

North (rebid): "*Yes I do! And with your 9 we have 26 combined points. Let's try for that 500-point bonus.*"

Notice the three different names of bids. The first person in an auction to make a bid makes an **opening bid.** His or her partner becomes the **responder,** and makes a bid called a **response.** The opening bidder then makes a second bid: a **rebid.** In fact, from that point on, all subsequent bids by either party are called rebids.

Now let's see how much you've learned. As an opening bidder, how might you plan to paint an accurate picture of your hand if you are dealt one of these hands?

Hand 1: ♠ A 3 2   ♥ 4   ♦ A Q 10 9 7 5 2   ♣ K 4

With 13 HCP and 3 points for length and no five-card major, you would have a 1D opening bid. Now, is there an outstanding feature of your hand, something that your partner might be very interested in knowing? Sure: your wonderful seven-card diamond suit. Remember that your 1D opening bid did not in itself convey very much in the way of specific information. All your partner knows is that you have four or more diamonds and 13 or more points. With your second bid, however—that is, with your rebid—you start painting a better picture of a hand rich in diamonds. You should plan on rebidding your diamond suit to emphasize its importance. If, for example, your partner responds 1H (and we'll get to what your partner means by this soon), you should plan to rebid 2D.

<u>N</u>	<u>E</u>	<u>S</u>	<u>W</u>
1D	p	1H	p
2D			

Hand 2: ♠ A Q J 7 5   ♥ K Q J 4 2   ♦ Q 9   ♣ 10

You have 13 HCP plus 2 length points. With two five-card suits—in this case, the spades and the hearts—we have learned to open the higher ranking of the two. Therefore, open 1S. Plan on a rebid that gives your partner a better feel for your hand. You have not one but two very good, long suits; let your partner know this. Having opened in spades, at your next opportunity, plan to rebid in hearts.

<u>N</u>	<u>E</u>	<u>S</u>	<u>W</u>
1S	p	2C	p
2H			

Here your partner responded with a bid of 2C, his suit, and you, with your rebid, gave him the two-suited feel of the hand.

An opening bid of 1NT consists of two parts: a very distinctive shape and a very narrowly defined HCP range. This is not true of a one-of-a-suit opening bid. As we've seen, suit openings tend to be more vague in these areas. But that's okay; they're supposed to be. They're intended only as starting points. When an auction begins with one of a suit, it is expected that it will take two or three bids to describe fully the strength and shape of a hand. Let's look at the following hand as an example:

♠ K 9   ♥ A Q 9 8 4   ♦ A K 3   ♣ Q 10 5

When you open this hand with a bid of 1H, you do so with the intention of eventually being able to tell your partner that you have five hearts, a no trump shape (5–3–3–2) and too many points (18 HCP + 1 LP) to have opened 1NT. No one bid in bridge could be expected to say all that. But a series of bids can.

Opening bids of one of a suit do have an upper limit and hence a definite range, just as an opening bid 1NT does. That limit is defined as 20 points. Thus **the range for opening bids of 1S, 1H, 1D, and 1C is from 13 to 20 points.**

The good news is that 13 and 20 are easy markers to remember: 13 is half of 26, the number of points you need to make game; and 20 is half of 40, the total number of points in the deck. The other good news is that, in the course of this entire book, you'll only have to remember three such ranges—and you've already got two under your belt.

These ranges are the building blocks of bidding. Along with the number 4 (the HCP value of an ace) and the number 26 (the amount of combined points it takes to make game), these ranges will be all you'll need to know to construct a series of bids for yourself and your partner that will describe any hand. So please, please, please, commit these two ranges to memory:

To open **1NT,** you must have from **15–17** HCP.

To open **1 of a suit,** you must have from **13–20** points.

Q: Which is stronger, in terms of points: an opening bid of 1NT or an opening bid of one of a suit?

A: It's a trick question! No matter which you chose, you got it right. An opening bid of one of a suit can be weaker than (if the hand has 13 or 14 points), equal to (if it has 15–17 points), or stronger than (with 18–20 points) an opening 1NT bid.

Opening range for one of a suit: 13 14 15 16 17 18 19 20

Opening range for 1NT: 15 16 17

▪ THE TRUMP FIT

You can never be too thin or too rich, they say—and you can never have enough wild cards. One of the criteria that go into your decision to play a hand in no trump or in a trump suit is: Does your side have *a lot* of one particular suit? If the answer is yes, then you might try steering the contract into that strain.

Now, what constitutes "a lot of"? Is six a lot of cards of one particular suit? Is seven? Eight? Nine?

Seven is the smallest number of cards of any suit you can have and guarantee that you have more than your opponents. Even so, a seven-card fit is a little close for comfort. With thirteen cards of each suit in the deck, if you and your partner have seven of them, your opponents have six. Clearly, seven is a pivotal number of cards; so let's take a minute to see if we should think about naming seven-card suits trump.

1. **Mathematically, an odd number of cards rates to break evenly.**

2. **Conversely, an even number of cards rates to break unevenly.**

These are very powerful and useful pieces of information to an attentive bridge player. Let's see what they mean. An *odd* number of cards (if, say, between you and your partner you have a seven-card fit) rates to break *evenly* (so that you and your partner split that suit 4 and 3—about as even as you can get). If you want to know the odds, the chances of such a near-even split are a full 62 percent. An *even* number of cards rates to break *unevenly*. When you have a seven-card fit, the six outstanding cards held by the opponents, rate to break 4–2 (unevenly) rather than 3–3 (evenly), 48 percent to 35 percent.

If you decide to play in a seven-card fit, where you hold four trumps and your partner holds three, look at the implications. Most of the time one of your opponents will also have a four-card or, heaven forbid, longer suit. You might wind up playing in his suit.

Now look at how dramatically these numbers change when we give your side an eight-card fit. With eight cards between you, the opponents are left with only five. From Rule 1 we learned that five, an odd number, rates to split evenly, 3–2, and it does so 68 percent of the time. So when you find yourself playing in an eight-card fit, where you and your partner each hold four trumps, rest easy. 68 percent of the time neither one of your opponents has more than a three-card suit.

With a seven-card fit, you only have one trump more than the opponents; but with an eight-card fit, you have three more. With a seven-card fit, you can wind up playing in the opponents' suit two thirds of the time. But with an eight-card fit, you will play in your own suit two thirds of the time. You can never be too rich . . .

With nine trumps between you and your partner, a full five more than the opponents, you have found the optimum trump length. The opponents' longest trump holding, four, can never be as long as yours, five (your nine-card fit will divide 5–4 most of the time). With so many more trump than the opposition, they will have a difficult time preventing you from using your trumps effectively.

So, after all is said and done, what is the minimum number of cards you need as a partnership in order to name a suit trump? The answer is eight. **Eight cards means you're holding a comfortable majority of the suit.**

In the following example, let's see a demonstration of just how powerful an eight-card trump fit can be.

Let's first try playing this hand in no trump:

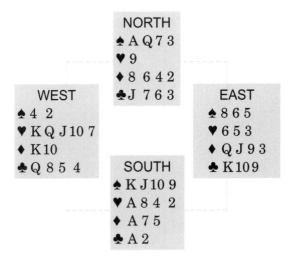

NORTH
♠ A Q 7 3
♥ 9
♦ 8 6 4 2
♣ J 7 6 3

WEST
♠ 4 2
♥ K Q J 10 7
♦ K 10
♣ Q 8 5 4

EAST
♠ 8 6 5
♥ 6 5 3
♦ Q J 9 3
♣ K 10 9

SOUTH
♠ K J 10 9
♥ A 8 4 2
♦ A 7 5
♣ A 2

Q: How many tricks will North–South be expected to make?

A: With 23 HCP and no length points, a total of 23 points, in no trump, all you can expect to make with this hand is seven tricks: four spade tricks plus your three aces as quick tricks.

Q: Now, playing the same hand with spades trump, how many tricks will North–South make?

A: Picture the step-by-step play of the hand. N–S still has the same winners—four spades and three aces, but with spades, they have the ability to turn their three heart losers into winners by trumping them with dummy's spades.

It may go like this:

West will lead the ♥K. South will win that trick with the ♥A. Immediately afterward, South will trump the ♥2 (that's trick two) with dummy's ♠3 and then go back to his (South's) hand with the ♦A, or the ♣A (trick three), in order to trump another heart (trick four) this time with dummy's ♠7. Then he'll return to his hand with the ♣A (trick five) in order to trump his last heart (trick six) with dummy's ♠Q. At this point, the North–South hands look like this:

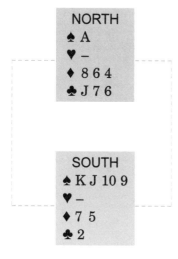

NORTH
♠ A
♥ –
♦ 8 6 4
♣ J 7 6

SOUTH
♠ K J 10 9
♥ –
♦ 7 5
♣ 2

With six tricks in the bag, they will win four more tricks with high trumps for a grand total of ten tricks (10 tricks = book + 4). In a major suit, 4 x 30 = 120 points. That's game—and bonus.

So we've watched the same hand yield dramatically different results. With only 23 points among your cards, there was no way even to think about contracting for game in no trump. Yet game in your eight-card spade fit was a snap. The moral of the story is clear and important: never, ever underestimate the power of an eight-card (or longer) major-suit trump fit. It's your easiest road to game.

▪ MAJOR SUIT BIDDING

So far, here are the four basic things we know about major suit bidding:

1. We know that when partner opens one of a major, he *guarantees* a five-card suit.

2. We know that, between us, we always want to try to find an eight- or nine-card major suit fit.

3. We know that when partner opens one of a major, he has between 13 and 20 points (HCP + length points).

4. We know that the easiest road to game is a 4S or a 4H contract (4 × 30 = 120 points).

As responder, then—as the partner of the opening one spade or one heart bidder—what do you do with all this information? Let's give you some idea how to respond.

Imagine that the auction goes like this:

N	E	S	W
1S	p	?	

You are South. Your hand looks like this:

♠ K 9 4 2   ♥ 8 7   ♦ A K 7 6   ♣ A 10 3

How many HCP do you have? Fourteen. How many length points? None. So you have fourteen points in the hand: the equivalent of an opening bid. When your partner North opens the bidding, he shows that he has at least 13 points. Partner's and your opening bids, in effect, face one another. Your 14 points added to his minimum of 13 comes to more than the 26 points you need for game: bonus time. You're certainly going to contract for game. But playing in what strain? Or, as we bridge players say, where?

You have four spades. Partner's 1S bid guarantees five spades. Together you have at least nine, more than enough (eight) for a trump fit. Therefore, you're going to game in spades. Remember, you earn 30 points a trick in the majors; 30 + 30 + 30 + 30 = 120; a four-level contract brings you to 100+ points. To bid game in spades, in other words, is to bid 4S. And that's your response in this auction: that's what you bid over your partner's 1S opening.

N	E	S	W
1S	p	4S	

One spade—four spades. Your 4S bid tells partner that between you, you have at least eight spades and 26 points. When raising your partner's major suit, not only are you agreeing on where the hand should be played—in the majors—but you're also saying how many points you have.

Here's your hand for our next example:

♠ K 9 4 2   ♥ 8 7   ♦ A 7 6 5   ♣ 10 9 3

You have 7 HCP and no length points: 7 points total. Like life, bridge doesn't always deal you a good hand. You've got to make the most of what you've got. So let's figure out how to do just that.

Again partner opens 1S. With this poor collection of cards, should you respond at all?

<u>N</u>	<u>E</u>	<u>S</u>	<u>W</u>
1S	p	?	

In our no trump discussion, do you remember what you did, as responder, when you were dealt from 0 to 8 points? You passed. Your 0–8 points, when combined with partner's 15–17 points, could *never* come to 26; there was no chance of game. So you didn't enter the auction. The possibility of game, remote as it may be, is what drives you to bid. With 9 points, you invited further research into the possibility of game by responding 2NT, urging partner to bid game if he had a maximum no trump of 17 points.

The same principle applies here, in trump bidding. If there is absolutely no possibility of game, pass. If there is even the most remote chance at game, **invite** your partner by bidding something.

So, with your measly 7 points, is there any possibility of game when partner opens 1S?

Yes. He didn't open 1NT. He's not limited to the 15–17 point range. He opened one spade: one of a suit. And the range for one of a suit, remember, is 13–20 points. So, when that range is added to your paltry 7 points, together you two could have as many as 27 points: more than enough for game.

Now, how likely is it that your partner has 19 or 20 points? Not very. But the fewer points you have, the more he could have! Be optimistic. Invite partner to bid game if he has a very powerful opening hand.

So what bid will communicate to partner "I have 3 or 4 spades with you, so together we should play in a spade contract; but I have a very weak hand with just enough points to keep the auction open?" What's the least you can raise his 1S bid without expressing overconfidence?

A bid of one and a half spades.

Just kidding. Don't go cutting cards in half. The "cheapest" spade bid you can make, when your partner opens 1S, is 2S. That says, "I like spades, partner, but bear in mind that my weak response of 2S could be based on as few as 6 points."

Here are two terms that we should use from now on: **Minimum Trump Support (MTS)** and **Normal Trump Support (NTS).** When partner opens one of a major, minimum trump support is three, which guarantees an eight-card fit (his 5 + your 3). Normal trump support when partner opens one of a major is four—which guarantees a nine-card fit (5 + 4 = 9).

As we did with no trump bidding, let's build a major suit bidding box to reflect what we know already. In each case below, it is assumed that the responder has at least MTS—that is, three- or four-card trump support for the opening bidder.

THE MAJOR SUIT BIDDING BOX			
Opener	Responder has:	Responder's bid:	Reason
1 spade (13–20 points)	0–5 points	pass	no chance at 26 combined points
1 spade (13–20 points)	6–? points	2 spades	outside chance at game, but opener needs a big hand
1 spade (13–20 points)	?–? points	?	?
1 spade (13–20 points)	13–?	4 spades	two opening bids facing each other: 13 + 13 = 26

Before we fill in the question marks, make sure that you understand the three responses listed:

1S–pass . . . Shows 0–5 points.
1S–2S . . . Shows 6 to some as yet undetermined number of points
1S–4S . . . Shows 13 to also some undetermined number.

Now, ready to proceed with a few questions that will give us our answers? Good.

Q: With MTS, when your partner opens 1S, what is the largest number of points you can have and not bid game?

A: 12. If you had 13 points, you would be able to guarantee 26 combined points and would bid game yourself.

Q: What bid sounds like "We're close, partner, very close to 4S?"

A: You guessed it . . . 3S. Three spades says, "I can't guarantee game, but I could have as many as 12 points."

Now let's try to fill in some of those question marks:

Q: What's the difference between a two-level contract and a three-level contract?

A: One level, obviously.

Q: What's a level?

A: A trick. One more trick is what makes the difference between contracting for eight tricks or nine tricks— that is, between a two-level contract or a three-level contract.

Q: What card is the equivalent of a trick?

A: An ace. That's the undeniable master card, and the master card can win a trick.

Q: And what's the value of an ace?

A: Four points.

So the difference between hand A and hand B below, is four points: an ace, one trick, and a contract level.

A. ♠ K 7 6 5   ♥ 5 4   ♦ K 9 7 6   ♣ 10 9 3
B. ♠ K 7 6 5   ♥ 5 4   ♦ A K 9 7   ♣ 10 9 3

In both cases, when your partner opens 1S, your intention will be to set the spade suit as trump. With hand A, we know to raise with this six-point holding from 1S to 2S. Hand B is exactly one trick stronger than hand A. So if we make the same response with A as with B, how is partner supposed to distinguish between the two? He can't.

When *raising your partner's suit, you tell your partner how many points you have by the level you choose to raise to.*

With hand B, then, tell your partner you have 10+ points. Instead of a 2S bid, jump-raise to 3S.

1S—3S. Making this jump in the auction says, "My hand is the equivalent of one trick stronger than a 2S bid." If 2S shows as little as 6 points, as it does, then 3S has to start at 6 + 4, or 10 points. We know that it ends at 12 points, because with 13 we must insist on game, 4S (13 + 13 = 26). The box can now be filled in.

THE COMPLETED MAJOR SUIT BIDDING BOX			
Opener	Responder has:	Responder's bid:	Reason
1 spade (13–20 points)	0–5 points	pass	no chance at 26 combined points
1 spade (13–20 points)	6–9 points	2 spades	outside chance at game, but opener needs a big hand
1 spade (13–20 points)	10–12 points	3 spades	a trick stronger than 2S, but not enough for a game
1 spade (13–20 points)	13–16	4 spades	two opening bids facing each other: 13 + 13 = 26 is a game bid

With no trump bidding, the key number was 9. With less than 9, you passed; with 9, you bid 2NT; with more than 9—that is, 10+ points—you bid 3NT.

With major suit bidding the key number is 10. I'll explain.

If I were to deal thousands upon thousands of hands, what do you think would be the average number of points that each person was dealt per hand? Ten points. After all, there are 40 points per deck, four players per hand. Ten points will be the average holding. So if you pick up a hand with less than 10 points, you feel cheated; you didn't get your fair share. Let's admit that. Let's say that with fewer than 10 points, you "hate" your hand.

So when partner opens the bidding one of a major and you have MTS and only 6–9 points, you *hate* your hand—but you have to bid anyway. This is a 2S bid. The bidding, between your partner and you, goes 1S–2S.

On the other hand, when you pick up a hand that contains 10–12 points, you've gotten just about your fair share. You're not nuts about the hand—after all, you can't guarantee game right off the bat—but it's not bad either. You *like* your hand. This is a 3S bid. The auction goes 1S–3S.

Finally, when you pick up 13 points, and your partner opens 1S, you *love* your hand. Of course you love it: you can guarantee game. This is a 4S bid. The auction goes 1S–4S.

Hate: 1S–**2S** . . . 6–9 points.

Like: 1S–**3S** . . . 10–12 points.

Love: 1S–**4S** . . . 13–16 points.[1]

In each of the following cases, partner opens 1H. What call do you make with each of these hands?

A.	♠ K 7 6	♥ K 9 4	♦ K 8 7 3	♣ K 10 2
B.	♠ A 4 2	♥ 10 4 3 2	♦ A K Q	♣ 7 6 5
C.	♠ 4 3 2	♥ K Q 4 2	♦ J 7 6 5	♣ 8 4
D.	♠ 4 3 2	♥ 10 9 8 4	♦ J 7 6 5	♣ Q 4

And the answers are:

A. You have 12 points, and three-card trump support (MTS). Jump to 3H.
B. You have 13 points and four-card trump support (NTS). You can guarantee game: jump to 4H.
C. You have 6 points and NTS. Raise your partner to 2H.
D. You only have 3 points. It doesn't matter what kind of support you have. You can't bid, so pass.

----

1. Notice that 13–16 is a 4-point range. With any more than that—i.e., with the equivalent of an ace more than 13—you are too strong to jump merely to game. The possibility of a slam must be investigated. Unfortunately, slam bidding is beyond the scope of this book. In general, my advice to you is if you think a slam exists, then bid it. No bid, no bonus.

▪ LOOK OUT FOR SHORTY

Let's put our newfound major suit bidding skills to the test.

Example 1.

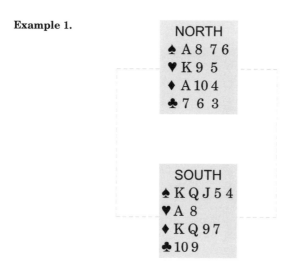

NORTH
♠ A 8 7 6
♥ K 9 5
♦ A 10 4
♣ 7 6 3

SOUTH
♠ K Q J 5 4
♥ A 8
♦ K Q 9 7
♣ 10 9

South, the dealer, has 15 HCP + 1 length point = 16 points; with a five-card spade suit and two doubletons, no trump is out of the question. Therefore, she opens 1S. North, with 11 HCP plus four-card support for partner's known five-card suit (it's a major) raises to 3S. South rebids 4S. Her 16 points coupled with North's 10, 11, or 12 (which he showed by jumping to three spades) comes to at least the 26 combined points they need to try for game in a major suit. Three passes end the auction.

Here's how the bidding looks:

S	W	N	E
1S	p	3S	p
4S	p	p	p

South will be declarer; she introduced spades, the strain in which the hand is going to be played.

Looking at the two hands in the previous example, try to determine how many tricks you can expect to make.

All told, North–South should make five spade tricks, two heart tricks, three diamond tricks and no clubs. That's ten tricks. South might be able to trump a fourth diamond in the dummy, which would create an eleventh trick. The system is vindicated! Game is bid and made—in this case, perhaps even with an overtrick to boot.

Now let's look at another hand.

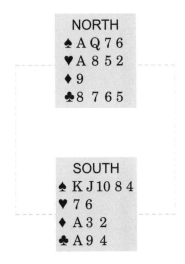

NORTH
♠ A Q 7 6
♥ A 8 5 2
♦ 9
♣ 8 7 6 5

SOUTH
♠ K J 10 8 4
♥ 7 6
♦ A 3 2
♣ A 9 4

The bidding proceeds:

S	W	N	E
1S	p	3S	p
p	p	p	

South deals and, with 12 HCP and 1 LP, opens 1S. North, looking at 10 HCP and NTS (4 trumps), raises to 3S. South passes. After all, North has shown 10, 11 or 12 points, coupled with South's absolute minimum opening bid total of 13 points; South reasons that game cannot be reached.

As the hand is played, South, the declarer, will make five spade tricks, one heart trick, three diamond tricks (two small diamonds will be ruffed in the dummy), and one club trick, for a total of ten tricks.

Should North–South be happy with this result? No. They stopped in 3S, they made 4S. It's a system disaster: they missed the bonus. In the bidding, they stopped in 3S, just as they were taught to. Counting again, 13 points for South and 10 for North comes to only 23, barely enough to make nine tricks, let alone the ten needed for game. But ten was what they made. If we were North–South, we'd be upset at not getting to game and would be questioning a system that failed to get us there.

Does this mean that we should scrap the system? Or does it mean that we might have overlooked something— something that's worth the three points we didn't think we had that would have brought us to the 26 needed to bid game, and that we should have counted in our initial calculations? Let's see: besides high cards and length, what was used in this hand to create tricks?

Shortness. We made use of the **shortness** in the dummy. That singleton diamond enabled us to trump two diamonds, creating two more tricks. If it normally takes 26 points to make ten tricks in a trump contract, then we can think of it as taking, on average, 2.6 points to make a trick. We created two tricks using that singleton: $2.6 \times 2 = 5.2$ points. That singleton diamond, in this hand, was worth a full 5.2 points!

But wait. Is shortness always worth points? And if so, why haven't we been taking account of it all along?

Let's say we played this last hand in no trump. What suit do you think the opponents would lead? Against no trump contracts, it's correct to lead your longest suit; the opponents' longest suit is always our shortest, and vice versa. The opponents, in this case, would attack diamonds. Is having a singleton when playing in no trump a benefit or a drawback? It's a drawback. In fact, it's our main weakness. Therefore shortness, when a hand is played in no trump, has no value.

When playing in a suit contract, on the other hand, shortness often provides us the opportunity to trump losers, thereby creating tricks. Shortness here most definitely has value. Will shortness always be worth something? Well, no. Look at these two situations. In each case, hearts are trump:

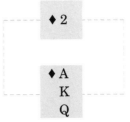

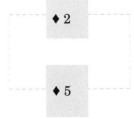

Is a singleton opposite an A K Q valuable? Of course not. Remember, we trump losers, not winners.

Is a singleton opposite a singleton valuable? Of course not. Once they're both played, there are no losers left in either hand to trump.

But both of these examples are extremes. In most cases, shortness has some value. Look at the hands below. Once again, hearts are trump:

	(A)			(B)			(C)	
♥ 7	♦ 3		♥ 7	♦ 2		♥ 7	♦ —	
6	2		6			6		
5			5			5		
♥ A	♦ 6		♥ A	♦ 6		♥ A	♦ 6	
K	5		K	5		K	5	
Q	4		Q	4		Q	4	

Q: Out of A, B and C on previous page, which diamond holding would you rather have?

A: C. The void in the North hand allows South to trump all three of his diamond losers with his little hearts.

In hand B, you could only trump two diamonds and you'd lose one.

In hand A, you could only trump one diamond and you'd lose two. In other words, the shorter the better.

Which of the following trump holdings would you prefer? Again, hearts are trump.

(A)			(B)			(C)	
♥	♦		♥	♦		♥	♦
7	2		7	2		7	2
6			6			6	
5			5				
4							
♥	♦		♥	♦		♥	♦
A	6		A	6		A	6
K	5		K	5		K	5
Q	4		Q	4		Q	4
J	3		J	3		J	3

Four trump is better than three trump, and three trump is better than two. In each case, you give the opponents a diamond in order to void the dummy. Seeing that it's your intention to trump diamonds in the dummy, your opponents will try to thwart your plan by returning a trump every time, thereby diminishing dummy's trump holding and lessening your ability to trump your losers. With four trump, as in hand A, you still have three trump left and can ruff all three remaining diamonds. But this can't be said of B or C. The longer the trump, the better!

Volumes have been devoted to discussing the exact value of all these various holdings. But here's a quick and easy way to remember the value of singetons and voids. Subtract the number of cards in your short suit from the number of trump, and that's its value. In example A on previous page, you have four trump and a singleton . . . 4 − 1 = 3. The trick taking value for a singleton with four trumps is 3 points, about the value of a king.

Try these out:

You hold ♥ A 4 2 and a singleton ♦ 3. The value of that ♦ 3 is 3 − 1 = 2. Now, what's the value of the short suit holding if you have ♥ A 4 2 and a void in diamonds? That void is worth 3: 3 − 0 = 3. And if you have ♥ A 5 4 3 and diamond void, that holding would be worth 4 points for shortness: 4 − 0 = 4.

Doubletons are sort of like stepchildren. They are worth, at most, 1 point and that is only when they're accompanied by *four* trump or more. In a hand containing ♥ A 4 2 and ♦ 7 6, that doubleton diamond would have no value: With only three trump you may not be able to both draw the opponents' outstanding trump and trump losers yourself. But if a hand contained ♥ A 4 3 2 and ♦7 6, you would count that doubleton as 1 point. If a hand contained ♥A 4 3 2 and *two* doubletons, you would still only count 1 shortness point.

In addition to high card points (HCP) and length points (LP) when playing in a trump contract we must also consider the value of shortness points (SP).

Now we know *how* and *why* to count shortness points. But *when*? Here's the key: Count shortness only after you are absolutely certain that the hand is going to be played in a trump suit. In a no trump contract, as we've seen, shortness doesn't count for anything; it's a weakness, not a strength. Only once you and your partner have agreed on a trump fit and discarded the idea of playing the hand in no trump—only then can you tally those shortness points and evaluate your hand accordingly.

Let's test you on this. Look at the sample hand below, in both cases listen to the opening bid and consider the value of the singleton heart.

♠	♥	♦	♣
K	7	J	A
9		10	6
7		9	5
6		8	2

First case: Partner opens the bidding 1S. How many points, if any, do you now count for shortness?

Second case: Your partner opens the bidding 1H. Do you count your shortness? If so, what's its value?

Answers:

1. Count your singleton heart, as you know you'll be playing in spades. 4 trump − 1 diamond = 3 points. Count 3 points for shortness. Add 3 SP to your 8 HCP. Your hand now is worth 11 points in all. Instead of raising your partner's 1H bid to the two level, as you would with 8 points, you must now factor in the trick-taking potential of that singleton (3 SP) and jump with 11 points to 3S.

2. Do not add any SP for your singleton. Your partner opened in hearts and you have only one heart. You don't have the necessary eight-card trump fit, so you're not going to be playing in hearts. You may even end up playing this hand in no trump, where shortness has no value.

Now, to conclude, let's go back to the example hand that got us started on this in the first place:

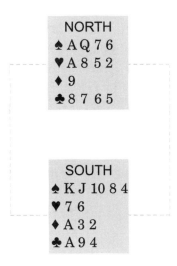

NORTH
♠ A Q 7 6
♥ A 8 5 2
♦ 9
♣ 8 7 6 5

SOUTH
♠ K J 10 8 4
♥ 7 6
♦ A 3 2
♣ A 9 4

This was the hand in which we failed to reach game yet easily made ten tricks.

When South opened 1S, North knew he would not be playing in no trump. (South's opening 1S bid guaranteed at least a five-card suit; with North's four spades North knows there are at least nine spades between them). Evaluating North's hand simply in terms of high cards brought us to 10 points. Now, however, we know to add 3 for the shortness (4 trumps – 1 diamond = 3 points). That makes 13 points **in support of** spades. (You only count shortness points when you can **support** your partner's trump holding.) With 13 points, we know to jump directly to game—4S. We'll make ten tricks—just as we did in the earlier example. But this time, we'll be in game and get the bonus.

The system is vindicated!

Notice how easily we reached the game level in spades. If we had been in no trump, we would have had to settle for a part score. Remember, in no trump we count HCP and LP only because shortness in no trump takes no tricks. In no trump we had 22 combined HCP and 1 LP, for a total of 23 points—well short of the 26 needed for game. In practice, in no trump, we could only have made the eight obvious tricks. This would get us a score of +70. But in a trump contract, shortness combines with length and high cards to give us three ways of making tricks. In a trump contract, we count anything that's not nailed down. HCP, LP, and SP, all count in our efforts to get to game.

And, just as you count HCP and LP in both partner's hands, so too do you count SP. We still start, then, with 22 HCP and 1 length point; but now, when no trump is ruled out, we add 3 for the singleton diamond in the responder's hand and 1 for the double heart in the opener's hand for a grand total of 27 points. The bid is 4S. And, when you make it the score is +620.

One last time, given all these examples, take heed:

The easiest path to game is to locate and play in your eight-card (or longer) major suit fit.

▪ HANDS-ON PLAY

In each of the four practice hands that follow, attempt to do the following:

A. bid the North–South cards.

B. look at West's opening lead, then plan the play. Remember: in trump contracts, the key is to understand when to draw trump.

Hand 1:

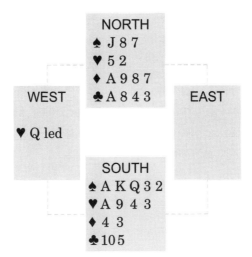

NORTH
♠ J 8 7
♥ 5 2
♦ A 9 8 7
♣ A 8 4 3

WEST

♥ Q led

EAST

SOUTH
♠ A K Q 3 2
♥ A 9 4 3
♦ 4 3
♣ 10 5

South deals, so he starts the auction. He has a 5–4–2–2 shape; therefore, he can already discount the possibility of opening 1NT. He has 13 HCP and 1 LP in that fifth spade; that's 14 points. With 13 or more, he must open the bidding. He has a five-card major, so he opens this hand 1S.

North has 9 HCP and MTS (minimum trump support). With her three spades and South's guaranteed five, they manage to reach the combined eight or more cards necessary to agree on a trump suit. Now, why agree right away on spades without first looking around for somewhere else to play? Because our object in bidding is to look for game. We know that game in the majors is the easiest game to reach. Agreeing on a major suit fit is half the battle. North found the easiest path to game as soon as South opened 1S. All that's left is to see if, between them, North–South has enough fire power—enough points—to attempt a four-level contract. Remember: that number is 26.

North has 9 HCP, zero LP and zero SP (doubletons only

count as one point when you have four or more trump). With 9 points and MTS, North can only raise South's 1S opening to the two level, no further. On his next turn, South passes because he cannot reach 26 points. South has the 14 points he started with, and gains 1 SP from his doubletons after North raises his suit and confirms that they are going to play in a trump contract. 14 + 9 (at most) does not come close to 26.

The opening lead is the ♥Q. Plan the play.

In a trump contract, if a partnership's trump holdings are unequal, I like to view the proceedings from the hand with the longer trump. I find that this makes it easier to count losers and winners. Therefore, let's count South's winners first. South probably has five spade tricks—the honors, plus one for length—in addition to the three outside aces. Those are his **top tricks**—the ones he would probably win even if this hand were being played in no trump.

Next, look around for shortness in the shorter trump hand. Remember, in order to create tricks, it is necessary to ruff losers in the short hand. Notice that there is a doubleton heart in dummy and four hearts in the South hand. This inequality is just what you're looking for: you plan on playing your A, followed by a low heart. This will create the void in the dummy that will allow you to try to trump your two losing hearts.

Instead of counting winners, another way of looking at the hand would be to start by counting losers. In some trump hands, this will be easier to see. By identifying your losers ahead of time, you may be able to devise a plan that allows you to trump or discard them. (My suggestion to you is that, time permitting, you look at the hand both ways.) You have two little diamonds in the South hand. One is covered by the ♦A in the North hand. The other is a loser. Same situation in clubs. Both face length in the dummy, so they cannot be trumped. The four-card heart suit has one winner and three possible losers; the dummy, however, contains only two hearts, which affords South the possibility, after losing one heart, of trumping two hearts in the dummy. South might make as many as five spade tricks, three aces and two ruffs in the dummy, for a total of ten tricks.

Now let's play the hand. Win the ♥A, and then give the opponents a heart trick right away. West wins the next trick and switches to a trump. This is a good play on the part of the defenders. Seeing as how you chose not to draw trump in favor of voiding the dummy's hearts, the defenders are onto you, so they go about shortening the dummy's ability to trump by drawing your trump! Win this return with the ♠A, ♠K, or ♠Q, and then trump a heart. You've now reached this position:

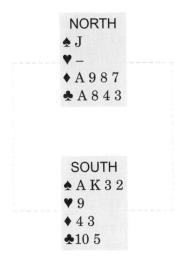

NORTH
♠ J
♥ –
♦ A 9 8 7
♣ A 8 4 3

SOUTH
♠ A K 3 2
♥ 9
♦ 4 3
♣ 10 5

You're now in the North hand. You have one trump left with which to ruff your last losing heart. But you're in the wrong hand with no quick way back to the hand that holds the heart. So what can you do? Say you play dummy's ♦A and follow it with a low diamond, planning to trump the third diamond, which would get you back into the declarer's hand. One of your two opponents will win the second diamond trick and shoot back a trump, forcing you to play dummy's ♠J, killing your ability to ruff your last heart. Nice defense! The opponents thus manage to hold you to five spades, three aces, and only one ruff in the dummy, for a total of nine tricks. Lucky for your side you didn't overbid to game, or else you would have gone minus.

The full hand was:

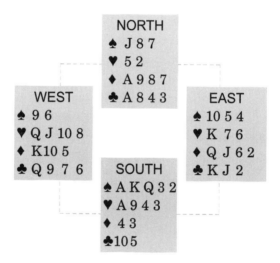

NORTH
♠ J 8 7
♥ 5 2
♦ A 9 8 7
♣ A 8 4 3

WEST
♠ 9 6
♥ Q J 10 8
♦ K10 5
♣ Q 9 7 6

EAST
♠ 10 5 4
♥ K 7 6
♦ Q J 6 2
♣ K J 2

SOUTH
♠ A K Q 3 2
♥ A 9 4 3
♦ 4 3
♣ 10 5

Had the defenders not shortened your trumps at trick three, you would have made an extra trick. This is a good illustration of why we do not count doubletons as shortness points when we hold only three trumps. Too often you don't get to use those trumps to their fullest potential.

Hand 2:

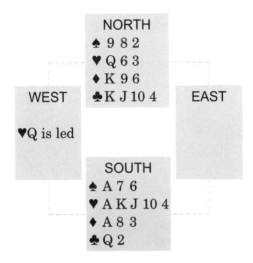

NORTH
♠ 9 8 2
♥ Q 6 3
♦ K 9 6
♣ K J 10 4

WEST

EAST

♥Q is led

SOUTH
♠ A 7 6
♥ A K J 10 4
♦ A 8 3
♣ Q 2

South deals. She has a 5–3–3–2 distribution, 18 HCP and 1 LP for a total of 19 points. That's the right shape, but too many points, for an opening bid of 1NT. So South opens the bidding with a call of 1H (five or more hearts; 13–20 points). North, holding 9 points (9 HCP, 0 LP, 0 SP) and three-card trump support (thereby guaranteeing 8 trump) raises you to 2H. South's 19 points and North's 9 are more than enough for South to contract for game by jumping to 4H.

The ♠Q is led. Plan the play: remember that you need ten tricks (book + 4).

That ♠Q is a good lead for the defense. It will knock out your spade stopper. As soon as they regain the lead, the opponents will cash two spade tricks. Your club suit can provide two discards (as you hold four cards opposite two cards), but that will be too late to help you with your spade problem. In order to set up those two club winners, you'll have to surrender the lead to the opponents' ♣A. As soon as that happens, they'll cash their two good spade tricks. Let's look at your holdings.

Count your winners: one spade trick, five heart tricks, two diamond tricks and three club tricks—that makes eleven. We know you have two spade losers and you are also going to lose to the ♣A. That's all you can spare. But you may also lose one diamond trick, and that makes four potential losers. On this hand it looks like you have eleven winners plus four losers. That's fifteen tricks—two more than there are! Don't panic; this happens often, especially in trump hands. Can we discard the diamond loser on one of our eleven winners? Yes. The club suit, which did not offer us immediate spade help, will provide us with a slow diamond discard if we can establish the suit before we cash the ♦A and ♦K.

Put all this information together and decide whether we should draw trump now or later. Ask yourself two questions: (1) Do we need to trump losers in the dummy? The answer is no. (2) Can we discard any spade losers before the opponents can cash them? The answer, again, is no. In this case, we'd better draw trump now, so that the opponents won't be able to ruff any of our good club tricks when we get around to establishing that suit.

Play three rounds of hearts (the missing five hearts split evenly, 3–2). Then drive out the opponents' ♣A. (Start by playing the ♣Q, so as not to block the suit.) You will have plenty of time to discard your losing diamond on an established club—that is, the three clubs that were promoted to master cards after you knocked out the ♣A.

When all's said and done, you will win one spade trick, five heart tricks, two diamond tricks, and 2 club tricks.

Here's the complete layout of the hand:

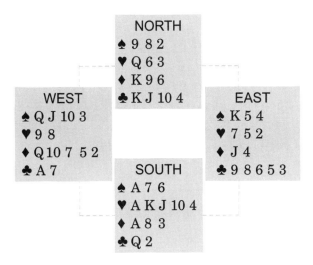

NORTH
♠ 9 8 2
♥ Q 6 3
♦ K 9 6
♣ K J 10 4

WEST
♠ Q J 10 3
♥ 9 8
♦ Q 10 7 5 2
♣ A 7

EAST
♠ K 5 4
♥ 7 5 2
♦ J 4
♣ 9 8 6 5 3

SOUTH
♠ A 7 6
♥ A K J 10 4
♦ A 8 3
♣ Q 2

Had you not drawn trumps when you did, West might have been able to ruff your third club for the fourth defensive trick, defeating your contract.

Hand 3:

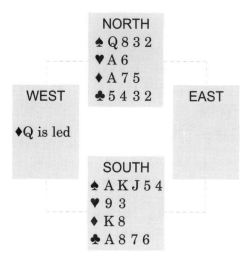

NORTH
♠ Q 8 3 2
♥ A 6
♦ A 7 5
♣ 5 4 3 2

WEST

♦Q is led

EAST

SOUTH
♠ A K J 5 4
♥ 9 3
♦ K 8
♣ A 8 7 6

South deals. He has 15 HCP, but his 5–4–2–2 shape precludes opening 1NT. Instead South opens 1S.

Bingo! North knows instantly that a beautiful nine-card major suit fit exists on this hand, so you know where the hand will be played. Now all that's left for North–South to do is to determine how many points they have between them and set the level of the spade contract. North has 10 HCP and 1 SP (that doubleton heart along with those four trumps), too strong for a single raise to 2S, which would show only 6–9 points in support. North must jump to 3S to show partner three- or four-card spade support and 10–12 points. South counts his points again now that he knows he'll be playing in a trump suit, adding a total of 1 point for the shortness in both red suits: 15 HCP + 1 LP + 1 SP = 17. 17 + the 10 to 12 points that North showed by jumping to 3S gets the two of you to at least 26 total points. South bids game, 4S.

The opening lead is the ♦Q. Plan the play.

North–South have five spade tricks, one heart trick, two diamond tricks, and one club trick for a total of nine winners. As for losers, they're looking at one heart and three club losers. In other words, they have one too many losers and one too few winners. They have to find a way to turn a loser into a winner.

Let's see: nothing can be done about their heart loser. They have equal length in both hands, so they can't trump it away; nor do they have any outside high cards on which to discard it. South can trump the dummy's third diamond, but that won't get them an extra trick because they will be ruffing it in the long hand. Therefore, if they are going to make the contract, it is up to the club suit to provide them with an extra trick.

They have eight clubs; the opponents have five. If the five outside clubs split evenly, 3–2 (as they rate to break about two thirds of the time), then the fourth club in each hand will be promoted, through length, to a winner.

Having thought through the hand, now put the plan into action. After winning the ♦Q lead, the first question that should occur to you is: when do you draw trump? The answer is *right now*. First, North–South have nothing to discard immediately, and second, they are not planning on using their trump to ruff anything. Win the lead in the South hand with the ♦K and play ♠A and ♥K, drawing the opponents' trump (the trump suit split 5–4–2–2). Now play the ♣A and a small club. Win the return and drive out the opponents' last club. If the club suit breaks 4–4–3–2 around the table, North–South will have their ten tricks.

The complete hand was:

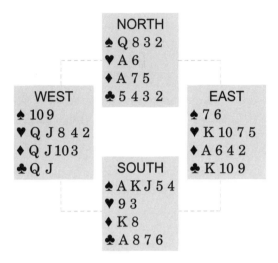

NORTH
♠ Q 8 3 2
♥ A 6
♦ A 7 5
♣ 5 4 3 2

WEST
♠ 10 9
♥ Q J 8 4 2
♦ Q J 10 3
♣ Q J

EAST
♠ 7 6
♥ K 10 7 5
♦ A 6 4 2
♣ K 10 9

SOUTH
♠ A K J 5 4
♥ 9 3
♦ K 8
♣ A 8 7 6

Notice that the ♦Q that West led was not from his longest suit (as it might have been, for instance, against a no trump contract), but rather from a shorter, stronger suit.

Hand 4:

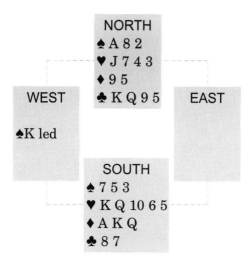

NORTH
♠ A 8 2
♥ J 7 4 3
♦ 9 5
♣ K Q 9 5

WEST

♠K led

EAST

SOUTH
♠ 7 5 3
♥ K Q 10 6 5
♦ A K Q
♣ 8 7

South deals. She is looking at a 5–3–3–2 distribution. With a no trump shape, but with only 14 HCP, she must discount the idea of opening 1NT. Instead she opts for a 1H opening.

North has 10 HCP. On learning that his side has at least a nine-card heart fit and therefore will not be playing this hand in a no trump contract, he counts one point for the doubleton diamond. That comes to 11 points. With four-card trump support and 11 points, North jumps to 3H.

South, now, has an easy decision. With 14 HCP and 1 LP and 1 SP—16 points in all—plus North's announced 10, 11 or 12 points, the partnership is now over the 26-point threshold required to bid a major suit game. South raises to 4H.

The ♠K is led. Plan the play.

Count the North–South winners. They have one spade trick, four heart tricks, three diamond tricks and one club trick (the K Q in dummy): that's nine winners. How about losers? They have two spade losers, one heart loser and one club loser: four losers in all. They must turn a loser into a winner.

Again, with that killer lead, the opponents have gotten off to a great start. If North–South try to draw trump, East–West will win the ♥A and immediately cash two spade winners. N–S would still have a club loser to go with those three, so E–W would beat them.

Is there any way to avoid this? Yes. There are three diamond winners in the declarer's hand, facing only two diamond cards in the dummy. This length inequality will provide a quick and necessary spade discard.

Delay drawing trump. Win the opening ♠K and play diamonds immediately. Now, you have to get a little lucky here. You have to hope that both opponents have three or more diamonds, or else they'll ruff one of these winners. If they do that, then you will not make your contract; but you can console yourself with the fact that you took your best and only shot at making the hand. The outstanding eight diamonds rate to break 4–4 or 5–3 about 90 percent of the time. Only 10 percent of the time will one of the opponents have two or fewer diamonds and be able to ruff one of your three winners, thwarting your plan to discard a losing spade. Ninety percent of the time you'll make ten tricks. This hand is one of those times.

On the third diamond, discard dummy's ♠2. Now you can draw trump. The opponents will win one spade, one heart and one club, and you'll make your 4H contract.

The complete hand was:

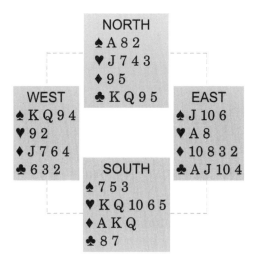

Notice that the opening ♠K lead was not from a three-card sequence. A two-card sequence against a suit contract is enough. Remember, against a suit contract, we are mainly interested in the first two rounds of the suit, as subsequent rounds are likely to get trumped by somebody.

By the way, on West's ♠K lead, when declarer calls for the dummy's ♠A, East should signal his approval of this lead by playing the ♠J. East knows that partner led from the ♠K Q—a two-card sequence—and since East is looking at the next two sequential cards and sees three little spades in the dummy, he should signal to his partner that it is safe for West to continue the suit should he regain the lead. From West's point of view, seeing East's dramatic ♠J discard can mean only one thing: that he has the ♠10. Otherwise, he couldn't afford to discard a potential trick.

EVALUATING YOUR HAND

▪ MINOR SUIT BIDDING

Bidding games in the minors—that is, playing in a contract of five diamonds or five clubs—is a last resort.

Obviously, it's harder to make a five-level (eleven tricks) contract than a four-level (ten tricks) contract. So if you are faced with a decision of whether to play 4S or 5D, all things being equal, you should always opt for the easier ten-trick contract: 4S. Why make it harder than it has to be?

Consider this hand:

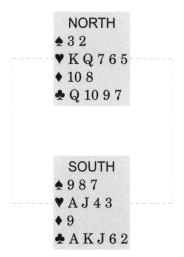

NORTH
♠ 3 2
♥ K Q 7 6 5
♦ 10 8
♣ Q 10 9 7

SOUTH
♠ 9 8 7
♥ A J 4 3
♦ 9
♣ A K J 6 2

When faced with two nine-card fits, a minor and a major, always try to steer the contract to the major. Look closely at this hand: Playing with either hearts or clubs trump, you have three losers—two spades and one diamond. You won't make 5C but you will make 4H. Can you see that?

More often, the decision before you isn't between five of a minor or four of a major, but between five of a minor and three no trump. In the previous chapter, we saw that when the choice was between four of a major and three no trump, we chose the major. The presence of a trump fit more than made up for the needed extra trick. This is not true in the minors. When making the five of a minor verses three no trump choice, opt for no trump. It is usually much easier to try for nine tricks in no trump than to try to create the *two* additional tricks needed to fulfill a five-level minor suit contract. The trump presence is just not enough to overcome this two trick differential. As an added incentive, we also have the relative luxury of being able to lose four tricks in a 3NT contract, instead of the only two afforded us in 5C or 5D.

> It takes 26 HCP + LP to make 3NT.
> It takes 26 HCP + LP + SP to make 4H or 4S.
> *But:*
> It takes **29 HCP** + LP + SP to make 5C or 5D.

As you might expect, raising your partner's one-of-a-minor suit opening bid to the two or three level requires the same number of points as raising his one-of-a-major to the two or three level.

> 1D—2D: this takes 6–9 points.
> 1D—3D: this takes 10–12 points.

Look at the following three hands and consider how you would respond to your partner's opening bid of 1D. Ask yourself how many points you have in support of partner's suit.

A.   ♠ K 7 5   ♥ 10 9 7   ♦ K J 8 3 2   ♣ 6 4

When you first picked up this hand you counted 7 HCP + 1 LP for your fifth diamond. As soon as partner opened 1D, your hand got better. Because of your known nine-card fit, your shortness, the doubleton club, gained some value. Add 1 SP to your original 8 points. With 9 points and good trump support raise your partner to 2D.

B.   ♠ Q 9   ♥ 10 9   ♦ A J 8 3 2   ♣ K 10 7 4

Here you have 10 HCP +1 LP +1SP. In support of diamonds you have 12 points. Raise partner's 1D opening bid to 3D.

C.　　♠ 7　　♥ 10 9 8　　♦A J 8 3 2　　♣K 10 9 4

You have 8 HCP, 1 LP, and 3 SP for the singleton spade. With 12 points in support of diamonds, raise partner's 1D opening to 3D.

Though raising partner's minor suit requires the same number of points as raising his major suit, it requires a different number of trump cards.

- When partner opens 1S or 1H, he guarantees a five-card suit.

- When partner opens 1D, only four cards are promised. In order to guarantee eight between you, to support diamonds you must have a minimum of four. MTS (Minimum Trump Support) for diamonds, therefore, is 4.

1D–2D . . . Opener may have four diamonds, responder must have four diamonds to raise.

- When partner opens 1C, only three cards are guaranteed. MTS, the least you need to guarantee eight between you, therefore is five. Let's look at this example:

♠A Q 4　　♥A 8 7 6　　♦Q 8 3　　♣Q 8 2

With 4–3–3–3 shape but only 14 HCP you're one point shy of a 1NT opening. With more than 13 points, you have to open. You only have four hearts, so you can't open 1H. You must, therefore, open this hand one of a minor. Remember which? When faced with the choice of two three-card minors, choose clubs. So, if by opening 1C, you're only showing three or more clubs, how many clubs must partner bring to the table in order to guarantee the eight-card fit necessary to suggest clubs as a trump fit? 8 – 3 = 5.

1C–2C . . . Opener may have three clubs, responder must have five clubs to raise. If your partner opens 1C, what would you bid with the following hand?

♠ K 8   ♥ 9 7   ♦ K 10 4 2   ♣ K J 6 5 3

You have 10 HCP, 1 LP, 1SP, and five-card support for clubs. With 12 points in support of clubs and NTS, raise 1C to 3C.

▪ MAJOR SUIT BIDDING

As noted at the start of this section, minor suit games require the most tricks and so are the least attractive to bid. Whenever possible look to the other strains, majors and no trump, before resigning yourself to those eleven-trick contracts. This decision to shy away from minor suit games will profoundly affect the bidding:

♠ 3 2   ♥ K 9 7 5   ♦ K J 7 5 3   ♣ K 10

Q : Partner opens 1D, you have five-card support plus 10 HCP + 1LP +1SP. What is your response?

A : You could raise to 3D; this looks like the perfect hand for it—beautiful trump support and 10–12 points. The "correct" call, however, is 1H! Before settling on a minor you must first explore easier paths to game.

Because we open only five-card majors, when partner opened 1D, he denied having five hearts. **But an opening bid of 1D doesn't deny that opener has four hearts.** With your 1H response and a four-card heart suit, you are setting the stage to try and uncover possible 4–4 major suit fits.

In the 1D–1H auction that we just had, you held the North cards. Let's give your partner, the 1D opener, the South cards:

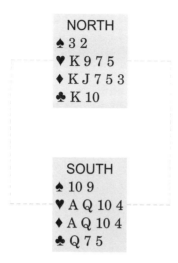

NORTH
♠ 3 2
♥ K 9 7 5
♦ K J 7 5 3
♣ K 10

SOUTH
♠ 10 9
♥ A Q 10 4
♦ A Q 10 4
♣ Q 7 5

With 14 HCP and a four-card diamond suit South indeed would open 1D. Between the N–S cards, a 5D contract would fail because N–S would lose two spades and one club. 3NT would fail too because N–S would lose one club and at least five spades. The *only* game contract that N–S can make is 4H. But how can you get to four hearts if no one even mentions the suit?

So mention it. **As responder, before you raise your partner's minor suit, show him a four-card or longer major.** If you don't, he'll assume you don't have one. Speak now or forever hold your peace. In the above example, partner opened 1D. Even with five lovely diamonds, restrain your natural impulse to raise diamonds. Suggest an easier strain to game. Enter a call of 1H.

<u>S</u>	<u>W</u>	<u>N</u>	<u>E</u>
1D	p	**1H**	

Your 1H *response*, remember, is not a 1H *opening bid*. Only a 1H *opening bid* requires five hearts. As a responder, bidding hearts—or, for that matter, any suit—shows *four* or more of them. Keep in mind why you are mentioning hearts in the first place. Since partner didn't open 1H, there can't be a 5–3, eight-card major suit fit. But a 4–4, eight-card fit could still exist. You're introducing your four-card heart suit hoping to hear that partner has one too. If he does, that combined eight-card fit will provide the easiest path to game.

S	W	N	E
1D	p	1H	p
2H			

With A Q 10 fourth of hearts, when partner hears your 1H response to his opening 1D bid, he knows an eight-card major suit fit has been found. His 2H rebid alerts you to that fact.

True, your diamonds are stronger than your hearts; but they will pull their weight anyway in the course of the play. They'd better—you're counting on five diamond tricks.

Imagine that you, the responder, hold the same hand as before:

♠ 3 2   ♥ K 9 7 5   ♦ K J 7 5 3   ♣ K 10

Once again, partner opens 1D; you respond 1H, looking for a 4-4 fit, partner now rebids 1S. What's going on?

S	W	N	E
1D	p	1H	p
1S			

What does that 1S rebid of partner's mean? Could he have five spades? No: if he did, he would have opened 1S. Might he be showing you four of them? Yes! Why? Because he wants to suggest spades as a possible trump suit, and because he doesn't have four hearts! If he did, he would have supported you by raising hearts.

Could you have four spades? In response to 1D, you bid 1H, showing four or more hearts. Did this deny four spades? Not necessarily. If you had four hearts and four spades, you would have mentioned hearts first because they come before spades in the suit ranking. What suit ranking? The order in which suits are bid in auctions, which goes from the lowest ranking suit to the highest:

$$\underrightarrow{\text{1C} \quad \text{1D} \quad \text{1H} \quad \text{1S} \quad \text{1NT}}$$

Bid your four-card suits up the line. Don't bypass one four-card suit in order to bid another. This way, by the time you reach 1NT, you will have been able to find or eliminate any 4–4 fit, thoroughly exploring all possible roads to game.

Let's look at a few examples of bidding up the line. In each scenario below you are the opening bidder. In each auction, decide what suits, if any, your rebid denies.

A.   1C–1D
         2D

You open 1C, partner responds 1D, and you raise to 2D. You are guaranteeing four or more diamonds and denying the presence of four hearts or four spades. If you had four cards of either hearts or spades, now would have been the time to alert your partner by bidding up the line. Instead, you've agreed on a minor suit and eliminated the major suits.

Your hand could be:

♠Q 6   ♥K 8   ♦A J 4 2   ♣A 9 8 6 5

Your hand cannot be:

    ♠ K Q 6 5   ♥ 7   ♦ Q 10 8 3   ♣ A Q 4 2

After all, with the second hand, you would have rebid 1S, still looking for a 4–1 major suit fit.

B.   1C–1D
        1H–2H

You open 1C, partner responds 1D, and you rebid 1H, showing four or more hearts—but not denying four diamonds. With her bid of 2H, partner confirms a 4–4 heart fit.
You could have:

    ♠ ——   ♥ K J 6 5   ♦ A 10 8 3   ♣ K Q 9 7 2

Remember to introduce your own major suit before thinking about raising partner's minor.

C.   1C–1D
        1S–2S

You open 1C, partner responds 1D, you rebid 1S—not denying four diamonds, but denying four hearts, and showing at least four spades. Partner confirms the spade fit.
You could *not* have:

    ♠ A 6 5 4   ♥ Q J 9 4   ♦ 6 5   ♣ A K 7

If you did, the auction would have sounded like this:

        1C–1D
        1H

D.   1C–1D
        1H–1S
        2S—

You open 1C, partner responds 1D, you rebid 1H, showing four or more hearts. Partner rebids one spade, showing four, and you confirm an eight-card fit in spades by raising his second suit—spades.

You could have:

♠A 5 4 3   ♥Q J 8 7   ♦9   ♣A Q 6 3

Notice that, in this auction, before you've even gotten to the no trump strain, you've managed to discuss every single suit and finally found a 4–4 spade fit.

In all these examples, we haven't talked about one very subtle, yet incredibly important point. While you and your partner were busy looking around for a place to play, you each kept bidding. Go back and review the auctions. No one passed until a place to play was agreed upon.

**When exploring at the one level,
all new suit bids by responder are forcing.**

Only a responder can force the bidding. Forcing means your partner, in this case the opener, must not pass. We haven't seen forcing bids before.

We know that when your partner opens one of a suit (meaning he has *at most* 20 points), and you have less than 6 points, *you may pass.*

When your partner opens 1NT (meaning he has at most 17 points), and you have less than 9 points, *you may pass.*

The reason both these opening bids were not forcing on responder was that they required responder to have a minimum number of points. If responder didn't have this requisite number and therefore knew game was unreachable, he was free to pass.

If the prescribed range for an opening bid is 13–20 points, is there also a prescribed range for the response? The range for a simple change of suit bid by responder on the one level is . . . ready for this? . . . 6 or *more*. There is no upper limit. (Well, technically it's 27 points because the opener supposedly had 13 for his bid, and there are only 40 points in the deck.) That being the case, whenever you open the bidding and your partner responds one of a suit, any contract from a part-score to a grand slam is possible. Because the range for a simple response is unlimited and the potential for game is alive, the opener must keep the auction going.

Let's compare the first one of a suit bid by opener and the first one of a suit response by partner: let's have the opening bid be 1C and the response be 1S.

Opening Bid: 1C . . . shows . . . three or more clubs and 13–20 points

Response: 1S . . . shows . . . four or more spades and 6–27 points

Between you, you could have as few as 19 or as many as 40 HCP. Subsequent bids by both parties will eventually narrow this range down substantially.

The point is, when you open the bidding, no matter how awful you think your opening bid is, when your partner changes suits you must respond.

Example:
You pick up ♠A ♥K J 9 3 ♦K 7 2 ♣J 9 6 5 4
12 HCP + 1 LP = 13 points

You have barely enough to open the bidding, but, quite correctly, you do. You open 1C. Your partner responds 1D. Can you pass? Can you be a little pregnant? A bid is either forcing or it's not. Responder's 1D bid is forcing. You must find a rebid. For all you know, your partner could be looking at this perfect companion hand:

♠K932 ♥AQ84 ♦AQJ65 ♣ —

In responding 1D to your 1C opening all partner was trying to do was locate a strain to play in. If you pass 1D, he'll make it for sure, but then you'll have missed out on possibly bidding and making a slam or grand slam in hearts or diamonds.

Now, let's go back to this hand from earlier in the chapter. You hold:

♠3 2 　♥K 9 7 5 　♦K J 7 5 3 　♣K 10

Your partner opened 1D. You rightly responded 1H (forcing), and partner rebids 1S. So what do you do now?

You should continue to try to describe your hand to your partner. By his opening bid, partner is showing four or more diamonds; with his rebid he denies four hearts and shows exactly four spades. He could have:

♠A K 6 4 　♥8 　♦Q 10 8 4 2 　♣A 9 3

Wouldn't he like to know that you have four or more diamonds with him and 10–12 points? Of course he would.

Pretend, for a moment, you didn't have four hearts. When partner opened 1D, what would you have bid? With five diamonds and twelve points you would have jumped to 3D. So that's what you do now. That's your rebid.

1D–1H
1S–*3D!*

By rebidding 3D, you are saying, "Partner, I first had to bid hearts; as you know, it's my job to investigate the possibility of a 4–4 major suit fit. But in truth, I really liked diamonds all along, and I'm jumping to the three level to show you that I also happen to like my hand (being that it's in the 10–12 point range)."

▪OPENER VERSUS RESPONDER

When I was first learning how to bid, I constantly confused the "opener" with the "responder" and often lost sight of the meanings of their respective rebids. For example, what's the difference, say, between these two 2S rebids?

(a)   1D–1S
           2S   and   **(b)**   1D–1H
                                        1S–2S

The difference lies in who did the rebidding. In (a) it's the opener, while in (b) it's the responder. So what does that tell us?

The opener, by definition, has 13 or more points (we think of him as the "big" hand);

The responder, meanwhile, could have as few as 6 or more (aka the "little" hand).

To highlight the difference, let's take a closer look at the above examples:

(a)   1D–1S
           2S

Opener rebids 2S. Opener's hand could be:

♠ K Q 7 2   ♥ 8 6   ♦ A J 9 4   ♣ K 7 6

Opener's 2S rebid sets spades as the trump suit and indicates a hand with a minimum of 13 points. **He opened:** he could have no less than 13 points.

(b)   1D–1H
           1S–**2S**

Responder rebids 2S. Responder's hand could be:

♠ K 9 7 2   ♥ 10 9 6 3   ♦ K 7   ♣ J 8 4

Responder's 2S rebid also sets spades as the trump suit, but this time indicates a minimum of only 6 points. **He responded**—he could have as few as 6 points. (Notice responder's first call of 1H with four hearts to the 10: any four-card major suit, no matter how measly the holding, can and should be mentioned as a possible trump suit.)

Responder's Rebids

Now while we're on the subject of rebids, what's the difference between the responder's 2S and 3S rebids in the following auctions?

1D–1H	1D–1H
1S–**2S**	1S–**3S**

The difference is a level—a trick, an ace, 4 points.

The 2S rebid shows 6–9 points: "I *hate* my hand but since partner, opener, could have as many as 20 points, I have to bid." (A typical hand for this action might be, example (b):

♠ K 9 7 2 ♥10 9 6 3 ♦K 7 ♣J 8 4

The 3S jump rebid, meanwhile, shows about an ace more . . . 10–12 points: "I *like* my hand but can't bid game, since I don't have 13 points." A typical hand—adding an ace to example (b)—would be:

♠ K 9 7 2   ♥ A 10 9 6   ♦ K 7   ♣ J 8 4

As responder, when your hand evaluates to 13–16 points, in support of your partner's opening bid, and game is a definite possibility, double jump to 4 of his major:

♠ K 9 7 2   ♥ A 10 9 6   ♦ K 7   ♣ A 8 4

1D–1H
1S–**4S**

When we talk about the relative strength of these three responses, we refer to them as:

A minimum response: 6–9 points (Hate)
An intermediate response: 10–12 points (Like)
A strong response: 13–16 points (Love)

Opener's Rebids

When responder jumps a level, he's showing extra strength. As opener when you jump a level you do the same:

1.	1D–1S		**2.**	1D–1S
	2S	and		**3S**

Once again, the difference is a level, a trick, an ace, 4 points.

As opener, your first bid showed no less than 13 points. To jump a level you need the equivalent of an ace (4 points) more than that. If you can open the bidding with 13 points, then in order to show a hand that's one trick stronger than the minimum (13 + 4 = 17) when raising partner's suit, jump a level.

A minimum opening bid: 13, 14, 15, or 16 points:

♠ K Q 6 4   ♥ 8 7   ♦ A J 4 3 2   ♣ Q 9
(13–16 points)

An intermediate opening bid: 17 or 18 points:

♠ K Q 6 4   ♥ A 8   ♦ A J 4 3 2   ♣ Q 9
(an Ace more: 17–18 points)

With the equivalent of 19 or more points in support of responder, a hand so big that even if your partner had only 6 points, the least he could have to keep the bidding open, game would be a distinct possibility, double jump to four of his major.

1D–1S
4S

A strong opening bid: 19 or more points:

♠ K Q 6 4　　♥ A 8　　♦ A J 4 3 2　　♣ A 9
(19+ points)

One last time. Both opener and responder have minimum, intermediate, and strong rebid ranges. Try not to confuse them. Opener's points start at 13. Responder's start at 6.

■ DISTRIBUTION

By now you should be comfortable with the reasons for bidding your four-card suits up the line this way:

1C–1D
1H–1S

Now let me throw you a curve. Let's say the auction progresses like so:

1D–*1S*
2D–*2H*

Responder for some reason chose to bypass his four-card heart suit, (yes, he does have a four-card heart suit) to bid his spades first. Got your thinking caps on? Why would he do that?

Could responder have a very good four-card spade suit and a very bad four-card heart suit, like . . .

♠ A K Q 3　　♥ 10 7 6 5　　♦ 3 2　　♣ Q 8 7

Nice try, but no. Even with this disparity in strength, we saw that responder should still mention his heart suit first. *Any* four-card major is biddable. So what is there about responder's spades that make them so much more attractive than his hearts? He must have *longer* spades than hearts. As in:

♠ A J 9 8 4   ♥ A 10 9 3   ♦ 3 2   ♣ Q 7

We bid four-card suits up the line. We never bypass a four-card suit to bid *another* four-card suit. By inference, when someone violates this rule, it is with the express purpose of showing at least a five-card suit. So, when you do bypass one suit to bid another and then come back and mention the bypassed suit, you are showing at least a 5–4 distribution. That is, at least five of the first bid suit, and at least four of the second bid suit. Notice that you could also be showing five of the first and five of the second. Do you recall the rule about bidding five-card suits? **With two five-card suits always bid the higher one first.**

Let's bid this hand as an example:

♠ A J 9 8 4   ♥ K Q 10 9 6   ♦ 4 2   ♣ Q

Partner opens 1D. As responder, first bid 1S, planning on rebidding your hearts later. Partner will play you for at least five spades and at least four hearts. If you get another chance to bid, show this 5–5 shape by *rebidding hearts*. Each time you rebid a suit it gets longer. But your first bid suit is always as long as, or longer than, your second bid suit. In this case, the longer your partner thinks the hearts are, the longer he'll know the spades can be.

1D–1S
2D

What is opener showing by rebidding diamonds? First, he's trying to show a minimum of 13–16 points (after all, he didn't jump to the three-level, which would have meant 17–18 points) and second, **extra diamond length.** An opening 1D bid shows only four diamonds; to show extra length, we rebid the suit.

Let's now put our newfound distribution skills to the test:

You, South open the bidding:

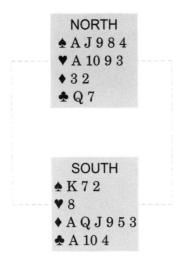

NORTH
♠ A J 9 8 4
♥ A 10 9 3
♦ 3 2
♣ Q 7

SOUTH
♠ K 7 2
♥ 8
♦ A Q J 9 5 3
♣ A 10 4

S		N
1D	–	1S
2D	–	2H
3S	–	4S

After the first round, 1D–1S, you rebid diamonds rather than raise spades. After all, responder guaranteed only four spades with her *response* of 1S. At this point in the auction, you still have 14 HCP, 2 LP, and no SP (as no eight-card fit has as yet been found and you still might be playing this hand in no trump, where shortness has no value).

When responder now makes a 2H rebid, you know that she had a four-card heart suit that she chose to bypass. The only reason to bypass a four-card heart suit is to show a longer spade suit. Your partner's shape, therefore, is at least 5–4, with at least five spades. Her five and your three-card spade support guarantees an eight-card or longer spade fit. It is now time to reevaluate your hand in terms of spades: 14 HCP, 2 LP, *2 SP* (3 spades – 1 heart = 2 SP). That's 18 points, *in support of spades*. Show an opening hand of intermediate strength by jumping a level to 3S.

North raises to game: 4S. His 13 points (11 HCP, 1 LP, 1 SP), coupled with your known 17 or 18 points, is more than enough (26) needed for game.

A classic auction. This is good stuff! Of course, it is just the start; it will take time and practice to put it all together. But if you understand these principles, you're well on your way to describing all the different hands that will be coming your way.

▪ BIDDING PRACTICE

In each example below, you are the responder, and the hand shown is yours. How would you respond, in each case, (a) if your partner opened 1C and (b) if your partner opened 1H?

1.
♠ 10 9 8 6
♥ Q 6 3   a. 1C–?
♦ 9 3   b. 1H–?
♣ A K 10 3

2.
♠ A J 5 2
♥ J 7   a. 1C–?
♦ Q 10 8 2   b. 1H–?
♣ 8 7 6

3.
♠ Q 7
♥ K 10 5 2   a. 1C–?
♦ K 4   b. 1H–?
♣ Q 9 5 4 2

4.
♠ K 4 3
♥ A 9 8 4   a. 1C–?
♦ A K 7 5   b. 1H–?
♣ 7 4

Answers:

1.   ♠ 10 9 8 6   ♥ Q 6 3   ♦ 9 3   ♣ A K 10 3

a. When your partner opens 1C, what do you know about his hand? Not much! A 1C opening is the most vague of all opening bids. It simply says that opener has three or more clubs and 13–20 points. It does, however, deny something very important. Partner does not have a five-card or longer major suit. If he did, he surely would have chosen to open 1H or 1S because half the battle is in trying to locate major suit fits.

As responder, your first job is to keep the auction open if the possibility of game exists. Your 9 HCP added to partner's 13–20 points makes this a very real possibility. Having decided to respond, your next job is to investigate possible strains in which to play the hand—always keeping an eye out for the major suits.

Even with ♣A K 10 3, you cannot support partner's club suit for two reasons. Your partner only guaranteed three clubs. With only four of your own, you cannot guarantee that the partnership has eight between you. More importantly, even if you had an eight-card club fit, your first job is to try to locate eight-card major suit fits, before retreating to no trump or a minor suit.

You have four spades. Your partner opened 1C. Could he have four spades? Yes. (His opening bid only denied his having *five* spades.) A 4–4 spade fit could in theory exist. Therefore, respond **1S.** Tell your partner you have four or more spades and 6 or more points. This asks partner to support spades if he too has four of them.

Notice your 1S response is almost as vague as your partner's 1C opening. As far as he's concerned, you could have the 9-point hand you actually have or this 18-point monster: ♠A K J 9 4 ♥3 ♦A K 4 2 ♣Q J 3. Your partner is still pretty much in the dark. You are just looking around for a strain to play in; clarification of how many points you have and what the rest of your hand looks like will have to come later.

b. Partner's opening 1H bid guarantees a five-card or longer heart suit and 13–20 points. With your 9 points, game is possible. You respond **2H.** With this bid you get to inform your partner of two important things: first, the existence of a combined eight-card or longer major suit fit, and second, the fact that in support of hearts your hand is valued at between 6 and 9 points. Your partner should now be in an excellent position to set the final contract, knowing both the strain and the combined point range of the hands. By your limiting, very descriptive bid of 2H, you turn over the final decision to your partner. What your partner does with this information depends entirely on the strength of his hand, leaving him to either pass with a weak opening bid or jump to game with a strong hand.

2.   ♠ A J 5 2   ♥ J 7   ♦ Q 10 8 2   ♣ 8 7 6

a. Respond **1D.** This shows four or more diamonds and 6 or more points. It does not deny four hearts or four spades, because diamonds are lower ranking than either major and get to be mentioned first.

Let's continue the auction. After you respond 1D, let's say partner comes back with a 1H rebid. Now what?

1C–1D
1H–?

Rebid 1S. You're still hoping to find a 4–4 spade fit. Partner could have:

♠K Q 7 6 ♥Q 10 4 2 ♦7 ♣A K Q 3

and a 4S contract would have a good play. Or partner could have:

♠K Q 7 6 ♥K 7 5 2 ♦7 ♣A K 5 4

and you'd still have an easy time making at least a 2S contract.

b. Respond **1S.** You are hoping that your partner opened with five hearts and four spades. Partner's hand could look like this:

♠ K Q 7 6 ♥ K Q 10 6 2 ♦ 7 4 ♣A 5

3. ♠Q 7 ♥K 10 5 2 ♦K 4 ♣Q 9 5 4 2

a. Respond **1H.** Plan on showing your four-card heart suit, and if partner doesn't raise your heart response, show him your five-card club fit with your next response.

1C–1H
1S–?

If partner comes back with a 1S rebid, jump-raise him to 3C. This will say, "Partner, I had 10–12 points and a good fit with you in clubs all along. I just had to stop off and show you my four-card major first."

b. Respond **3H.** With nine or more combined hearts, bring your partner in on the good news. Confirm hearts as the trump suit. With 10 HCP, one length and one for shortness (the doubletons with four-card support), you can jump raise your partner to 3H to show your strength (10-12).

4.   ♠ K 4 3   ♥A 9 8 4   ♦A K 7 5   ♣7 4

a. Respond **1D.** Yes, you have an opening bid, and you're dying to show your partner how strong a hand you have, but be patient. First figure out what strain you're going to be playing in. Then show him the strength of your hand. You can't do everything with one bid.

We'll continue the auction to show you what might happen after your 1D response.

First, your partner must rebid something. Your bid of 1D was 100 percent forcing. It showed 6 or more points, with no upper limit. (Don't confuse this six-or-more situation with the 6–9 point range you are more familiar with. When *raising* parnter's suit, 1S—2S, you show 6–9 points. When simply *changing* suits on the one level, 1C–1D, you show 6 or more points.)

Say your partner chooses to rebid 1H. Not only can you now show him that you too have four hearts, you can also reveal your strength. You are going to support hearts. Recount your hand, adding extra points for any shortness.

You started wtih 14 HCP; now add 1 SP for the doubleton club. With 15 total points you are within the 13–16-point range for an immediate jump raise to 4H. As responder it is your duty to make sure that when you know the values for game exist, you force the auction to game. Partner's opening showed 13+ points; you had 15. You have eight hearts between you. You know you must be in a 4H contract. Bid it.

1C–1D
1H–4H

Say the auction went like this instead:
1C–1D
1S–?

Now what?

You both had an opening bid. You both tried to find the easiest path to game in a major suit, but you don't have a fit. So you settle for the next best thing: jump directly to 3 NT. This says, "Partner, we have at least 26 points between us and we don't have an eight-card major fit." As responder, you've fulfilled your duty to see that game is bid.

b. If your partner opens 1H, you can jump directly to **4H.** This shows 13–16 points and at least MTS (3+ hearts). If your partner has a big hand (17 or more points), maybe you'll get to slam (twelve tricks), or even grand slam (all thirteen tricks). The intricacies of slam bidding are beyond the scope of this beginner's book, but my advice is this: if you think you can make it, go ahead and bid it.

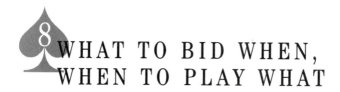

WHAT TO BID WHEN, WHEN TO PLAY WHAT

▪ NO TRUMP REVISITED

Let's say your partner opens 1NT. You, meanwhile, are not looking at much:

♠ J 10 9 8 7 6   ♥ 3 2   ♦ 3 2   ♣ 4 3 2

You have 1 HCP, 2 LP, and that's about it: 3 points total. Let's give your partner 16 HCP for his 1NT opening; even when you donate your 1 HCP to his cause, it's still going to be rough going if you leave him to play in no trump. The opponents have him outgunned 23 HCP to 17 HCP.

But wait, you say. *What about my six-card spade suit? That must count for something. Maybe we can make some long-suit tricks?*

Let's see if you're right. Give your partner a fairly typical no-trump holding and see how he does opposite your hand:

♠ A 5   ♥ A 8 7 6   ♦ A 9 6 5   ♣ A 10 9

That's 16 HCP, with a 4–4–3–2 distribution: a perfect 1NT opening.

two hands? (2) What's the *smallest* number of tricks you can expect to make? Take your time.

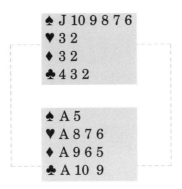

The answer to *both* questions, as it turns out, is four! How do you propose to use that nice, long spade suit? You can't. You can't bridge across. There are no entries to the hand with the long spade suit. The result, then, is dismal: All you'll make, as declarer, are your four aces. Your 1NT contract will fail by three tricks for a score of – 300.

Now, what if instead of a no trump contract, we found ourselves playing in a spade contract? What would be the most and least tricks that you could win?

The most would be eight, the least seven.

You'd make eight tricks if the spades were divided like this:

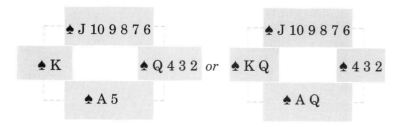

If the opponents' outstanding five spades contained a
stiff K or Q, or a K Q tight, you'd lose only one spade trick.
You'd make five trump tricks (spades) and three aces for
eight tricks. If you were playing in a two-spade contract,
you'd have a legitimate chance of making it and going +60.
Even if you had to lose two spade tricks, you'd still make
four spades to go along with your three aces. In either
event, you'd make a heck of a lot more tricks playing in 2S
than in 1NT.

Now all we need is a bid to get us to 2S.

When partner opens 1NT, and you have too few points
to entertain the idea of playing in game but have a long
five- or six-card suit, take your partner out of 1NT by bidding two of your suit.

	1NT–2S
or	1NT–2H
or	1NT–2D
but *not*	1NT–2C:

2C, as you will see, means something else.

That's how easy it is to play in two of your suit. Even
with that pitiful 1 HCP hand, you smugly bid 2S when
partner opens 1NT. This is a **command to pass.** It says,
"Partner, I heard you open 1NT. I know you can have as

many as 17 HCP and four spades—big deal. Your 17 and my 1 or 2 or 3 can't come close to the 26 we need for game. I'm in a better position than you to know this. You should respect my decision not to play in 1NT but to play in 2S. I don't want you bidding any more. Please pass. Thank you."

These two-level bids are sometimes called **shut out** or **close out** bids. 1NT, 2S or 2H or 2D closes out the auction. When do you use them? When your partner opens 1NT and your hand is worth less than the 9 points needed to invite game (17 + 0 to 8 cannot equal 26).

Please note: This is nothing like a 1S–2S response, even though it gets the auction to the same place. 1S–2S leaves open the possibility of the auction continuing. Raising your partner's suit shows that the chance for game still exists. If it didn't, you would have passed his 1S opening.

1NT–2S says, "Partner, my only other option was to pass your 1NT opening bid, and let you suffer and fail dismally in that contract."

You've seen shut out bids before. Strange as it seems the 3NT response in the auction 1NT–3NT is a shut out bid. It says, "Partner, I believe I'm looking at enough of a hand to make nine tricks in no trump, but not enough to investigate slam (a twelve-trick contract). Please pass." Even more strange sounding is the auction 1NT–7NT. No one ever calls the grand slam bid of 7NT a shut out bid, but it is. It's the highest bid in bridge. Even if your partner wanted to continue bidding, he couldn't. Shut out bids, you see, are not always weak. They come in all sizes. It is important to recognize them when they do occur.

Let's change that previously weak responder's hand to a game-going hand with a six-card major suit:

♠ A J 10 9 5 4   ♥ A 3   ♦ 3 2   ♣ J 10 9

Now you, the responder, have 10 HCP and 2 LP. This time, when partner opens 1NT, his 15–17 points combine with your 12 to give you the opportunity to play for game. But where?

Partner cannot have a void or singleton: he opened 1NT. He must have at least two spades. Your six spades plus his, equal an eight-card major suit fit.

Therefore, jump directly to game in spades: 1NT–4S is the entire auction.

4S is another shut out bid. It says, partner let's try to make 4S, period.

Imagine now that you hold the following hand:

♠ A J 10 7 4　　♥ A 8 3　　♦ 3 2　　♣ J 10 9

When your partner opens 1NT, and you have a five-card major and enough points to go to game, all you need to know is: Which game, 4S or 3NT?

Partner opens 1NT. Consider your options.

If partner has three or four spades, you want to pay in your combined eight- or nine-card major suit fit. If he has only two spades, you want to play in 3NT. In order to find out how many spades he has, just ask him:

1NT–*3S*

A bid of 3S says, "We're in game, partner: I have *exactly five spades* and 10 or more points. I'm asking you to pick which game to play in. If you have three or four spades, then put us in 4S. If you have two spades, then put us in 3NT. It's up to you."

The bid of 3S in this auction is the exact opposite of a shut out bid; it's a **forcing bid;** it cannot be passed. It asks partner a question and demands an answer.

These three suit bids (1NT–2S, 1NT–3S, 1NT–4S) are among the oldest bids in bridge. They've been around so long because they are uncomplicated and they work. That said, consider what to do when partner opens 1NT and you have a hand like this:

♠ A Q 9 4   ♥ A J 8   ♦ 3 2   ♣ J 10 9 8

If partner has four spades, go for game in an eight-card major. If he doesn't, play in 3NT. Unfortunately, all our spade bids are busy meaning other things. 1NT–2S, –3S, and –4S all show at least a five-card suit. How, then, can we get to show a four-card major?

Let's take a better look at the situation:

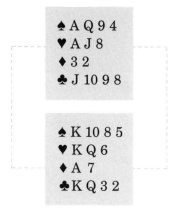

♠ A Q 9 4
♥ A J 8
♦ 3 2
♣ J 10 9 8

♠ K 10 8 5
♥ K Q 6
♦ A 7
♣ K Q 3 2

You are North. Partner opens 1NT. With 12 HCP, you can raise to 3NT. Playing in no trump, your opponents will most likely lead their longest suit, which in this case is diamonds. After a diamond lead, 3NT has no play—you have but eight quick tricks, four spades, three hearts, one diamond—even with 17 HCP opposite 12 HCP. Yet a 4S contract would be a walk in the park. Somehow, though, getting there isn't.

How can we show a four-card spade suit? In the 1930s, this was a major problem. And bridge theorists solved it, rather ingeniously, by *creating* a bid. They decided to take a bid that was not very important and use it instead for another, more important purpose. The bid they chose was **2C.** This bid, in effect, asked partner to bid a four-card *major* if he possessed one. It goes like this:

1NT–2C:	"Partner, I have a four-card major; do you?"
2S:	"Yes I do; I have a four-card spade suit."

or

1NT–2C:	"Partner, I have a four-card major; do you?"
2H:	"Yes I do; I have a four-card heart suit."

Note that the bid of 2C over the 1NT opening bid no longer has anything to do with clubs. A bid that sounds like one thing but means something entirely different is called a **conventional bid**. Oftentimes conventions are named after their developers or, as in the case of the 2C bid, the first person to bring it to national attention. Sam Stayman, playing in partnership with Murray Seiler, had this honor. **The Stayman Convention**—or, more simply, **Stayman**— is one of the oldest and most widely used conventions in bidding.

Whenever a bid becomes conventional, its natural meaning becomes lost. You can no longer use 2C as a shut out bid, as you can with other two-level bids:

1NT–2D, or 2H, or 2S all say, "Partner, I want to play in these contracts. Please pass."

1NT–2C says, "Partner I have a four-card major. Do you?"

Here are some Stayman applications:

Q: In all of the following cases, partner opens 1NT. What is your call with each of these hands?

1. ♠ K 8 7 6	2. ♠ K 9 7	3. ♠ 8 7
♥ A 9 7 5	♥ K 8 7	♥ 10 9 8 5
♦ 5	♦ A Q	♦ A K Q
♣ Q J 9 4	♣ J 10 9 8 7	♣ Q 8 4 2

A: 1. Bid 2C. You're looking for a 4–4 major suit fit.

2. Bid 3NT. You don't have four of either major suit. However, with 13 HCP + 1 LP you have enough to bid game.

3. Bid 2C. Even with this poor four-card heart suit, if an eight-card fit is found, it will be your best shot at game.

Q: Imagine you open 1NT and your partner responds 2C. In each of the following three hands, how do you plan on answering his query?

	1.		2.		3.	
	♠ K Q 10 2		♠ K Q 2		♠ K Q 7	
	♥ Q 8 7 4		♥ Q 10 3		♥ J 9 4 3 2	
	♦ A 9		♦ K 7 6		♦ A 10 8	
	♣ K Q 3		♣ A K 9 8		♣ A Q	

A: 1. With two four-card majors, I like to bid the lower-ranking of the two majors. Some experts bid the stronger one. It doesn't much matter. What matters is the follow-up. To review: you opened 1NT; partner bid 2C, Stayman. Say, like me, you decided to show your four-card heart suit rather than your four-card spade suit, so you rebid 2H.

Partner now jumps to 3NT. What's going on?

You	Partner
1NT	2C
2H	3NT

Partner has to have a four-card major: he bid Stayman. If it's not hearts, then he must have four spades. Show him your 4–4 fit. Bid 4S.

His hand, as it turns out, is:

♠ A J 8 7
♥ K 5
♦ 7 6 5
♣ A 9 6 2

2. With no four-card major, when partner bids 2C over your 1NT opening, bid **2D**. **2D** says nothing about diamonds, in fact: *it's a conventional response*. It just says, "Partner, I do not have a four-card major."

There are three possible responses to Stayman (2C): I have a four-card spade suit (2S); I have a four-card heart suit (2H); or I don't have a four-card major (2D)— diamonds being the only suit left on the two-level available for response.

3. You can open 1NT with a *bad* 5-card major and a no trump shape (in this case, 5–3–3–2). Treat those weak hearts as a four-card suit. When partner bids 2C, respond 2H.

Entire books have been devoted to Stayman auctions and their dynamics. Many players seem to fall in love with conventions—there are all sorts of them—and love to talk about them. They're perfect icebreakers at bridge parties. All you have to do is go up to a player and, batting your baby blues, inquire, "Can you help me with Stayman?" You're odds-on to get an enthusiastic response.

▪ NO TRUMP RESPONSES: A QUICK REVIEW

Q: Partner opens 1NT. With each of the hands below, what is your response?

1.	♠ Q J 9 4 3	2. ♠ K 9 4 3	3. ♠ 8 4
	♥ 9	♥ 9 5	♥ K 9 5 4
	♦ J 9 8 3	♦ A 9 8 3 2	♦ A 9 8 3
	♣ 7 6 5	♣ K 4	♣ Q 10 7
4.	♠ J 9 8 6 4 2	5. ♠ K 9 4 3 2	6. ♠ K Q 9 4 3
	♥ K 5	♥ K J 8 7 5	♥ 6 5
	♦ A 9 8	♦ K 6	♦ A K 8 3
	♣ K 4	♣ 10	♣ 6 5

A: 1. Bid 2S. Even with only five spades, it is better to be in 2S than 1NT, because of the extreme weakness in two of your suits. Remember, 2S is a drop-dead bid: partner must pass.

2. Bid 2C, Stayman. Then, if partner responds 2S to your 2C, bid 4S. If partner bids 2D instead, saying that he doesn't have a four-card major bid, then bid 3NT. In both cases you have enough material to bid game.

3. Bid 2C, Stayman. Then, if partner responds 2H, jump to 4H: you have 9 HCP and 1 SP. If partner bids 2D, on the other hand, rebid 2NT to show you have only 9 points. (With no suit fit you lose the 1SP you got when you found an eight-card fit.) Note that before you knew Stayman, this auction would have gone: 1NT–2NT.

4. Jump right to 4S. Partner's got at least two spades. There's your eight-card fit. You've got more than enough points for game.

5. Jump to 3S. Remember, always bid the higher-ranking of two five-card suits. (Once again, note the difference—four-card suits are bid up the line.) If partner bids 3NT, do *not* pass. He opened 1NT: he can't have two doubletons. If he has a doubleton spade, he must have at least three hearts. Bid 4H.

6. Jump to 3S. If partner bids 3NT, then pass. Yes, you have two weak doubletons, but partner's 16 or so points aren't in spades or diamonds. They have to be someplace. Hope for the best.

▪ THE PLAY OF THE CARDS REVISITED

What card should you play and when should you play it? At this point in your lessons, some things are falling into place nicely, but you're still left with some big questions, that being one of the biggest. As you'll see from the examples below, it all depends on where you are in relation to dummy, what cards you can see, and what cards you must imagine. Before we get to the examples, bear in mind this one basic rule: **If possible, high cards are meant to take other high cards.**

I. When There Is an Honor in Dummy

Say you are East, and you find yourself defending a 3NT contract. The auction is very straightforward: South bids 1NT, North jumps to 3NT. After careful consideration, your partner West decides to lead the ♠3. The dummy comes down. For now we'll just concentrate on spades:

♠Q 5 4

♠3   ♠A 10 7 (you)

♠ ?

After studying the hand, the declarer calls for the ♠4. What should you play, and why?

To answer this, you must first ask yourself a series of specific questions:

Q: Why did my partner choose to lead a spade?

A: Presumably it was his longest and strongest suit. When defending against no trump contracts, it is usually best to lead from your longest and strongest suit in order to establish one or two long-suit tricks for your side. Partner's longest suit must contain at least four cards.

Q: Why did my partner specifically lead the ♠3?

A: Because his spade suit is long but broken (nonsequential) and because he has an honor in the suit—the jack or higher. When you want to show your partner that there's something substantial in the suit and you would like the suit continued, lead a low card. When your suit is long but weak, you lead the second highest card you hold.

Here are four long spade holdings. Let's try to determine when you'd lead the ♠3 and when you wouldn't:

1. ♠ 9 7 6 3
2. ♠ J 7 6 3
3. ♠ 9 7 6 3 2
4. ♠ K 10 8 3 2

In 1 and 3, both weak long suits, lead the second highest card from both holdings—the ♠7. Partner knows that you're leading from length, not strength. In 2 and 4, lead the ♠3 to show you have a more substantial holding. In this particular hand, your partner may have been leading from a holding similar to 2 or 4.

Q: What is the declarer holding?

A: Approach it like a detective. Use the clues in hand to fill in that blank. The dummy has ♠Q 5 4, and you have ♠A 10 7; your partner's ♠3 lead indicates that she has at least a four-card suit headed by the jack or better. The declarer is left with—at most—a three-card suit that at most could have an honor but in fact may be much weaker. Here are several possible spade holdings that fit this conclusion:

a. ♠ K 8 2   b. ♠ J 8 2   c. ♠ K 8

d. ♠ J 8   e. ♠ 9 8 2   f. ♠ 9 2

Remember, the declarer opened 1NT and cannot have a singleton or void in spades.

Now we are ready to tackle the main questions. What card do you play when your partner leads the ♠3 and declarer calls for the ♠4 and why? You only have three choices: ♠A, ♠10 or ♠7. Let's observe what happens when you try each of the three cards against the six possible holdings that the declarer could have:

a (1)

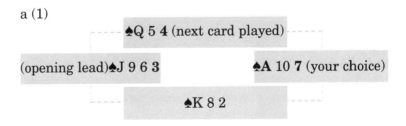

♠Q 5 4 (next card played)

(opening lead)♠J 9 6 3   ♠A 10 7 (your choice)

♠K 8 2

In this example, we've given the declarer the ♠K. Say you choose to play the ♠A. Declarer will play a low card and save his king for later. What cards did your ♠A beat? The declarer's ♠4 and ♠2. Not much to brag about. More importantly, now that you've wasted your ♠A on these little spot cards, how many tricks is the declarer going to make in spades? Two: the ♠Q and ♠K.

a (2)

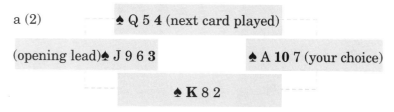

This time try the ♠10. The declarer will play the ♠K and win the trick. Can he win a subsequent trick? This is how the cards will look after the first trick has been played:

Your ♠A sits over the dummy's ♠Q. If declarer plays a spade to the ♠Q, your side will take three tricks in the suit. If your partner gets the lead and sends the ♠J or ♠9 through dummy's ♠Q, your side again will take three tricks. In both cases, declarer is held to only one trick.

By inserting your ♠10, you saved your ace for dummy's ♠Q. That's the card your ace is meant to take, seeing to it that the ♠Q can't take a trick. Your job is to force the declarer to commit the ♠Q. Remember your old friend the tenace? You had the ♠Q surrounded by your ♠A and ♠10, and your partner was on lead. These were the two conditions necessary to take the finesse. You just didn't recognize it as such. Rest easy—three quarters of the bridge-playing population doesn't either.

a (3)

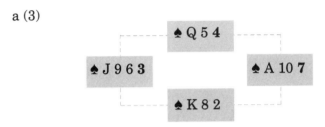

Now let's complete the picture by showing what would happen if you played the ♠7. Declarer would win the trick with the ♠8! Right away you should see that this isn't good bridge. Finesses are taken with the cards surrounding the card in question, not some random low spot card.

On your own, try each of the other five possible holdings for the declarer (b–f). You should be able to see that by inserting the lower card of the tenace position you cannot lose. You may not gain anything (as in b and d) where the declarer is entitled to win a trick no matter what, but you will not embarrass yourself as in examples e and f, where by spending your ♠A on the dummy's ♠4—playing it "on air"—you allow declarer to make a second trick with that ♠Q that he never could have made had you inserted the ♠10 for a finesse.

II. When There Is No Honor in Dummy

Again, the auction goes 1NT–3NT. Again, your partner leads the ♠3. This time you are holding the ♠K 10 7 and the dummy has ♠8 7 4.

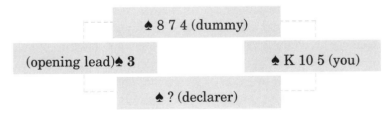

Declarer calls for the ♠7.

Q: Do you play the ♠K or do you insert the ♠10?

A: Partner is leading from a four- or five-card spade suit headed by an honor. Isn't this the same situation that we just had? Not at all. What card is your K 10 tenace surrounding? You can't trap a card in your tenace unless your opponents have an honor for you to try to capture, and there isn't one in the dummy. In the previous example, you saved your ace for the dummy's queen. In this example, what are you saving your king for? The ♠8? **When there is nothing in dummy to capture, go right up with your highest honor.** Maybe you'll trap whatever is on your left *under* your partner's tenace position. Picture this layout:

Trick one: ♠ 3, ♠7, ♠K, ♠2.
This is what's left:

Now you are on lead. Whichever card you return traps South's ♠Q in your partner's ♠AJ tenace position. The declarer makes no spade tricks. If you inserted the ♠10, declarer's ♠Q would win a trick he didn't deserve.

My students are always worrying about "wasting" their

king in this situation. But there is nothing to save it for. If the declarer has the ace or the ace and queen, your king is never going to win a trick anyway.

♠ 8 7 4

♠ J 9 6 3   ♠ K 10 5

♠ A Q 2

Declarer in this situation is *always* entitled to two tricks. It's when declarer *doesn't* have the ace that *not* playing the king could be deadly.

III. When You Play Before Dummy

♠ Q 7 6

♠ A 5 4

You are West. Unlike our previous examples, this time you play before the dummy. You don't have the comfort of seeing what the opponents do first.

Let's again say the auction went 1NT by South—3NT by North, but this time, we are several tricks into the play.

Declarer has just played us his ♠3.

Q: Do you play your ♠A or not, and why?

A: If you play your ♠A, what will it capture? Declarer's ♠3 and dummy's ♠6. If you save it, might it capture something more significant?

Aces are meant to take honors. If you reserve your ♠A here, it will be sitting *over* whatever honor is in South's hand when South tries to take a subsequent trick with his high card.

Let's fill in the two missing hands from our example:

Play this out. First see that if you grab declarer's ♠3 with your ♠A, N–S will come to two tricks. Then see what happens when you let dummy's ♠Q win the first trick and save your ♠A for his ♠K. You will hold N–S to only one trick. Even if declarer didn't hold the ♠K, but held a lesser honor, it amounts to the same thing:

By not playing your ♠A on air (declarer's ♠3), you and your partner can prevent declarer from winning a single trick. Had you played your ♠A on declarer's ♠3, you would have freed up his ♠J, allowing it to win a trick.

Here are some exercises on when to play your honors. Do your best, but remember that this is a tough topic that takes years of practice to master. Everybody has trouble with it at first!

In each case, assume South is the declarer. For now, I'll let you see all the cards. Afterwards you might try tackling them with both declarer's and your partner's hands hidden, as they will be in actual play.

Q:

1.

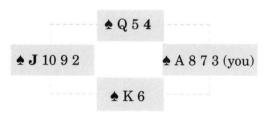

West leads the J and North plays low. Do you play the ace?

2.

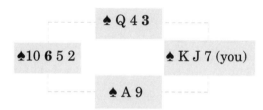

West leads the 6 and North plays the 3. Do you play the K or the J?

3.

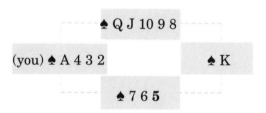

South leads the 5. Should you play your ace?

4.

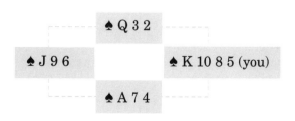

North leads the Q. Should you play your king?

5.

North leads the Q. Should you play your K?

A: 1. No. Your partner must have led from a sequence. Let his J knock out South's K and save your A for North's Q.

2. Play your J. It's as high as you need. The only card South can have that beats your K or J is the A. Let the J force out declarer's A. Save the K for North's Q.

3. No. Play low at the first trick and wait to see where the king is. If South has the king, save your ace for it. If your partner has the king, you want to be sure it's not a singleton.

4. Yes. Play your K. Your K is there to get the Q in dummy. When you're presented with the queen, you should take it. If you don't cover the Q with the K, declarer will make two tricks.

5. No. This is the hardest one because it looks just like example 4. Let your partner's A beat North's Q. You should save your K for the second honor in the sequence. Otherwise you will free the J to take a trick.

■ HANDS-ON PLAY

You are South. Here's the deal:

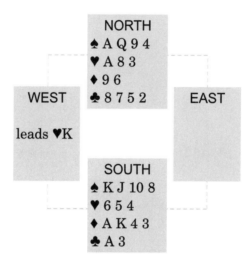

NORTH
♠ A Q 9 4
♥ A 8 3
♦ 9 6
♣ 8 7 5 2

WEST

leads ♥K

EAST

SOUTH
♠ K J 10 8
♥ 6 5 4
♦ A K 4 3
♣ A 3

The Bidding: You have a 4–4–3–2 distribution and 15 HCP. If it walks like a duck and quacks like a duck . . . You have a 1NT opening bid. North has just enough points for game (10 points). Before committing the hand to a no trump game, he should check whether his four-card spade suit faces the same in partner's hand. North bids 2C, Stayman, which asks, "Partner, do you have a four-card major?" You reply by bidding 2S, which says, "Yes, I have a four-card spade suit." Note that both your and North's hands each add a point on because you each have a doubleton. Only North is able to realize this, because only he knows of the definite eight-card spade fit. By the time you hear about it, it's too late for you to do anything about it. But nonetheless it does exist. The combined point count jumps from 25 HCP to 25 + 2 SP, or 27 points in all. And what a difference those two extra points can make! North bids 4S, and everyone passes.

The Play: The ♥K is led by West. Plan the play. Count your winners. In no trump, you would have eight winners: four spades, one heart, two diamonds and one club. More importantly, you would have no possibility for a ninth trick. In other words, had you elected to play this hand in 3NT, you would not have made your contract. But you didn't. You found your spade fit. Now let's see if that's going to pay off.

With spades trump, let's look at your winner and loser situation: eight winners, five losers: two hearts, two diamonds, and one club. In 4S, we can only afford to lose three tricks.

Can you turn two of those losers into winners? Yes, by trumping diamonds in the dummy. We plan on eight tricks from high cards and two from ruffing, for the ten we need. Putting this plan into action requires some thought. What if one opponent is short in diamonds? They may ruff, or overruff, your trick. You should try to prevent this. You need only two trump in dummy to ruff your two losing diamonds; therefore, you should draw two rounds of trump, leaving the opponents with as few as possible. You should win the ♥K lead, play your little trump (♠4) over to your hand (now all your trumps are master cards) and draw one more round of trump. Only now do you touch diamonds. Play the ♦A, ♦K, then ruff the ♦3 in the dummy. Come back to your hand with the ♣A and ruff your last diamond.

At this point, if all went well, you will have eight tricks. Your two high trumps will win the ninth and tenth tricks.

The complete hand looked like this:

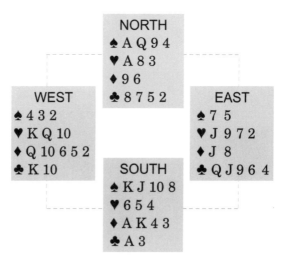

NORTH
♠ A Q 9 4
♥ A 8 3
♦ 9 6
♣ 8 7 5 2

WEST
♠ 4 3 2
♥ K Q 10
♦ Q 10 6 5 2
♣ K 10

EAST
♠ 7 5
♥ J 9 7 2
♦ J 8
♣ Q J 9 6 4

SOUTH
♠ K J 10 8
♥ 6 5 4
♦ A K 4 3
♣ A 3

If you had failed to draw trump and instead played the ♦A and ♦K and ruffed a diamond carelessly with the ♠4, East could have defeated you by overruffing this trick with the ♠5 or ♠7.

Notice you couldn't be 100 percent safe. Before trumping diamonds, you couldn't draw all the opponents' trump because that would have left you with only one trump. You needed to ruff two diamonds. You had to risk the possibility of one of your opponents being very short in diamonds and having three or more trump. Had that been the case, you would have failed. Nevertheless, this was a much better contract than the hopeless 3NT contract you could have been in.

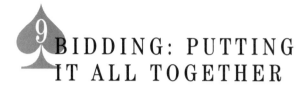

9 BIDDING: PUTTING IT ALL TOGETHER

■ I. RESPONDER'S THINKING

WHEN YOUR PARTNER OPENS 1 OF A MAJOR, AND YOU HAVE TRUMP SUPPORT (3+)		
Partner opens	What you're holding	What you respond
1H or 1S (13–20 points)	You have 0–5 points.	Pass
1H or 1S (13–20 points)	You have 6–9 points. You hate your hand, but you have to bid.	2H or 2S
1H or 1S (13–20 points)	You have 10–12 points. You like your hand.	3H or 3S
1H or 1S (13–20 points)	You have 13–16 points. You love your hand.	4H or 4S

WHEN YOUR PARTNER OPENS 1 OF A MINOR AND YOU HAVE TRUMP SUPPORT		
Partner opens	What you're holding	What you respond
1D (4-card suit)	0–5 points	pass
1D (4-card suit)	6–9 points and 4+ diamonds	2D
1D (4-card suit)	10–12 points and 4+ diamonds	3D
1C (3-card suit)	0–5 points	pass
1C	6–9 points and 5+ clubs	2C
1C	10–12 points and 5+ clubs	3C

I hope by now you are fairly comfortable with these structures. The idea is not to memorize them, but rather to understand them. I ask my students to build these boxes for themselves over and over until they make sense and *they own them*. Here's how I teach them to do it:

*A one of a major suit opening shows 13–20 points. The smallest number of points I need to be able to have 26 between us is 6 . . . that must be a 1H–**2H** auction. The least I need to guarantee 26 is 13 . . . that must be 1H–**4H**. The auction 1H–2H is one trick weaker than 1H–3H; a trick is an ace or 4 HCP. If 1H–2H can be made with as little as 6 HCP, then if I have 10 points and want my partner to know I'm a trick stronger than the 1H–2H hand, I have to make a bid that sounds one trick stronger . . . 1H–**3H**.*

There's a little more to completing the picture, but I hope you're getting the idea. If you build the structure again and again, the logic behind it takes hold. This is your foundation, make sure it's sound.

■ THAT ELUSIVE EIGHT-CARD MAJOR SUIT FIT

Let's review and try to cement some of the principles of suit bidding we introduced in chapter 7.

When your partner opens one of a major, how do you respond when you have trump support and how do you respond when you don't? Alternately, what do you do when your partner opens one of a minor?

- If you have 0–5 points, pass. Game cannot be reached.

- Do not support your partner's minor suit until you are sure no eight-card (or longer) major suit fit exists.

- Bid your four-card suits up the line.

- With five-card or longer suits, bid your longest suit first (on the one level).

- With two five-card suits, bid the higher-ranking suit first (on the one level).

Practice Bidding

1. ♠ 10 9 8 6
   ♥ K 9 6 3
   ♦ 3
   ♣ A K 10 3

a: If your partner opens 1C, what do you respond?
b: How do you respond to an opening 1H bid?

a. 1C–*1H*. When you first pick up your hand, try to get the *feel* of it: 10 HCP, 4–4–4–1 shape, two four-card majors, and something we haven't talked about yet. Your hand is rich in tens and nines. These cards pull more weight than twos and threes and as you gain experience, they'll begin to take on more of a role in evaluating your hand's strength. With this hand, when partner opens 1C you must respond. Partner could have as many as 20 points, so with your 10, game is a very real possibility.

Since your partner did not open 1S or 1H, you know that she does not have a five-card major (if she has five clubs and five hearts or spades, she would open the major, the higher ranking of the two five-card suits). Therefore you know there's no way you can have a nine-card major suit fit. But you might have a 4–4 major suit fit. You have four spades and four hearts, and your partner just might have four hearts or four spades. Before you think about raising clubs (which you shouldn't do with only four anyway, since opener may have as few as three clubs), you need to explore this possible eight-card major suit fit. So bid 1H—your first four-card suit up the line. This is your initial response and as such it doesn't say everything. It simply tells your partner that you have *4 or more hearts* (remember, only the *opening bid* guarantees five or more of a major) and *6 or more points* (not 6–9 points; when raising partner's one of a suit bid to two of his suit you need 6–9 points. Here you're just exploring—looking around for the easiest road to game).

Let's suppose, to your delight, your partner raises you to 2H, confirming an eight-card fit. You now know the strain; you need to know the level (partial or game). In support of hearts, has your hand gotten any better? You bet. That singleton diamond, which had no value until now, jumps to 3 points (4 trump-1 singleton); you're going to be playing in a trump suit. Those 3 SP, added to the 10 points your hand originally was worth, brings the value of your responding hand to 13. Added to partner's minimum of 13 (he opened), brings you to that magic 26. With an eight-card fit and at least 26 points jump directly to game in hearts—bid 4H.

b: 1H–*4H*. You have four-card heart support. Your partner is guaranteeing five or more. Right away, there's your nine-card major suit fit. You're happy—half of your work is already done. You and your partner have found the right strain to play in. Now all you have to do is find out what level you're going to play. Before you respond, take a moment to reevaluate your hand. Because you know you will not be playing in no trump, along with your high card points you should now add 3 points for shortness. This brings your total to 13 points in support of hearts. *With 13–16 points and normal trump support (NTS),* your response to an opening 1H bid is 4H.

2. ♠ A 9 5 2
♥ J 7 4
♦ K 10 8 2
♣ 8 7

a. If your partner opens 1C, what is your response?
b. What if your partner opens 1H?

a. 1C–*1D*. You have 8 HCP. You must respond. Your partner doesn't have a five-card major, or he would have opened with it. He may, however, have four of a major suit. You have a four-card major. At some point you will have to talk about it. Now is not the right time. Since you have two four-card suits, you bid them in order (up the line). Respond 1D— *which shows four or more diamonds and 6 or more points.* Your partner's hand could be: ♠ K 7 ♥ 9 5 ♦ A Q J 3 ♣ A K Q 9 5. The best game contract would be 5D.

Let's continue the auction. Over your 1D response, opener rebids 1S. He is showing four spades and 13–20 points. There's your major suit fit. You've got 8 HCP + 1 SP (the doubleton club with four trumps). That comes to 9 points in support of spades. Raise your partner to 2S which shows 6–9 points, in support of spades.

b. 1H—*2H*. You have three hearts, and your partner guarantees at least five. There's your eight-card fit. In support of hearts you only have your original 8 points (the doubleton with three-card support has no value). Raise partner to 2H. This shows 6–9 points and 3+ trumps.

3. ♠ 7
   ♥ Q 5 2
   ♦ K 9 5 4
   ♣ K 9 5 4 2

   a. If your partner opens 1C, what is your response?
   b. What if your partner opens 1H?

a. 1C–*3C*. With no four-card major of your own, when partner denies a five-card major by his opening 1C bid, no eight-card major suit fit can exist. You are reduced to playing this hand in either clubs or no trump. You have 8 HCP + 1 LP + 3 SP (partner opens 1C), *you should jump to 3C immediately, which would show 10–12 points, at least five clubs and no four-card major.*

b. 1H–*3H*. Partner's five hearts plus your three gives you your eight-card major suit fit. That's half the battle. In support of hearts add 2 SP for the singleton spade: 8 HCP + 1 LP + 2 SP = 11 points. *Jump to 3H, which shows 10–12 points and 3+ trump support.*

4. ♠ K 4 3
   ♥ A 8 7 4
   ♦ A J 7 6 5
   ♣ 6

a. If your partner opens 1C, what is your response?

b. What if your partner opens 1H?

a. 1C–*1D*. With 12 HCP + 1 LP, and your partner opening the bidding, game somewhere (26 points) is assured. You only have to make sure you make bids that are forcing, that is, that your partner can not pass before game is reached. Diamonds are your longest suit. Bid 1D. This simple change of suit shows 6 or more points, four or more diamonds and is 100 percent forcing.

Let's continue the auction. Say your partner now rebids 1H. As opener this shows exactly four hearts and 13–20 points. With four-card support, you are going to raise hearts; you just have to figure out to what level. Recount your points. In support of hearts you have 12 HCP + 1 LP + 3 SP, a total of 16 points. Jump to 4H which, as responder, shows 13–16 points and four-card support for trumps. Partner already knows from your 1D initial response that you also have at least four diamonds. She's starting to get a pretty good idea what your hand looks like.

b. 1 H–*2D*. Are you wondering why I didn't say 4H? Well, with four-card trump support, 12 HCP, 1 LP and 3 SP, you know you're going to game. You should be careful not to go too fast. Sure, you can jump directly to 4H. But then you may miss a slam or grand slam. To paint a picture of your hand start with 2D (new suit is forcing), then over whatever partner rebids, jump to 4H. Partner's hand could be: ♠A 9 ♥K Q 9 6 2 ♦K Q 3 ♣9 8 7. Twelve tricks in hearts is probable. As in **a** it can't hurt to show your partner both your hearts and your diamonds.

▪ TWO OVER ONE BIDS OR GETTING *TWO* HIGH

Do you remember the significance of these numbers?

NUMBER OF TRICKS	NUMBER OF HCP
6 or 7	20
7	22
8	24
9	26

They are the number of combined HCP your partnership needs to be able to make the corresponding number of tricks in no trump. If you've forgotten, that's where 26 points for 3NT came from. In bridge scoring, 26 is the most important number. In bridge bidding that number is 24, the points required to make a contract of 2NT. Let's see why.

Your partner opens 1S. You hold:

♠7 4   ♥K 4 3   ♦K 9 8 7 6   ♣J 9 2

With 7 HCP + 1 LP, you must respond. Partner promises five spades, but your two are not enough to guarantee eight. You can't raise your partner. OK. You have a five-card diamond suit, so you show her that you like diamonds, but you can't bid them on the one level. So you bid 2D. Now your partner, who happens to not like diamonds, doesn't have another suit to show. She has only 13 or 14 points. But she cannot pass. Your new suit bid, remember, is forcing. So she does the best she can and rebids 2NT. She could have:

♠Q J 8 3 2   ♥A Q 5   ♦10 4   ♣A 10 8

Now what? Are you going to make 2NT? Let's see, partner has 13 HCP +1 LP or 14 points. You have 8. That's 22 combined points. Looking at the chart, we see that 22 is just enough to make seven tricks in a no trump contract. In 2NT you're way outgunned. With no eight-card fit anywhere, you've also got nowhere else to go. You're going minus on this hand.

Q: What went wrong? How did you wind up getting so high?

A: Your partner opened 1S and you raised to the two-level with 2D—an eight-trick contract that requires 24 points. Partner's opening bid guaranteed only 13 points. Your hand, to make a two-level contract, would have to contain 11 points, which you don't have. In the absence of a suit fit, you have to prepare for the eventuality of playing in no trump. Let's go back and see what bid you should have made over your partner's 1S bid.

♠7 4   ♥K 4 3   ♦K 9 8 7 6   ♣J 9 2

Again, with 8 points, you can't pass. You can't raise spades, and you can't bid anything on the two level. Doesn't leave you with many choices, does it? The only bid left is 1NT. And that's the bid to make.

Over 1S, a bid of 1NT says:

1. I *don't* have 11+ points (or I would have bid something at the two level).

2. I *don't* have three or more spades with you (or I would have supported spades).

I DON'T . . . I DON'T

What 1S–1NT does say about responder's hand:

1. She has 6–10 points.

2. She has at least eleven cards in the three other suits.

Over 1H, a bid of 1NT says:

1. I *don't* have 11+ points.

2. I *don't* have three or more hearts with you. And . . .

3. I *don't* have four or more spades (or I would have bid one spade)

I DON'T . . . I DON'T . . . I DON'T.

With all these "I don'ts" we are left with a pretty good idea what the responder *does* have.

1. She has 6–10 points

2. She has at least 8+ minor suit cards (since she has at most three spades and two hearts)

This is what the responder's hand might look like:

♠ 7 4, ♥ Q 2, ♦ K J 10 7 5 2, ♣ Q 8

Over 1D, a bid of 1NT says:

1. I don't have 11+ points.

2. I don't have 4+ diamonds (or I would have raised diamonds).

3. I don't have four hearts or four spades.

So what *do* you have with all these **don'ts?** Clubs. Your hand might be:

♠7 4, ♥Q 9 4, ♦K 8 3, ♣Q J 10 7 2

Finally, let's look what it means to bid 1NT over an opening bid of 1C:

1. I don't have 11+ points.

2. I don't have four spades, four hearts, or four diamonds

Therefore, you must have four clubs; you can't have five because you would have raised clubs. That leaves you with exactly a 4–3–3–3 hand with four clubs:

♠J 9 5 ♥Q 8 3 ♦7 6 5 ♣A J 10 7

1C–1NT 1D–1NT 1H–1NT 1S–1NT

These responses show more of what responders don't have than what they do have.

The response of 1NT to the bid of one of any suit is really a lot of DON'TS. You can remember this because of the word's last two letters: NT . . . as in doNT.

Nowhere is this more true than of one of a major–one no trump:

Say partner opens 1S with:

♠Q 10 9 6 3   ♥A Q 2   ♦10 9   ♣A Q 7

You, as responder, have one of these two hands:

a.   ♠8   ♥K J 9 7 3   ♦8 6 4   ♣K J 8 2

b.   ♠7   ♥K 9 3   ♦K 8 7 6 5 3 2 ♣J 2

What is your bid with either hand? That's right. . . . 1NT.

Q: Do you want your partner to pass and have you play there?

A: In 1NT, with hand **a,** the opponents might take two or three spades and four or five diamonds. Maybe you'll make 1NT; maybe you'll go down one or two. But what if you found your 5–3 heart fit with your partner? You'd make nine or ten tricks with no problem.

Same with hand **b.** Maybe you'll make 1NT. But you'll have no problem making ten or even eleven tricks in your 7–2 diamond fit.

You can't get to either of these beautiful trump fits if partner passes you in 1NT. So added to all our previous 1NT DON'TS, comes this final one: If your partner bids 1S and you respond 1NT, it says to your partner, "I **don't** want to play here. Bid something, even if you don't have another suit of even four-card length."

In both cases, your partner should rebid 2C, his lowest ranking three-card suit. You would then get to bid your long suit. With hand a, this is how the auction would look:

OPENER	RESPONDER
1S	1NT
2C	2H
pass*	

With hand b, the auction would go:

OPENER	RESPONDER
1S	1NT
2C	2D
pass†	

As with 1S–1NT, when partner opens the other major 1H and you respond 1NT, you **DON'T** want to be left there either:

♠A 3 2   ♥Q 10 9 6 3   ♦Q 9   ♣A Q 7

---

*Opener knows responder has less than 11 points. No game is possible.

†Again, the opener knows that there is no way to reach game.

With this hand, when partner answers 1NT to your 1H opening, you know he has at least eight cards in the minors. Why? Because he can't have more than two hearts and three spades. He's asking you to bid your best minor. Respect his wishes, rebid 2C.

Let's give him this hand:

♠4   ♥5   ♦K J 10 5 4 3 2   ♣K 10 6 5

You'll make about six tricks in no trump; but in diamonds you'll make eleven (game). If you pass your partner's 1NT response, how are you going to get to the right part score, game, or slam? In this case the auction would sound like this:

YOU (OPENER)	PARTNER
1H	1NT
2C	3D*
5D	pass

Over a one of a major opening, treat a 1NT response as a command to bid at least one more time.

■ EXERCISES

Q:

1. This is your hand:

♠Q 5 ♥9 5 ♦9 8 2 ♣K Q 9 8 6 5

---

*Notice this jump from 2C to 3D. This shows a good six- or seven-card suit and just less than 11 points. If partner had 11 or more points he would have bid 2D over 1H, but he didn't. He started with a response of 1NT. Now all his subsequent bids are limited by that bid.

a. Your partner opens 1D. What do you respond?

b. Your partner opens 1S. What do you respond?

Answers:

a. Bid 1NT. You can't show your clubs on the two level with only 7 HCP. But your partner will know you have clubs. What else could you have? Your 1NT response denies four spades, four hearts, or four diamonds. Partner *can stay* in 1NT if she thinks it's right. She may have a balanced hand, like this:

♠K 9 7 2   ♥A 10 3   ♦Q J 7 4   ♣A 7

b. Bid 1NT. Now your partner *can't leave you there* because she doesn't know what your shape is. If she rebids 2D or 2H, you will take her back to 2S. She'll know you didn't have three spades because you didn't raise spades. You'll have to play in a 5–2 fit. Worse things can happen. If partner should rebid 2C, raise to 3C.

Q:
2. This is your hand:
♠K 8 4   ♥Q 8 6   ♦J 10   ♣A J 10 7 4

a. Your partner opens 1D. What do you respond?

b. Your partner opens 1S. What do you respond?

Answers:

a. With 11 HCP +1 length, you could bid 2C. A jump to 2NT is also a possibility. If 1D–1NT shows 6–10 points, then 1D-2NT should show 11 or 12. (More on this later in the chapter.)

b. As in part a you have a choice of bids. A jump to 3S does express your values and shows 3+ support. But you could also start with a bid of 2C, which would automatically show 11+ points, and then you could bid spades next time at the cheapest level. This would give your partner the flavor of your hand a little better than the immediate jump to 3S, but either is acceptable. As you get more into the game you'll see that you are often faced with these kinds of choices. Neither answer is right or wrong. The subtleties of choice are what makes the game so rich.

Q:

3. This is your hand:

♠A J 4 3   ♥J 7 3 2   ♦A Q 8 4   ♣2

a. Your partner opens 1D. What do you respond?

b. Your partner opens 1S. What do you respond?

Answers:

a. Simply bid 1H, your cheapest four-card major. If partner raises you to 2H, jump to 4H (12 HCP + 3 SP). If instead, your partner rebids 1S, jump to a game in spades. Remember, always bid four-card suits in order, no matter how weak the suit is, and you'll be sure not to miss any possible strains to play in.

b. Jump right to 4S. In support of spades you have 12 HCP + 3 SP = 15 points. Your partner opened the bidding, so you must insist on a game. The jump sets the trump suit and shows 13–16 points in support of spades. It is *not* a shut out bid. With 17+ points, partner can look for something grander if he wishes, like a slam or a grand slam.

▪ II. OPENER'S THINKING

Just as responder's first rebid begins to define his HCP and shape more clearly, so too does opener's second bid. An opening bid of one of a suit, especially one of a minor, is a very vague bid. It can show anywhere from 13–20 HCP and in the case of clubs as few as three or as many as eight cards of the suit. The opening hand can contain voids or singletons or be absolutely flat. It's your job as the opener to find a way to help your partner understand what type of hand you hold. With your second and sometimes third bids, you try to narrow the HCP ranges and define more exactly the shape and texture of your hand. You will try to paint a picture for your partner. Unlike an opening bid of 1NT, where the responder knows pretty much what's in your hand and consequently makes almost all the important decisions, when someone opens one of a suit it is never clear which partner is going to set the final contract. Both partners must endeavor to describe their hands as best they can. Let's see how this works:

▪ OPENER'S REBIDS

With Minimum Strength (13–16 points)

a.	♠ Q 2	♥ J 9 3	♦ A Q 10 9 6 2	♣ K 8
b.	♠ Q 2	♥ J 9 3 2	♦ A Q 10 9 6	♣ K 8
c.	♠ Q 3 2	♥ J 9 3	♦ A Q 10 9 6	♣ K 8

Each of these three hands has two things in common. Each is an opening 1D bid, and each has between 13–16 points. Just as a four-point range defines the weakest responding hand (6–9 points), so too it defines the weakest opening hand. The weakest hand you can open with is 13 points; the four-point range for this hand would be 13–16 points. **Any opening hand of less than 17 points (that**

is, within a trick of 13) is considered to be in the minimum range.

Say you open the bidding 1D with each of these three hands, and each time your partner responds 1H. (Remember, that 1H bid is 100 percent forcing.) I'd like you to think about the different ways you might go about telling your partner that, although you opened the bidding and have at least 13 points, your hand isn't much stronger than that. In the auction, 1D–1H, what might you select as your rebid with each of these hands?

a. With hand a, you should rebid **2D** to show both the extra length of your diamonds and the weakness of your opening bid. When you opened 1D, you showed only four cards. Each time you rebid a suit, your partner will assume you have a longer and longer suit. The simple raise to the two level, the cheapest level that you could rebid diamonds on, shows the hand's minimum strength: you have 12 HCP + 2 LP for a total of only 14. Notice you don't support hearts because in responding 1H, you partner only promises a four-card suit.

b. With this hand, you should rebid **2H**. You've found at least an eight-card heart fit. That's much more important than rebidding your diamonds. In support of hearts, you have minimum strength for an opening bid: 12 HCP + 1 LP + 1 SP = 14 points.

c. With this hand you could rebid 2D, since you have a hand in the minimum range and a lovely five-card suit. But there's a more descriptive bid available to you. With a 5–3–3–2 shape, you didn't open 1NT because you didn't have enough points. Now you can tell your partner this. **Rebid 1NT.** This tells your partner that you have 13 or 14 points (not 15,16 or17) and a no trump shape. It also denies four hearts or four spades. This 1NT rebid is the absolute weakest rebid that you can make as an opening bidder. It shows no more than 14 HCP.

With Intermediate Strength
(17–18 points)

Now let's add an ace to each of these three example hands and see how that affects the bidding:

a.	♠ A Q	♥ J 9 3	♦ A Q 10 9 6 2	♣ K 8
b.	♠ A Q	♥ J 9 3 2	♦ A Q 10 9 6	♣ K 8
c.	♠ A Q 3	♥ J 9 3	♦ A Q 10 9 6	♣ K 8

Again, you open 1D and again your partner responds 1H.

a. With 18 points, (16 HCP + 2 length) you are too strong for a minimum rebid of 2D. Jump a level to 3D. After all, you're an ace, one trick, stronger than a minimum opening.

b. In support of hearts you have 18 points (16 HCP + 1 length + 1 shortness). Jump to 3H to show your added strength.

c. This is a trick question. You really have no good rebid. This hand should have been opened 1NT. Any subsequent action that you take will be predicated on this fact. Partner will never guess that you have a 1NT opening bid, because if you did have it you would have opened with it. For example, you can't rebid 1NT because, as we just saw in the section on minimum rebids, that's how you show 13 or 14 points. You can try 3D, but that doesn't give the feel of a flat (5–3–3–2) hand. Partner will play you for longer diamonds and shortness in one or two places (like hand a). And finally you can't jump to 2NT. Although that would show the shape of your hand, partner would play you for more HCP, 18 or 19.

If you forget to open 1NT, your goose is cooked. You have no accurate way to recover. You'll have to lie a little and hope for the best.

Let's use this opportunity to build a **flat opening bid structure of all hands from 13 to 26 HCP:**

To show a flat hand that's too weak to open 1NT, open one of a suit and plan to *rebid NT at the cheapest level:*

♠ A Q 2   ♥ Q 9 2   ♦ K J 7 4   ♣ Q 8 3

With this 14-point hand, open 1D. If your partner bids 1H (or 1S), rebid 1NT; if instead partner bids 2C, rebid 2NT. This shows all flat opening hands of less than 15 HCP, because—

With 15, 16 or 17 HCP we *open 1NT:*

♠A Q 2   ♥Q 9 2   ♦K Q J 7   ♣Q 8 3

With 18 or 19 HCP, the next higher range, open one of a suit and *jump to 2NT.*

♠A Q 2   ♥Q 9 2   ♦K Q J 7   ♣A 8 3

Here if you opened 1D, and your partner bids 1H (or 1S), jump to 2NT; if instead partner bids 2C, you would again have to jump in NT to show your strength—rebid 3NT.

With 20–22 HCP, half the deck, simply open 2NT.

♠A Q 2   ♥Q 9 2   ♦K Q J 7   ♣A Q 3

For now with hands that are flat and bigger (23–26 points), you should open 3NT. There are better methods for showing these huge hands, but they are beyond the scope of this book. You can console yourself with the fact that they come up very rarely.

■ REVIEW

In each example that follows, see if you can get the partnership to the right contract. Check your bidding against our "suggested" auction. West is the opening bidder in each case.

1.	WEST	EAST	**2.**		WEST	EAST
	♠A J 5 3	♠K 6 2			♠ A J 6 5	♠K 10 4 3 2
	♥K 6 4 2	♥Q 9 3			♥K Q 8 2	♥A 6
	♦8 3	♦K 7 2			♦A J 7 3	♦9 6 4
	♣A Q 4	♣J 8 6 5			♣4	♣J 9 2

3.	WEST	EAST	**4.**		WEST	EAST
	♠A J 5 3	♠Q 10 6 4			♠A Q J 7	♠K 6 2
	♥K 6 4	♥A J 5 2			♥K Q 6 4	♥J 9 7 3 2
	♦8 3	♦7 5 2			♦ ——	♦Q 3 2
	♣A Q 5 3	♣J 8			♣A J 7 6 5	♣10 8

5.	WEST	EAST	**6.**		WEST	EAST
	♠A J 2	♠10 8 7 3			♠A J 4	♠8 5 2
	♥K 8 5 4	♥A 6 2			♥K Q 2	♥J 8 3
	♦9 6 2	♦K J 5			♦8 5 3	♦K Q 6 2
	♣A Q 3	♣10 8 6			♣A K J 8	♣7 4 3

7.	WEST	EAST	**8.**		WEST	EAST
	♠Q	♠K 10 4 2			♠A 6 2	♠8 3
	♥A J 5	♥Q 8 3			♥J 7	♥K 9 5 2
	♦7 5 4	♦A 10 8 2			♦8 5	♦A J 7 4
	♣A K J 10 7 3	♣8 5			♣A K J 6 3 2	♣8 7 4

Here are the suggested auctions:

1.

W	E
1C	1NT
pass	

West is too weak to open 1NT. East's has 6–10 points and no four-card diamond, heart or spade suit. With 14 HCP and no more than 10 for partner, West throws in the towel (26 points can't be reached).

2.

W	E
1D	1S
3S	4S

West has 15 HCP but with a 4–4–4–1 hand, not NT shape. West's jump to 3S shows 17–18 points and four-card support. East has 8 HCP + 1 LP + 1 SP. Added to West's 17–18 that's enough for game.

3.

W	E
1C	1H
1S	2S
pass	

East bids 2S to show 6–9 points. West, having 14 HCP +1 SP = 15, doesn't have enough with East's maximum 9 to make game.

4.

W	E
1C	1H
4H	

East's response shows four or more hearts and six or more points. In support of hearts, West has 17 HCP + 1 LP + 4 SP (count these *after* a fit has been found) = 22 points.

Twenty-two plus whatever East has is enough for game. (A more advanced way for opener to show this huge hand would be: over East's 1H response, jump to 2S (forcing) and then support hearts. When you bid three suits, jumping in one, you show 20+ points and a singleton or a void! The actual auction might have gone this way—

    1C–1H
    2S–2NT
    4H or pass

5. W   E
    1C   1S
    1NT   pass

West didn't open 1NT. He's showing 13–14 points and a no trump shape. East must then pass, because with her 8 points plus West's 13–14, they can't make game.

6. W   E
    1C   1D
    2NT   pass

West opens 1C because his hand is too strong to open 1NT. He then jump rebids 2NT to show 18–19 points and a flat hand, with no four-card major. East passes, because with her puny 6 points and West's 18 or 19, 26 still can't be reached.

7. W   E
    1C   1D
    3C   3NT

East responds 1D, the next four-card suit up the line. West's 3C bid shows 17–18 points, at least five clubs (usually six), and denies four-card diamond support and possession of a four-card major. East rebids 3NT because all the suits have stoppers and between them they have 26 or 27 points.. Notice East does not rebid 3S because West has already denied a four-card suit.

8. W   E
    1C   1D
    2C   pass

West's 2C rebid shows 5+ (usually 6) clubs, no diamond fit, no four-card major and at most 16 points. East's 8 + West's, at most, 15 will not reach game.

▪ HANDS-ON PLAY

Practice Hand 1

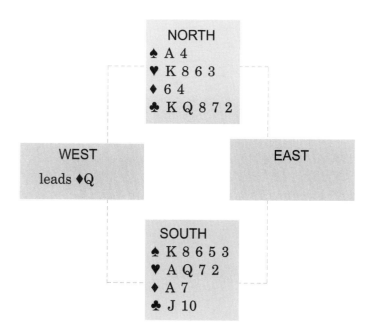

NORTH
♠ A 4
♥ K 8 6 3
♦ 6 4
♣ K Q 8 7 2

WEST
leads ♦Q

EAST

SOUTH
♠ K 8 6 5 3
♥ A Q 7 2
♦ A 7
♣ J 10

The Bidding: South deals. She has 14 HCP + 1 LP. She opens 1S. North has 12 HCP + 1LP = 13 points. He starts thinking about game. With 11 or more points, North is free to go to the two level in a new suit. He bids his longer suit first—2C. South completes the description of her hand by bidding her second suit, 2H. North, in supporting partner's hearts, adds 1 SP for the doubletons, raising his total to 14 points. With South's 2H call, North knows what strain to play in and how high. With at least 27 total points and eight hearts between them, North insists upon game—and jumps to 4H. Notice how the heart suit was introduced and agreed upon relatively late in the auction.

The auction went like this:

S	W	N	E
1S	p	2C	p
2H	p	4H	p
p	p		

The Play: The opening lead is the ♦Q. Plan the play. North–South have two spades, four hearts, one diamond and potentially four club tricks. They have the ♣A loser and, after this ♦Q lead, one diamond loser. That's two losers but eleven possible winners—one more than is required for a 4H contract. All that's left is proper technique.

This is what North's strategy will be: Win the diamond lead, then immediately draw trump. This allows you to go about establishing your club suit without fearing that one of the opponents will trump your winners. Play ♣J, ♣10, unblocking honors. The opponents can take their ♣A and ♦K whenever they want.

The complete hand looked like this:

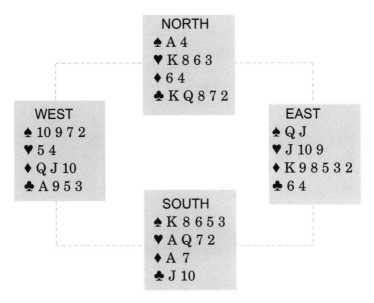

NORTH
♠ A 4
♥ K 8 6 3
♦ 6 4
♣ K Q 8 7 2

WEST
♠ 10 9 7 2
♥ 5 4
♦ Q J 10
♣ A 9 5 3

EAST
♠ Q J
♥ J 10 9
♦ K 9 8 5 3 2
♣ 6 4

SOUTH
♠ K 8 6 5 3
♥ A Q 7 2
♦ A 7
♣ J 10

Notice that against a suit contract, West did not lead fourth from longest, nor did he bang down his ♣A. He saved the ace for something better—perhaps a king or queen.

Practice Hand 2

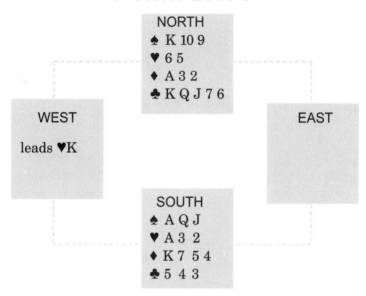

NORTH
♠ K 10 9
♥ 6 5
♦ A 3 2
♣ K Q J 7 6

WEST

leads ♥K

EAST

SOUTH
♠ A Q J
♥ A 3 2
♦ K 7 5 4
♣ 5 4 3

The Bidding: You are South. You have a 4–3–3–3 distribution and 14 HCP. You're one point shy of a 1NT opening bid. You open the bidding 1D. Partner responds 2C, showing 11+ points. With your rebid, you want to tell your partner that you have a no trump shape but were too weak to open 1NT right away. The way to do this is to bid 2NT (the cheapest level at which to bid NT). Your partner raises you to game by bidding 3NT, and this ends the auction.

The auction went like this:

S	W	N	E
1D	p	2C	p
2NT	p	3NT	

The Play: West leads the ♥K. Plan your play. You have three spade tricks + one heart + two diamonds = 6 quick tricks. In order to come to the nine tricks you need to make your contract, you'll need to establish the club suit for at least three winners. In leading hearts, your opponents attack your weakest suit and drive out your ♥A—your only stopper in the suit. Your next task will be to drive out *their* ♣A stopper, but in so doing, you'll be giving them the chance to play out the rest of their hearts. You were originally missing eight hearts. If those split 4–4, it would be no problem. You would lose three hearts and one club, but you would still make your contract. But if the hearts split 5–3 (which is more likely, since they are likely to break unevenly), then you will lose four hearts and a club and go down. Do you see any way of increasing your chances of preventing this?

Take a minute to think it through.

If the person with the ♣A also has five hearts, you are going down. There's no way out. But if the person with the ♣A has only two or three hearts, you can cut his ability to reach his partner's long hearts by ducking both the first and second heart leads.

This is the heart/club scenario you're hoping for:

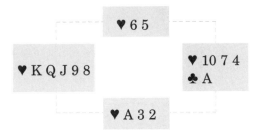

♥ 6 5

♥ K Q J 9 8

♥ 10 7 4
♣ A

♥ A 3 2

If East started with 3 to the ♥10 and the ♣A (see above), ducking the ♥K lead and the ♥Q continuation allows you to win the third round and safely give East the lead with the ♣A. He will then have no hearts left with which to bridge across to his partners' established suit. The opponents will take only two hearts and a club. You will win the other ten tricks.

The complete hand looked like this:

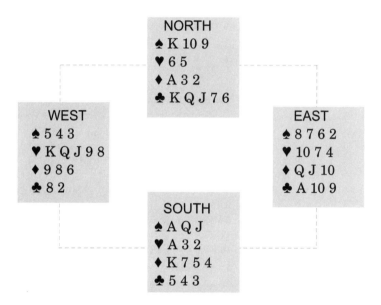

NORTH
♠ K 10 9
♥ 6 5
♦ A 3 2
♣ K Q J 7 6

WEST
♠ 5 4 3
♥ K Q J 9 8
♦ 9 8 6
♣ 8 2

EAST
♠ 8 7 6 2
♥ 10 7 4
♦ Q J 10
♣ A 10 9

SOUTH
♠ A Q J
♥ A 3 2
♦ K 7 5 4
♣ 5 4 3

We call this type of play **cutting defenders' communication.** You should consider this type of ducking play any time the opponents attack your shortest suit.

COMPETITIVE BIDDING

*I have to be honest with you. I've been pro-*tecting you. I've taught you how to open the bidding and how to respond to an opening bid. It's been fun. But we've chosen to ignore the fact that there are competitors at the table who might want to bid against us, well, competitively. And half of the time these very same competitors will be you! Are you going to just sit there and let them have their polite little auction? Or are you going to disrupt it and get in a few bids of your own?

What we've been doing so far is called **constructive bidding**—you and your partner have been left to your own devices. Now it's time to learn **competitive bidding**—the most heated, high-stakes part of bridge, where everyone gets in the fray, mixing it up; where subtle decisions promise success or failure, and experience, devious tactics and brilliant strategy become your most powerful allies.

After the opponents open the bidding, there are only two ways for you to enter the auction: **the overcall** or **the takeout double.**

▪ 1. THE OVERCALL

Imagine for a moment that you, West, pick up the following hand:

♠ A 3 2   ♥ 7 6   ♦ K Q J 9 3   ♣ A 10 4

After counting your points and looking over your options, you're all set to open 1D—when suddenly South, the dealer, to your right, opens 1C ahead of you. Life's not fair. There can be but one opening bidder per hand and you're not it. So what's left to do? Do you curl up into a ball and wait out the auction in silence?

Of course not! You jump right in and bid your diamonds anyway. Over the opening bidder's call of 1C, you **overcall** with 1D. You're not opening, you're overcalling, and from now on, in this auction, you'll be known as the overcaller.

After all, you've got 14 HCP and 1 LP. Your hand could be as good as or better than South's. Just because he happened to open first doesn't mean his side has more points than yours. What if the high card points that remained in the deck were divided as below?

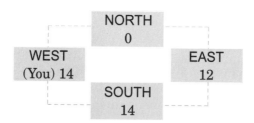

Even though the opponents opened the bidding, your side, with 26 combined points, would have a good play for game!

Let's look at another example of overcalling. Here's the first round of the auction, starting with North's opening bid:

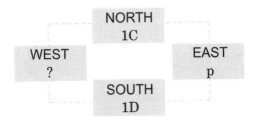

You are West. Both opponents, as you can see, have bid. So what? If you find a good reason to bid, jump right in. Say, for instance, that this were your hand:

♠ 9 4   ♥ A Q J 10 4 2   ♦ A Q   ♣ 7 6 5

You and your partner might still be able to make a contract of two or three hearts. So overcall 1H. Even if it turns out that the opponents have you outgunned, and it's not your hand, if your partner found herself on lead, wouldn't you want her to lead a heart—especially in a no trump contract? Of course you would. Overcall 1H and show the way.

An overcall, like an opening bid of 1NT, has a very definite shape and range. To be precise: the suit you are overcalling, *whether it be a minor or a major,* **must be 5 cards long** and must be substantial in strength; **the HCP range must be between 10 and 18 points.** Notice the word "must." This is also the third, and last, range you *must* commit to memory.

Let's take a minute to explore and explain the two conditions of an overcall.

A substantial (good) five-card or longer suit:
What does a "good" or "substantial" five-card suit look like? Well, not like this: Q 8 7 4 2. More like this: K Q J 9 6. Or this: A J 10 9 4. Or even this: Q J 10 9 6. Notice the Q J 9 or the J 10 9 interior portion of the suit. This is referred to as the **internal quality** or **internal strength** of a suit. A suit with internal strength takes tricks, no matter what.

When you overcall a suit, your partner should be able to count on you for at least three or four tricks in that suit.

10–18 point range:

This point range is extremely important when considering whether to overcall. Note: A good way to remember this range is that it's approximately 3 points weaker than the range for an opening bid (13–20).

Q: The opponent on your right opens 1D. Which of the following hands is *not* an overcall of 1S?

A.	**B.**	**C.**
♠ K Q 10 8 4	♠ A Q 10 9 8	♠ J 7 4 3 2
♥ A K	♥ A 7 4	♥ A 9 8
♦ 3 2	♦ 4 3 2	♦ Q 4 2
♣ K Q 7 4	♣ 9 5	♣ K J

Answer:

(C) You have 11 HCP, but your suit stinks. J 7 4 3 2 is not a substantial enough holding to support an overcall. Meanwhile, Hand A is about as strong as you can be, with 17 HCP and a powerful spade suit. Hand B is about as weak as you can be but still overcall, with only 10 HCP but a good five-card spade suit.

2-Level Overcall

If you find that you must go to the two level to overcall, you need one trick more in strength than you would need for a one level overcall. You would then be contracting for a minimum of eight tricks rather than the seven you needed when you overcalled on the one level. To try to make an eight-trick contract requires an additional trick in strength, either in the form of four more HCP (an ace) or one more card in length (a strong **six**-card suit).

No Trump Overcall

Say you pick up:

♠Q J 3   ♥A K 2   ♦K J 9 3   ♣Q 10 8

You are all set to open 1NT, when your RHO (right hand opponent) opens 1D. Don't let that stop you. Go ahead and overcall 1NT. Overcalling 1NT is exactly like opening 1NT but for a few differences: same no trump shape, same 15–17 HCP (though now you can go as high as 18 points). The only major difference is that the overcall of 1NT guarantees at least one stopper in the suit with which your opponent opened the bidding. For example, we were able to overcall in the above hand because we had no trump shape (4–3–3–3), no trump strength (16 HCP) and plenty of stoppers in the diamond suit.

The rules for overcalling are strict but straightforward. Overcalling itself is easy. Responding to your partner's over-call is easy, too, if you understand what you're trying to do. Remember when you first learned to raise partner's 1NT opening to 2NT or 3NT, you did so with a minimum of **9 points.** Why? Because partner's 15–17 point range pre-cluded *the possibility of game (26)* with any less than that. Similarly, when you raise partner's opening bid of one of a suit, you do so with no less than **6 points.** Why? Because partner can't have more than 20 points. 20 + 6 = 26. The *possibility of game* exists as long as you have at least 6 points.

The possibility of game is what keeps the auction mov-ing forward. When partner overcalls one of a suit, or 1NT, he could have as many as 18 points (10–18 points). There-fore, you are obligated to keep the bidding open with **8 or more points:** 8 + 18 = 26.

Q: Imagine that you have each of the hands below. In each case, partner overcalls the opponent's opening bid of 1D with a bid of 1H. As responder (to your partner's overcall) what action, if any, do you take?

A.	B.	C.
♠ Q J 9 8	♠ Q J 3	♠ A 7 4 2
♥ K 7 4	♥ 7 4	♥ Q 10 8 3
♦ 9 8 3	♦ A Q 9 7	♦ 9
♣ A 8 2	♣ Q 10 4 2	♣ A Q 8 6

Answers:

A. Raise to 2H. With your 10 points, if partner has a strong 16, 17 or 18 point overcall, game is possible. If partner has a minimum overcall (10–13+ points), he will pass 2H.

B. Bid 1NT. This shows about 8–11 HCP and only two-card support for partner's overcalled suit. Your partner has a good suit and at least 10 HCP. The addition of your 11 HCP gives you 21 HCP—more than your opponents. Your side should be declaring the hand. You also have stoppers in diamonds (your A and your Q) in the suit opened. If partner has a strong overcall (15+ points), he'll put you in 3NT!

C. Jump right to 4H. With 12 HCP and 3 SP, game is a real possibility. Remember, the weakest your partner can be is 10 HCP and 1 LP (in that five-card suit), for 11 total points. His 11 and your 15 (in support) = 26.

■ 2. THE TAKEOUT DOUBLE

Here it comes. I always save it for last: the single most misunderstood, most misused and most exciting bid in bridge, the **double**.

The double is so exciting because when it's used properly, it swings more points one way or another than any other bid. It commands attention. And it forces your partner—and your opponents—to sit up and think. At the same time, the double is misunderstood and misused for one very simple reason. Based on when it comes in an auction, it can have thirty-seven different meanings!

That's no exaggeration. Thirty-seven and counting. As we speak, bridge theorists are no doubt hard at work on thirty-eight. Don't worry. There are methods to deal with all this madness.

For the first year or two of your bridge-playing career, you won't need to worry about all thirty-seven various meanings. Two will suffice. They cover about 80 percent of all doubling situations. By the time you're ready to deal with the other thirty-five, there will probably be three or four new ones anyway. See what you have to look forward to!

Up until the early 1970s, there were only a handful of doubles. The first, the **penalty double,** dates back to games like bid whist and other forerunners of bridge. Bridge simply borrowed this wonderful bidding tool and expanded it.

Basically, the penalty double is the equivalent of a policeman. It keeps everyone in line and attempts to dispense justice and punishment. It usually occurs at the end of an auction, when the opponents have reached a fairly high level (a contract entailing nine tricks or more), and it's the reason that absolutely every hand doesn't end up at the game level with bonus in mind. We haven't discussed how a double affects the results since chapter 4. Here's a quick review.

Imagine that you're sitting North, and West, your RHO, opens the bidding 1NT. After you pass, East jumps to 3NT. This gets passed around to you. You take another look at your hand:

♠ 9 8 7   ♥ J 5   ♦ A K Q J 10 4   ♣ 4 2

Wait a minute: the opponents are not going to make nine tricks. Since West is the declarer, you will be on lead and will take the first six tricks. You know you have their contract beat. Therefore, you say, "Double," meaning, "I doubt you are going to make what you bid."

If, after the double, the auction finishes with every other player at the table passing (they each get another turn to bid), then you would simply cash your six-card diamond suit, and defeat 3NT by two tricks.

Here's how the auction looks:

W	N	E	S
1NT	p	3NT	p
p	**double**	p	p
p			

Down two tricks is a penalty of – 200; but down two *doubled* is – 500. In comparing these two results, you start to appreciate the power of the penalty double.

At the beginning of the twentieth century, a new use and meaning was found for the word "double." Here's the classic example. Say you hold:

> ♠ A 10 9 4
> ♥ K Q 7 2
> ♦ 8
> ♣ A J 6 3

You're all set to open the bidding 1C when the opener on your right beats you to the punch by opening 1D. Do you curl up into a ball and wait out the auction in silence? Of course not!

We've just learned how to handle this situation. With 14 HCP, it could be your hand; so you'll just overcall a . . . a . . .

a what? A vital condition of overcalling is that you must have a good five- or six-card suit. And I don't see one, do you? So, what to do. You could cheat and bid a four-card suit. After all, it's not really cheating, just exaggerating. Just this once. Let's see. Say you bid—you overcall—1H, and everyone else passes. So you find yourself playing in a contract of 1H. The dummy comes down:

WEST (Dummy)	EAST (You)
♠ K 8 5 3 2	♠ A 10 9 4
♥ J 8	♥ K Q 7 2
♦ 9 7 5 4	♦ 8
♣ Q 10	♣ A J 6 3

You're in a 4–2 heart trump fit. Maybe you'll make five or so tricks. Notice that if spades were trump, you'd have a good shot at making ten or eleven tricks. Why didn't your partner respond 1S to your 1H overcall? Because with only 6 points, he knew there was no game. Your overcall was limited, remember, to 18 points. He's not supposed to bid with less than 8 points. Did you expect him to cheat a little too on the same hand?

Wouldn't it have been nicer to have a bid at your disposal that said, "Partner, I have shortness in the opponents' suit (diamonds), **tolerance** (at least 3 cards) for *all* the unbid suits, and—like opener—I also have the HCP equivalent of an opening bid"? Conveying all this information would paint a pretty clear picture for partner, wouldn't it?

Well, that's what a call of double says in this situation. When your partner hasn't bid yet, or has done nothing but pass, and the opponents are just getting started, a double is not meant for penalties. It simply says, "Partner, I want you to bid a suit the opponents haven't."

The following examples illustrate take out doubles at work in auctions:

1.

<u>E</u>	<u>S</u>	<u>W</u>	<u>N</u>
1H	double		

This double says you have no more than one or two hearts, you have at least three spades, three diamonds, and three clubs, and a total of 13 or more points.

2.

<u>E</u>	<u>S</u>	<u>W</u>	<u>N</u>
		1C	p
2C	double		

This double says you're short in clubs, you have tolerance for the other three suits and the values for an opening bid.

3.

<u>E</u>	<u>S</u>	<u>W</u>	<u>N</u>
		1C	p
1D	double		

This double says you are short in the opponents' suits (clubs and diamonds). You have 4 or 5 cards in each of the other two suits and values for an opening bid.

Let's give you this hand:

♠ J 7 2   ♥ 9 8 3   ♦ 10 4   ♣ K 9 7 5 2

In the following example you're South. East deals and opens 1S. You pass. West, on your left, raises this to 2S. Your partner now steps in with a double that gets passed to you. What should you do? Here's the auction:

E	S	W	N
1S	p	2S	double
p	?		

First of all, ask yourself: "What kind of double is this?" Can this be a penalty double? Let's see. Before your partner's first bid, the opponents happily bid and raised their own suit. Sounds like they have eight or nine spades between them, and 22 or so points. You have three spades and 4 points. That leaves your partner with one or two spades (shortness) and about 14 or 15 points (an opening bid). That's no penalty double. That must be the other kind of double.

Great, so it's not a penalty double. So what? I only have 4 points. Do I have a problem here? Don't I have to pass? Don't I need 6 or 8 or some other number of points to respond?

Gets confusing, doesn't it?

The answer is rather surprising. Let's step back a minute and see what's going on. Let's picture four hands that are consistent with the bidding thus far:

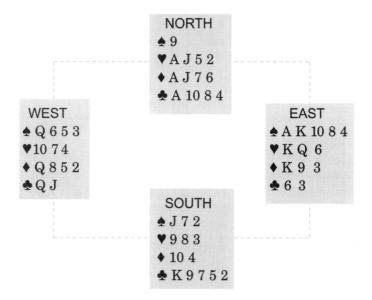

NORTH
♠ 9
♥ A J 5 2
♦ A J 7 6
♣ A 10 8 4

WEST
♠ Q 6 5 3
♥ 10 7 4
♦ Q 8 5 2
♣ Q J

EAST
♠ A K 10 8 4
♥ K Q 6
♦ K 9 3
♣ 6 3

SOUTH
♠ J 7 2
♥ 9 8 3
♦ 10 4
♣ K 9 7 5 2

You're South. This was the auction so far:

E	S	W	N
1S	p	2S	double
p	?		

Let's see what happens if you *pass* the double. West will also pass. Three passes end the auction. The contract becomes 2S doubled. (We will soon see how the double affects the score.) Even though this double was not intended as a penalty double, because it was followed by three passes, in effect it became one. Now will the opponents make 2S?

They will make five spade tricks, two hearts, and at least one diamond: that makes eight. That's enough. So passing the double allows them to make a contract of two spades doubled.

How is that scored? Making 2S is worth 60 points. Sixty doubled is 120. One-hundred-twenty is the **contract value** of two spades doubled. Remember where contract points go: below the line.

We	They
	50
	500
	120 → Bonus time!

One hundred twenty is more than 100; therefore, they get the 500-point game bonus. In addition, as if this weren't enough, any time you double the opponents and fail to beat them, they receive an additional 50 points for being insulted (no kidding). So, all told, how much is two spades doubled worth? A full 670 points. That's a long way from the 60 points earned by making a contract of two spades undoubled.

When partner doubled the opponents' two-spade bid, he wasn't saying he wanted to play in two spades doubled. He was asking you to "take him out" of 2S doubled, take him out to one of the other three suits that he promises tolerance for. 1S–p–2S–*double*, in effect, says, "Partner, I'm begging you: *please* take me out of this contract. Just bid your best suit, and we'll give it a try." Hence the name for this type of double: the **takeout double**.

Let's see what would have happened had you followed your partner's wishes and taken the double out to 3C, your best suit. In the play, you'd have made five club tricks plus your two aces—that's seven tricks—and eventually you'd be able to trump two spades in the dummy, for a grand total of nine tricks. You would have actually made your contract! If the opponents had foolishly doubled you, it would have been your turn to go +670: a 1,340-point swing! I told you at the start of this section that doubling gets exciting.

So what's the moral of this story?

When partner makes a takeout double, you must abide by his wishes and *take him out by bidding something*. In fact, the worse your hand is, the more imperative it is that you come up with a bid! In other words, **to respond to your partner's takeout double, you need *zero or more points*.**

Responding to the Takeout Double

Remember, when your partner makes a takeout double, he shows at least the values of an opening bid of 13 points, but he could be a lot stronger. There really is almost no upper limit. Assuming that the opening bidder has 13 points, the takeout doubler could theoretically have as many as 27. Normally the takeout doubler has about 14 or 15 points; so does the opening bidder. That leaves only about a dozen or so points between the other two players at the table; it's rare for the partner of the doubler to have more than eight points. But sometimes it happens.

For instance, look at these two hands:

A.	B.
♠ K Q J 2	♠ 10 9 8 4
♥ 8 7 5	♥ 8 7 5
♦ A 10 8 4	♦ J 10 8 4
♣ 3 2	♣ 3 2

Note that hands A and B have the same shape: 4–4–3–2. Hand A has 10 HCP; B has 1 HCP. In both cases, you are South and the auction has proceeded as below:

W	N	E	S
1H	double	p	?

We just learned that it was imperative to take your partner out of 1H doubled, even with a hand like Hand B— which contains only 1 HCP. We have two four-card suits. To introduce spades, we only have to bid at the one level. Our call, then, is 1S.

Let's continue the auction. Say that West passes. What should partner be thinking about?

Imagine that partner has a typical takeout double of a 1H opening. Here's his hand:

♠ A 7 6 5   ♥ J 6   ♦ K Q 7   ♣ A 9 5 4

Partner has 14 HCP, shortness in hearts, tolerance for all the other suits.

Here's the auction so far:

W	N	E	S
1H	double	p	1S
p	?		

Your partner says to himself, "I made a takeout double, I forced my partner to bid." It was like I held a loaded gun to his head and said "bid." The best he was able to do was to choke out a minimum 1S bid. He could have a complete **yarborough** (a zero-point hand). My 14 points and his possible zero aren't quite enough to get to 26. I'd better pass."

Now look at Hand A, a 10 HCP hand. When partner makes a takeout double, you must somehow convey to him the fact that you like your hand, that there is a good chance for game. That you don't have a hand like Hand B. You'd better not bid 1S! 1H–double–pass–1S is a bid you make when you're forced to bid with nothing but four spades in your hand. Here you want to tell your partner you have something better, that you like your hand. **Jump to 2S.**

The range for this jump starts at around **8 points** and goes up to **12 points.** With 13 points, just bid a game. By doubling, partner shows enough points for an opening bid. If you also have an opening bid, then game must be contracted for (13 + 13 = 26).

Say you have a hand of:

♠ K Q J 2   ♥ 8 7 5 2   ♦ A 10 8 4   ♣ 2

When partner makes a takeout double of 1H, jump directly to 4S. You have 10 HCP and in support of spades, 3 SP (with your singleton club).

Now, how do you remember to jump with 8 or more points? You don't have to memorize it. Here's the trick: I've already asked you to remember the overall range of 10–18 points; that's the third crucial bidding range to remember, after the no trump range of 15–17 and the one-of-a-suit range of 13–20. The maximum number of points for an overcall, once again, is 18; therefore, in order to *respond* to an overcall we need a minimum of 26 – 18 = *8* points. And that 8 is the same number you need to jump the bidding "over" a takeout double.

For example, imagine that you picked up the following hand:

♠ 2   ♥ 8 7 5 2   ♦ A 10 8   ♣ K J 7 6 5

Partner makes a takeout double of 1H. Should you bid 2C, or should you jump to 3C?

With 8 HCP and an outside singleton worth 3 points, game is a very real possibility. Keep the auction going: jump to 3C. This shows between 8–12 points. If partner has more than the 13-point minimum for a takeout double, game is a possibility in 5C or even 3 NT.

Try another example. Your hand is as follows:

♠ K 7 6 5   ♥ Q 4 2   ♦ J 7 2   ♣ J 4 2

You have 7 HCP. Your partner doubles an opening 1D bid. Unless partner has more than eighteen points, there's no possibility of game. Do not encourage him. Pick your best suit and respond as cheaply as possible: Bid 1S.

Try these:

Say you are South and the auction proceeds:

W	N	E	S
1H	double	2H	?

Q: How would you respond to your partner's takeout double with each of the following hands:

A. ♠ J 7 4 2   ♥ 8 7 4   ♦ K 4 3 2   ♣ 8 6

B. ♠ A J 7 4   ♥ 8 7 4   ♦ K 4 3 2   ♣ 8 6

C. ♠ A 6   ♥ 8 7 4 2   ♦ 4   ♣ K Q 9 8 7 3

Answers:

A. When East bids, he removes the double. Therefore, you're under no obligation to bid. You pass. This way, you show less than the 8 points you would need to bid 2S.

B. With 8 points, bid 2S. Notice that this is what you would have bid had East passed.

C. Jump to Game in clubs (5C). Partner has, at most, one heart card. (Were you listening to the bidding? West showed five or more hearts, East showed three or more—which doesn't leave too many for your partner to have.) Your hand has a value of about 15 points: 9 HCP + 2 LP + 4 SP. Added to partner's 13+ points, this brings your side's strength to right around the 29 points you need for eleven tricks.

■ HANDS-ON PLAY

Practice Hand 1

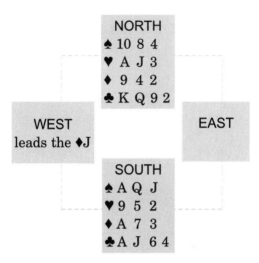

NORTH
♠ 10 8 4
♥ A J 3
♦ 9 4 2
♣ K Q 9 2

WEST
leads the ♦J

EAST

SOUTH
♠ A Q J
♥ 9 5 2
♦ A 7 3
♣ A J 6 4

The Bidding: You are South. East on your right opens 1D. You were preparing to open 1NT and so are a little surprised at this turn of events. How does East's opening bid affect your choice of bids? In this case it doesn't. A 1NT overcall on your part shows an opening 1NT hand with the suit opened firmly stopped (you have the ♦A stopper). Overcall 1NT. With 10 HCP and 1 LP, partner raises you to 3NT. This ends the auction.

The auction went like this:

E	S	W	N
1D	1NT	p	3NT

The Play: West leads the ♦J. Plan your play. You have one spade trick + one heart + one diamond + four clubs. You need at least two more tricks. They can come from finesses in spades if East has the ♠K. But does he have it?

A lazy approach to answering the question would be to assume he does, since he opened the bidding. But let's see if we can definitely place the ♠K with East.

You have 16 HCP, and your partner has 10—26 between the two of you. That means the opponents have 14 between them. West's ♦J lead might be his only point, since East needed all 13 remaining points to open the bidding. Therefore East has the ♠K. With that little bit of thought you have definitely placed the ♠K with East. Now all you need to do is make sure that it doesn't take a trick. To take a finesse, you must force East to commit his spade position *before* you do. You must play spades from the dummy first and lead through East. In order to get to the dummy, you can use your beautiful solid club suit for transportation purposes. Win the opening with your ♦A. At trick two, play the ♣4 to the ♣K. (This does not violate our policy of always trying to go after our potential first. We are playing clubs in order to try to establish winners in our potential suit.) At trick three play the ♠4 and if East wisely pays a low card, insert your ♠J. When this wins, cross back to dummy with the ♣Q and repeat the finesse. In all, you will take three spades, one heart, one diamond and four clubs for nine tricks.

Here's the complete hand:

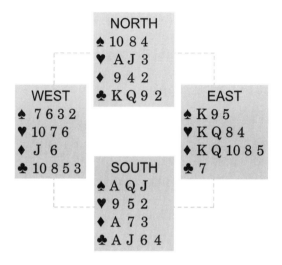

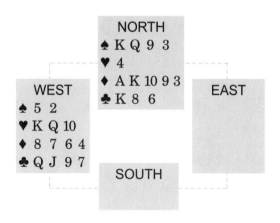

Practice Hand 2

The Bidding: You are West. North (whose hand you cannot see at this time) opens the bidding 1D. Your partner overcalls 1H, South chimes in with 1S. With 8 points and three beautiful trumps, you have just enough to raise your partner's 1H overcall to 2H. North ends the auction with an abrupt jump to 4S.

The auction went like this:

N	E	S	W
1D	1H	1S	2H
4S			

The Play: You lead the ♥K. The dummy comes down. Everyone follows to the first heart trick. Plan your defense.

Picture your partner's hand. For his overcall he needed to have a good five-card suit, say A J x x x, and 10 or more HCP. It looks as if he has to have either the ♠A or the ♣A for his bid. If it's the ♠A, then declarer has the ♣A and on defense you will probably take no more than two tricks, both major suit aces. Declarer will be able to draw trump, trump one or two hearts, and establish the diamond suit for four winners. In all, declarer will make three spades, one or two ruffs, four diamonds, and two clubs for ten or eleven tricks.

If, however, your partner has the ♣A, you may be able to take three quick club tricks before declarer discards them on those powerful diamonds. Switch immediately to the ♣Q and try to trap dummy's ♣K.

The complete hand looked like this:

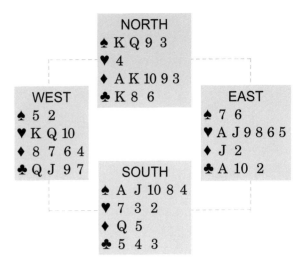

NORTH
♠ K Q 9 3
♥ 4
♦ A K 10 9 3
♣ K 8 6

WEST
♠ 5 2
♥ K Q 10
♦ 8 7 6 4
♣ Q J 9 7

EAST
♠ 7 6
♥ A J 9 8 6 5
♦ J 2
♣ A 10 2

SOUTH
♠ A J 10 8 4
♥ 7 3 2
♦ Q 5
♣ 5 4 3

Had you not switched to the ♣Q, declarer would have drawn trump and discarded his losing clubs on the diamonds. Declarer would actually come to five spades, two ruffs and five diamonds for a total of twelve tricks! Your thoughtful club shift produced a three-trick swing in the outcome, holding declarer to nine tricks and defeating his 4S contract.

Practice Hand 3

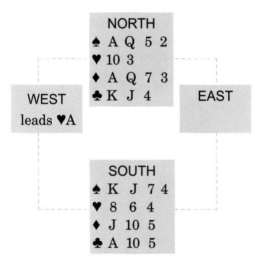

NORTH
♠ A Q 5 2
♥ 10 3
♦ A Q 7 3
♣ K J 4

WEST
leads ♥A

EAST

SOUTH
♠ K J 7 4
♥ 8 6 4
♦ J 10 5
♣ A 10 5

The Bidding: You are South. West deals and opens 1H. Your partner makes a takeout double. This gets passed to you. Your partner, by his double, said he was short in hearts, had tolerance in all the other suits and had at least the strength of an opening bid. Remember how many points you need to respond to this double: zero. You must respond. In this case, with 9 points you want to respond. If with zero you'd bid 1S, with this hand you should jump to 2S, showing 8+ points. Partner with 16 HCP + 1 SP (the doubleton hearts) jumps to 4S which ends the auction.

The auction went like this:

W	N	E	S
1H	double	p	2S
p	4S	p	p

The Play: West leads the ♥A. Plan the play.

In any competitive auction, the first thing you should do after the dummy comes down is review the bidding. This fixes in your mind who has what. In this case your left-hand opponent opened the bidding. Between you and your partner you are looking at 25 HCP. Clearly West has almost all the outstanding points.

Your diamond suit offers a finessing situation. Given the chance, you should plan on leading the ♦J and forcing West to commit his ♦K. If he doesn't, you should intend to repeat the finesse. Notice if West doesn't play his ♦K on your ♦J or ♦10, you will make four diamond tricks, not three. Your club suit offers a choice of finesses. Missing the ♣Q, you can finesse either East or West for it. Again, from the bidding, you should choose West. Now, put this all together.

At trick one, West leads the ♥A, then continues with the ♥K at trick two, which holds the lead. At trick three he plays a third heart, forcing you to trump it in the dummy. You draw three rounds of trump finishing with the ♠K or ♠J. West, unable to follow suit on the last round, discards a low heart.

At trick seven you lead the ♦J. West covers with the ♦K, and you win with the ♦A. Now comes the key play. Play a club to your ♣A and finesse the ♣J on the way back. It wins, as you expected. All together you make four spades + one ruff + three diamonds + three clubs for eleven tricks. All you lose is the ♥A, K.

The complete hand looked like this:

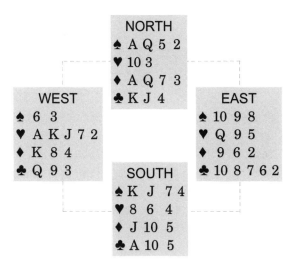

NORTH
♠ A Q 5 2
♥ 10 3
♦ A Q 7 3
♣ K J 4

WEST
♠ 6 3
♥ A K J 7 2
♦ K 8 4
♣ Q 9 3

EAST
♠ 10 9 8
♥ Q 9 5
♦ 9 6 2
♣ 10 8 7 6 2

SOUTH
♠ K J 7 4
♥ 8 6 4
♦ J 10 5
♣ A 10 5

Notice again how the bidding virtually "placed" the ♣Q for you and allowed you to play the suit correctly.

LET'S PLAY

You can pore over dry tomes on the game of bridge, do all sorts of exercises, study the bridge column in the paper, write up a bunch of bidding flash cards and carry them around with you; but you will never *really* learn to play bridge until you start playing. If you're doing this with friends or planning on joining a group, that's perfect. But if you're alone and want to start playing, here are a few suggestions:

1. The Yellow Pages. Check out local bridge clubs. Ask about novice games, practice sessions, or any program they have for beginners.

2. Call the American Contract Bridge League (ACBL), in Memphis, Tennessee. They have a list of every affiliated club in the country (about 2,000). The number is 1-901-332-5586 or http:// www.acbl.org.

3. Try programs written for the computer. Ask the ACBL for suggestions for beginners.

4. Visit O.K. Bridge Interactive, on the Net. 1-619-490-6770 or http://www.okbridge.com.

5. Visit my Website: //www.bridge–nyc.com.

Bridge is a game. The best way to get better is not to worry about getting better. It's meant to be played, and enjoyed, on all levels. Don't get discouraged. After twenty years of teaching beginners, I can assure you, you'll have fun at every stage of your bridge education. After all, it's not brain surgery. It's bridge, baby.

CHEAT SHEETS

■ BIDDING IN A NUTSHELL

No-Trump Openings and Responses

All no-trump openings (1NT, 2NT, 3NT) must have one of these three flat shapes:

4–3–3–2
4–4–3–2
5–3–3–2

No-Trump Point Ranges

To show a flat hand with 13 or 14 high card points:
Open one of a suit and rebid no trump at the cheapest level.
For example: a) 1D–1H b) 1S–2C
 1NT **2NT**
To show a flat hand with 15–17 HCP:
Open 1NT.
To show a flat hand with 18 or 19 HCP:
Open one of a suit and jump rebid in no trump.
For example: a) 1D–1H b) 1D–2C
 2NT **3NT**

To show a flat hand with 20–22 HCP:
Open 2NT.
To show a flat hand with 23–26 HCP:
Open 3NT.

Responding to 1 NT Openings

1NT–**pass**	(0–8 points)
2NT	(exactly 9 points)
3NT	(10–15 points)
1NT–**2D, 2H, 2S**	(five- or six-card suit and 0–8 points)
1NT–**3H, 3S**	(five-card suit and 10+ points)
1NT–**3C, 3D**	(five-card or longer suit and 10+ points)
1NT–**4H, 4S**	(six-card or longer suit and 10+ points)
1NT–**2C**	Stayman—asks opener to bid a four-card major if he has one, or to bid 2D if he doesn't

Major Suit Openings and Responses

1M (1H or 1S) shows five or more cards and 13–20 points

1M–**pass**	(0–5 points)
1M–**2M**	(6–9 points, *hate*)
1M–**3M**	(10–12 points, *like*)
1M–**4M**	(13–16 points, *love*)
1M–**1NT**	(6–9 points)
1M–**2NT**	(10–12 points)
1M–**3NT**	(13–16 points)

Minor Suit Openings and Responses

1C shows a three-card or longer suit and 13–20 points
1D shows a four-card or longer suit and 13–20 points

1m (1C or 1D)–**pass**	(0–5 points)
1C–**2C**	(6–9 points and five-card club support)
1D–**2D**	(6–9 points and four-card diamond support)

1m–3m   (10–12 points and five-card club or
                             four-card diamond support)

Overcalls

A good five-card suit and 10–18 points
Responses:
1D—1H—p—**2H**   (8–11 points, 3+ trumps)
1D—1H—p—**3H**   (12–14 points, 3+ trumps)
1D—1H—p—**4H**   (15+ points, 3+ trumps)
1D—1H—p—**1NT**   (8–11 points, stopper in diamonds)
1D—1H—p—**2NT**   (12–14 points, stopper in diamonds)
1D—1H—p—**3NT**   (15+ points, stopper in diamonds)

Takeout Doubles

*Shortness in the opponents' suit, tolerance (three or four cards)
 in all the unbid suits, at least an opening bid (13+ points)*
Responses:
1D–double—p–1H   (0–8 points, four-card or longer suit)

1D–double—p–2H   (9–12 points, four-card or longer suit)

1D–double—p–4H   (13+ points, four-card or longer suit)

1D–double—p–1NT   (8–10 points)

1D–double—p–2NT   (11–12 points)

1D–double—p–3NT   (13–15 points)

# GLOSSARY

above the line—where points won for overtricks, penalties, and bonuses are recorded on the score sheet

auction—a series of bids that determines the final contract

balanced hand—a hand containing no voids, singletons, and at most, one doubleton. The three patterns to meet these criteria are the no trump shapes: 4–3–3–3; 4–4–3–2; and 5–3–3–2.

below the line—where points won for making contracts are recorded on the score sheet

bid—a call in an auction that promises to take a certain number of tricks in the play

book—the first six tricks won by the declaring side

call—any action (passing, bidding, or doubling) taken during an auction

cash—to play a card

competitive bidding—auctions in which both sides bid

constructive bidding—auctions in which only one side bids

contract—the final bid in the auction that commits declarer to make a specified number of tricks in a particular strain

deal—the even distribution of the fifty-two cards

declarer—the first person to name the strain in which the final contract is to be played. Also, the person who will try to fulfill the contract by using both his own and dummy's cards.

defenders—the partnership that opposes declarer and tries to defeat the contract

discard—a played card that is not of the suit led nor of the trump suit

distribution—the number of cards held in each suit by a player or partnership

double—a bid that expresses an intent to defeat the opponents' contract and inflict a heavier penalty for the loss

doubleton—a holding of two cards in a suit

drawing trump—the playing of trump cards until there are none left in the opponents' hands

dummy—declarer's partner. Also, the hand that is placed faceup on the table after the opening lead

entry—a card that provides a means of winning a trick in a particular hand

face cards—the king, queen, and jack

finesse—an attempt to win a trick with a card lower ranking than one held by the opponents

forcing bid—a bid that compels partner to bid again

game—a total trick score of 100 points

game contracts—3NT, 4S, 4H, 5C, 5D

grand slam—a contract for all thirteen tricks

HCP—abbreviation for high card points

high card points—ace = 4; king = 3; queen = 2; jack = 1

hold-up (ducking)—refusing to take a trick, often with the intent to disrupt the opponents' communication

honors—the ace, king, queen, jack, or ten.

jump—a bid that skips a level (e.g., 1H—3H)

lead—the first card played to a trick

limit bid—a bid that promises no more than a certain amount of points. For example, 1S—3S. . . . 3S promises no more than 10–12 points.

major suits—spades and hearts

minor suits—diamonds and clubs

no trump—a contract where the play is conducted without a trump suit

opening lead—the lead to the first trick, made by the player (defender) to the left of the declarer

opening the bidding—making the first bid in an auction (pass is not a bid)

overcall—a bid made after an opponent has opened the bidding

overtrick—a trick won by the declarer's side in excess of those contracted for

part score (partial)—a contract with a trick score worth less than 100 points

pass—a call in an auction that expresses the player's desire not to bid or double

pass-out—a deal on which none of the players opened the bidding and which requires that a new hand be dealt

penalty—a bonus awarded to the defending side for defeating a contract

penalty double—a double made to increase the size of the penalty, in the expectation that the doubled contract will fail

point count—the method of hand evaluation whereby a numerical value is assigned to the trick—taking features of the hand. These include high cards, length, and, in the case of trump contracts, shortness.

promotion—the increase in the status of a card as higher-ranking cards in that suit are played

raise—support of partner's suit by bidding that suit at a higher level, often with the purpose of confirming that suit as trump

rebid—1. bidding the same suit a second time
2. a second bid by any player

responder—the partner of the opening bidder, or the partner of the player who makes an overcall or takeout double

ruff—trump

sequence—three or more cards adjacent in rank, the highest usually being an honor. There are also broken sequences, which contain a gap between the middle and lowest card of the sequence (Q J 9) and interior sequences in which the equals are accompanied by a higher-ranking card (A J 10 9)

signal—information imparted by a player to his partner by the choice of card played or a bid in an auction

singleton—a holding of one card in a suit

slam—a contract for twelve or thirteen tricks

spot card—a card below the rank of an honor

Stayman—an artificial response of 2C to an opening bid of 1NT, which signals partner to bid a four-card major if he has one

stopper—a card certain to take a trick that interrupts the opponents' ability to take a string of tricks in a suit

strain—suit

suit—hearts, diamonds, spades, or clubs

takeout double—a double that signals partner not to pass but to choose a strain in which to play

tenace—two cards in the same suit, one of which ranks two degrees lower than the other, e.g., A-Q; J-9; 7-5.

trick—four cards, one contributed from each player, starting with the player on lead and going in a clockwise direction. The highest card of the suit led wins, unless a trump card is played.

trump—the suit named in the final contract, more powerful than any other suit

trumping—playing a trump on a trick, permissible only after one is void in the suit being led

unblock—play that allows the uninterrupted run of a long suit, usually accomplished by cashing the high cards from the short suit first

undertricks—tricks that the declarer has bid but failed to win

void—a suit in which no cards are held

yarborough—a very weak hand

Jeff Bayone has owned and operated the Manhattan Bridge Club for over twenty years, where he has taught or supervised the teaching of over 3,000 novice and intermediate players. He is a Life Master five times over, and has won numerous regional and sectional victories, including the National Non-Life Master Pairs in Las Vegas. He lives in New York City.

To learn more about the Manhattan Bridge Club, visit their Website at www.bridge–nyc.com.